Luke

TEACHING CHRIST IN ALL OF SCRIPTURE

Head, Heart, Hand Bible Studies

- Ezra and Nehemiah — *The Good Hand of Our God Is upon Us*
- Isaiah — *The Holy One of Israel*
- Luke — *That You May Have Certainty concerning the Faith*
- Romans — *The Gospel of God for Obedience to the Faith*
- 1 Peter, 2 Peter, and Jude — *Steadfast in the Faith*

Luke

That You May Have Certainty concerning the Faith

Sarah Ivill

Reformation Heritage Books

Grand Rapids, Michigan

Luke
© 2022 by Sarah Ivill

Reformation Heritage Books
3070 29th St. SE
Grand Rapids, MI 49512
616-977-0889
orders@heritagebooks.org
www.heritagebooks.org

Printed in the United States of America
22 23 24 25 26/10 9 8 7 6 5 4 3 2 1

Library of Congress Cataloging-in-Publication Data

Names: Ivill, Sarah, author.
Title: Luke : that you may have certainty concerning the faith / Sarah Ivill.
Description: Grand Rapids, Michigan : Reformation Heritage Books, 2022. | Series: Head, heart, hand bible studies | Includes bibliographical references.
Identifiers: LCCN 2022017278 (print) | LCCN 2022017279 (ebook) | ISBN 9781601789495 (paperback) | ISBN 9781601789501 (epub)
Subjects: LCSH: Bible. Luke—Textbooks. | BISAC: RELIGION / Biblical Studies / New Testament / General Epistles
Classification: LCC BS2596 .I95 2022 (print) | LCC BS2596 (ebook) | DDC 226.4—dc23/ eng/20220613
LC record available at https://lccn.loc.gov/2022017278
LC ebook record available at https://lccn.loc.gov/2022017279

For additional Reformed literature, request a free book list from Reformation Heritage Books at the above regular or email address.

Contents

Contents

A Note from Sarah

Many women today are drowning in despair, flailing their arms in futility, and sinking in seas of sin and suffering. They reach out to false, futile saviors, clinging to things or relationships that are as capable of saving them as sticks floating in the sea and the wind that crashes with each wave. This is tragic, especially because the lifeboat that could secure them to the heaviest anchor is right in front of them. But they continue to try to save themselves, shirking the secure way.

Perhaps no one has told them that the lifeboat, the Word of God, is their very life because it reveals Jesus Christ, the anchor of their souls and the One to whom all Scripture points. Only as women are steeped in the Scriptures that point them to the Savior will they swim in hope, surf waves in security, and stand on shore anchored to the truth.

Let us return to being women of one Book above all others. If you have time to read only one book, make it Scripture. Then, if you have time to read more, you will be well trained to tell the difference between what merely tickles your ears and what mightily transforms your heart.

My love for teaching the Bible was inspired by my hunger to study it. Longing for the "meat" of God's Word and finding it lacking in so many churches today, I enrolled in Bible Study Fellowship after graduating from high school. It was there that I realized my desire to attend seminary and was influenced and encouraged by a strong, godly woman and mentor in my life to attend Dallas Theological Seminary (DTS). During this time I was leading women through in-depth Bible studies and caught a glimpse of how much women desired to be fed the depth of God's Word. This encouraged me even further to receive an education that would best prepare me to deliver God's Word to women who hungered for the truth.

After graduating with my master of theology from DTS, I took a position as assistant director of women's ministry at a large church where I served under a woman who shared my passion to teach the "meat" of God's Word. Within the year, I had assumed the role of director and delved into teaching the Bible in an expository and applicable manner. After three years I resigned in order to stay home with my first child. During those years at home, the Lord used my experience in seminary and ministry to lead me back to my roots and fully embrace Reformed theology. Raised for the first half of my childhood in conservative Presbyterian churches, I had been grounded in the Reformed faith and catechisms from an early age. But from middle school on, I was not in Reformed churches. The question in my twenties then became, What do I really believe?

One of the first steps on my journey was contacting a Reformed seminary and asking for a list of books covering everything I had missed by not attending a Reformed seminary. That began my reading of some of the most renowned Reformed theologians in the world. It was during those days that the question of what I really believed was finally answered, and I began teaching women based on my understanding of Reformed theology. In fact, that is how my first Bible study came to be written. I had the incredible privilege of teaching that first study to a wonderful group of women for a morning Bible study at our Presbyterian Church in America (PCA) church. And it was from their encouragement and exhortation that I submitted the study for publication.

I want to encourage you as you embark on the study of Luke. As you read, ponder what the Bible has to say about the depth of our sin and the judgment we deserve, and rejoice at the wonders of grace and salvation. In every chapter keep your eyes on Jesus, the one to whom all Scripture points, and worship Him for the work of salvation that He has accomplished for you through the power of the Holy Spirit, to the glory of God the Father. *Soli Deo gloria!*

Acknowledgments

I wish to thank those in my life who have been a part of this writing process.

Thank you to Reformation Heritage Books, especially Jay Collier for his interest in this project, Annette Gysen for her excellent editorial work, and Dr. Beeke for reviewing the manuscript.

Thank you to the pastors of Christ Covenant Church (PCA) for faithfully proclaiming the word of God each week. I especially want to thank the women (you know who you are!) who have encouraged me to keep writing Bible studies and have faithfully prayed for me.

Thank you to the men and women of Dallas Theological Seminary who taught me what it means to be a gracious student of Scripture and who instilled in me the importance of expository teaching and the love of God's Word.

Thank you to Westminster Theological Seminary as well as Reformed Theological Seminary and the professors who have served there. The many books that the professors have written and recommended as well as the many online class lectures and chapel messages have been of tremendous benefit to me. They have taught me what it means to see Christ in all of Scripture and to understand more deeply the history of redemption and the beautiful truths of Reformed theology.

Thank you to my mom and dad, David and Judy Gelaude, who have always supported me in my love of the Word and encouraged me to do that which the Lord has called me to do. I love you both more than words can express.

Thank you to my husband, Charles, who has always given me his love, support, and encouragement in the writing process and in what the Lord has called me to do.

And thank you to my children—Caleb, Hannah, Daniel, and Lydia—whose smiles, hugs, and prayers are a constant source of encouragement to me as I pray for the next generation of believers to love the Lord and His Word with all their hearts and minds.

Finally, thank you to my heavenly Father, to my Lord and Savior Jesus Christ, and to the Spirit, who helps me in my weakness. To the triune God be the glory for what He has done through me, a broken vessel and a flawed instrument, yet one that is in the grip of His mighty and gracious hand.

Introduction to This Study

It is my sincere hope that you are excited about studying Scripture, particularly the book of Luke. It is also my sincere desire that this study will help fuel your excitement. In this introduction I have provided three resources that I hope will prove beneficial to you. First, I have provided an overview of how to use this Bible study. Feel free to adapt my suggestions for the context in which you will be using this study. I want this study to be a help to you, not a hindrance!

Second, I have provided an overview of the history of redemption and revelation. When we study Scripture, it is sometimes easy to get so focused on the original context that we forget to pull back and study a passage with regard to its redemptive-historical context (which considers the question of where we are in salvation history). I hope this overview gives you a sense of the overarching story of Scripture.

Finally, I have provided an overview of what it means to study Christ in all of Scripture. You may wonder why this is necessary for a New Testament book like Luke, but as I will explain, people often teach these books in a legalistic or moralistic way, focusing more on what we are to do than on what Christ has already done for us. It is crucial we connect the passages to Christ first so that we understand our salvation is by grace alone through faith alone.

How to Use This Bible Study

This study is organized into four main parts:

(1) *Purpose:* This brief section introduces you to the passage you will be studying and is meant to guide you into how the lesson applies to your head (knowledge about God), your heart (affection for God), and your hands (service for God). Although it is brief, this is a significant section to read since it tells you in a nutshell what the lesson is all about, giving you the big picture before studying the finer details.

(2) *Personal Study:* This section of questions is meant to help you dig deeply into God's Word so that you might be equipped to worship God, work for His kingdom purposes, and witness for Him to a watching world. To assist you in your study, you may want to have a good study Bible and concordance close at hand. I would encourage

you not to get overwhelmed by the questions or think you have to answer every one of them, but to relax and enjoy the study of God's Word.

(3) *Putting It All Together.* This section is meant to help answer any lingering questions you may still have after your personal study time and assist you in tying things together from the lesson questions. It will prove helpful in cementing in your mind everything you've previously studied and will better prepare you to process things together with your Bible study group.

(4) *Processing It Together.* This section of questions is meant to help you study the Bible in the context of community, sharing what you have learned together so that you might sharpen one another, encourage one another, and pray for one another. Group leaders: Ideally, the women have worked through the previous three sections before coming together as a group. Your first gathering might be a time of fellowship and a discussion of the introduction to the book. Then you can assign the ladies the homework for the first lesson. Encourage them to read the purpose, work through the personal study questions, and read through "Putting It All Together." Remind them to relax and enjoy the study, encouraging them to come to the group time regardless of whether their homework is complete. You may want to star certain questions from your personal study that you want to cover in the group time, as well as highlight any sections from "Putting It All Together" to discuss. I would recommend reviewing the "Purpose" at the beginning of your group time as well. Don't forget to begin and end with prayer and to foster a warm and inviting environment where women can grow together in thinking biblically, being grounded in the truth, and living covenantally, being anchored in the covenant community.

Now that we have taken a look at how this study is organized, let's turn our attention to the big story of the Bible so that we might have a better grasp of the bigger context in which Luke fits.

An Overview of the History of Redemption and Revelation

God has chosen to enter into a covenant relationship with His people. He is the covenant King; we are the covenant servants. As our covenant King, He acts in history, bringing about both His word and His works and providentially ensures that the faith is passed from generation to generation. As His covenant servants, we are to obey His word.

It is only in Christ that the covenant King and the covenant servants meet. Christ is both the Lord of the covenant and the Servant of the covenant. He has come as Lord to extend grace and mercy to God's rebellious servants, and He has come as the Servant of the covenant to perfectly fulfill what God's people could never do, thus bringing blessing to all those who place their faith in Him.

Amazingly, our covenant King has chosen to dwell among His people. Throughout redemptive history we see a progression of God dwelling with His people. First, we observe Him dwelling with Adam and Eve in the garden. Then we see Him meet with His people in the tabernacle and then the temple and dwell with them there. But the climax is when Jesus came to earth and tabernacled among us, fulfilling God's promise, "I will take you as My people, and I will be your God" (Ex. 6:7). When Christ returns He will consummately fulfill this promise as we dwell with the triune God in the new heaven and the new earth forever (Rev. 21:3).

If we are to understand the overarching story of Scripture, we need to recognize the different covenants in the history of redemption: the covenant of redemption, the covenant of works, and the covenant of grace. What theologians call the *covenant of redemption* is described in Ephesians 1:4, which teaches us that God the Father chose us in Christ "before the foundation of the world, that we should be holy and without blame before Him." The Father has appointed our redemption, the Son has accomplished it, and the Holy Spirit applies it.

In Genesis 1–2 we learn of God's covenant with Adam before the fall. This covenant established a relationship between the Creator and the creature that involved *worship* (keeping the Sabbath day holy), *work* (ruling and multiplying), *woman* (marriage and procreation), and the *word of God* (God gave Adam a command when He put him in the garden of Eden to work it and keep it. He could eat of any tree in the garden except one, the tree of the knowledge of good and evil. God told Adam that if he ate of that tree he would die; if he obeyed, he would live). Theologians refer to this prefall covenant with Adam as the *covenant of works*, the *covenant of life*, or the *covenant of creation*.

Tragically, Adam failed to obey, and all mankind fell with him in this first sin. But God sounds a note of grace in Genesis 3:15: death will not have the final word. God promises that He will put enmity between the serpent and the woman, between the serpent's offspring and the woman's offspring. The woman's offspring would bruise the serpent's head, and the serpent would bruise His heel. This is the gospel in seed form. Ultimately, the woman's offspring is Christ. Christ defeated sin and death on the cross, triumphing over all His enemies.

Along with God's blessed promise to the woman that she would continue to produce *seed*, or offspring, the greatest of which is Christ, He also told her that she would experience the curse of *sorrow* with regard to children and the curse of *struggle* with regard to her husband.

God spoke a word to Adam also. He promised the man that he would receive the blessing of *sustenance*. But he would also experience the curse of *sweaty toil* and the *separation of soul and body* in death. Theologians call this postfall covenant the *covenant of grace*. The Westminster Larger Catechism 31 states, "The covenant of grace was made with Christ as the second Adam, and in him with all the elect as his seed." Titus 3:4–7 provides a good summary of this covenant: "But when the kindness and the love of God our Savior toward man appeared, not by works of righteousness which we have done, but according to His mercy He saved us, through the washing of regeneration and renewing of the Holy Spirit, whom He poured out on us abundantly through

Jesus Christ our Savior, that having been justified by His grace we should become heirs according to the hope of eternal life." The covenant of grace includes God's post-fall covenant with Adam (Gen. 3:15), Noah (Gen. 6:17–22; 8:20–22; 9:1–17), Abraham (Gen. 12:1–3; 15:1–21; 17:1–2), Moses (Exodus 19–24 and Deuteronomy), and David (2 Samuel 7), as well as the new covenant, all of which are fulfilled in Jesus Christ (Jer. 31:31–34). Let's take a closer look now at each of these covenants, as well as some other important events that were occurring in redemptive history, so that we have a better grasp of the story of salvation.

After the note of the gospel of grace is sounded to Adam and Eve in Genesis 3:15, we learn of God's covenant with Noah recorded in Genesis 9. The Lord promises that as long as the earth remains, seedtime and harvest, cold and heat, summer and winter, and day and night will continue. This is amazing grace, for it promises that there will be an earth on which the history of salvation will unfold. Just think if there had been no day for Jesus to be born in Bethlehem or to die on the cross!

God's covenant with Noah also promises that though the righteous will be saved, the wicked will be judged, a theme that is predominant all through Scripture. God's original purposes of worship, work, and woman in the prefall covenant with Adam are renewed in the context of the history of redemption. God's covenant with Noah can be summarized by the following: God's *glorious grace* alongside His *glorious justice;* the *genealogical aspect* of the covenant (God will deal with families, not just individuals); the *goodness* of life; and the *general grace* extended to all mankind, including the universe. The sign of this covenant, the rainbow, is most appropriate, then, as it shines God's grace in the midst of the cloudy storm of judgment.

In Genesis 12, 15, 17, and 22, we learn of God's covenant with Abraham, which is later renewed with Isaac and Jacob. First, God promises His *presence.* The crux of the covenant of grace can be summed up in one phrase, "I will walk among you and be your God, and you shall be My people" (Lev. 26:12). Second, God promises Abraham a *people;* God would make him a great nation. Third, God promises Abraham a *posses-sion;* He would give His people the land of Canaan. Fourth, God promises Abraham that he has a bigger *purpose* than he could ever imagine. The nation that came through his seed was to point others to the Lord so that all the families of the earth would be blessed.

In Exodus, we learn of God's covenant with Moses, the mediator of the law God gave to Israel, which can be summarily comprehended in the Ten Commandments. This is the beginning of the theocratic nation of Israel.[1] God brought His people out of slavery in Egypt and into a relationship with Him as servants of the Holy God. As such, they were to be a kingdom of priests and a holy nation (Ex. 19:6). We learn in both Leviticus 26 and Deuteronomy 28 that if they were obedient, they would receive bless-ings (Lev. 26:1–13; Deut. 28:1–14), but if they were disobedient, they would receive

---

1. By a theocratic nation, I mean that Israel's earthly kings, priests, and prophets recognized God as the true King, and as such served to interpret and enforce His laws for the people.

curses (Lev. 26:14–46; Deut. 28:15–68). One of these curses, the greatest, was exile from the land. But even toward the end of Deuteronomy, we see that God made provision for restoration after the exile, which involved the new covenant (Deut. 30:1–10; see also Jer. 31:31–34; Ezek. 37:21, 26).

In fact, Deuteronomy 28–30 is the "CliffsNotes" version of the rest of the Old Testament. First comes blessing, climaxing in the reign of King Solomon (1 Kings 8:24). Then come curses, ultimately resulting in exile from the land (2 Chron. 36:17–21). All the prophets refer to the covenant blessings and curses as they prophesy to Israel and Judah, giving them messages of judgment as well as holding out the hope of blessing. Though the prophets declare that exile is inevitable, they also declare God's faithfulness to His covenant, keeping the promise of the new covenant before them (Deut. 30:1–10; Jer. 31:31–34; Ezek. 37:21, 26).

After Moses died, the Lord raised up Joshua to lead the people into the promised land, which was the place where God would dwell with His people in the temple. Up to this point in redemptive history, the garden of Eden and the tabernacle had been the places where the Lord had temporarily dwelt with His people. The entire book of Joshua centers on the entry into and conquest of the land.

But then Joshua died, and in the book of Judges we see that the people failed to conquer the land as they should have. Instead, they did what was right in their own eyes because there was no king in Israel. The books of Judges and Ruth anticipate the beginning of the monarchy in Israel with King Saul and King David.

In 2 Samuel 7, God makes a covenant with David concerning an eternal kingdom with an eternal Davidic king. First, God promises David a *position*, taking him from being a shepherd of sheep to making him a shepherd king over his people with a great name. Second, God promises David a *place*. Israel would be planted in the land of Canaan. Third, God promises David *peace*. In their own place, Israel would have rest from their enemies. Finally, God promises David *progeny*. The Lord would raise up David's offspring and establish his kingdom forever.

The period of the monarchy climaxes in King Solomon, when the promises are fulfilled in Solomon's prayer of dedication (1 Kings 8:24). Sadly, it didn't take long (within Solomon's reign) for the monarchy to take a turn for the worse (1 Kings 11). Following Solomon's death, the country actually divided into the Northern Kingdom (Israel) and the Southern Kingdom (Judah) in 931 BC (1 Kings 12:16–24).

Elijah and Elisha preached to the Northern Kingdom during this time. Although there were a few good kings, the majority of kings in both Israel and Judah did evil in the sight of the Lord and led the people into rebellion as well. In His grace and mercy, God raised up prophets during this time to prophesy to the people of coming judgment so that they would turn and repent of their wicked ways. Hosea and Amos preached to the Northern Kingdom, while Isaiah and Micah preached to the Southern Kingdom. Joel, Obadiah, and Jonah also preached their messages during this time.

Tragically, the Northern Kingdom did not listen and was taken into captivity by the Assyrians in 722 BC.

A little over one hundred years later, the same thing happened to the Southern Kingdom, except it was the Babylonians who took them into captivity. This involved three different deportations in 605, 597, and 586 BC. In the second of these deportations, Jehoiachin, the last true Davidic king on the throne, was taken, along with the royal family and all the leading classes in Israel, to Babylon. God's promises seemed to be thwarted.

But again, in God's mercy, He raised up both Daniel and Ezekiel to prophesy to the people during the exile (Jeremiah was still prophesying during this time as well). Daniel and Ezekiel spoke messages of both judgment and restoration to the exiles. God would still be faithful to His covenant promise; He would be their God, and they would be His people. Both Jeremiah and Ezekiel spoke of the promised new covenant (Jer. 31:31–34; Ezek. 37:21, 26), inaugurated by Christ during the last Passover (which was also the first Lord's Supper) with His disciples before His death.

The new covenant involved seven different promises. First, God promised His people would *return* to the land of promise. Second, God promised a *restoration of the land.* Third, God promised a *realization* of *each of His previous promises* to Adam, Noah, Abraham, Moses, and David. Fourth, God promised a *renewed heart.* Fifth, God promised the *removal of sin.* Sixth, God promised a *reunion of Israel and Judah under one ruler,* Jesus Christ. Finally, God promised the *realization of redemption* (this was the final covenant, and, as such, it secured redemption).

Following the exile, God raised up the prophets Haggai, Zechariah, and Malachi to continue speaking to His people. Though there is a small fulfillment of a restored temple, people, and land under the leadership of Zerubbabel, Ezra, and Nehemiah, the promises of God could not be completely fulfilled until Jesus Christ came. As Paul so eloquently says, "All the promises of God in Him are Yes, and in Him Amen, to the glory of God through us" (2 Cor. 1:20).

The Gospels record for us the amazing truth of the incarnation. Jesus came to earth as a baby, lived a life of perfect obedience, died for the sins of God's people, was raised as the firstfruits of the resurrection, and ascended to the Father. Acts 2 records that the Holy Spirit was sent on the day of Pentecost to renew the church and establish it by His power.

The new age was inaugurated through Christ and His church, but it awaits its consummation until Christ returns to bring the old age to a complete end with the final judgment and usher in the new heaven and the new earth. In the meantime, the church is to fulfill the Great Commission: "And Jesus came and spoke to them, saying, 'All authority has been given to Me in heaven and on earth. Go therefore and make disciples of all the nations, baptizing them in the name of the Father and of the Son and of the Holy Spirit, teaching them to observe all things that I have commanded you; and lo, I am with you always, even to the end of the age.' Amen" (Matt. 28:18–20; see also Luke 24:47–49).

As we study any passage of Scripture, it is important for us to keep this overview of the history of redemption and revelation in mind. After studying the original context of the passage, we must ask the question, How does this text relate to the history of redemption? In other words, where is it in progressive, redemptive history? Then we must ask, How does this text relate to the climax of redemptive history—the life, death, resurrection, and ascension of our Lord and Savior Jesus Christ? The latter question leads us to the next section we need to consider in order to teach Christ in all of Scripture.

A Christ-Centered Interpretation of Luke

The story of Jesus begins in the Old Testament in the opening chapters of Genesis with the account of creation. As the apostle John so eloquently says, "In the beginning was the Word, and the Word was with God, and the Word was God. He was in the beginning with God. All things were made through Him, and without Him nothing was made that was made. In Him was life, and the life was the light of men. And the light shines in the darkness, and the darkness did not comprehend it" (John 1:1–5). Paul echoes this truth in Colossians 1:15–17: "He is the image of the invisible God, the first-born over all creation. For by Him all things were created that are in heaven and that are on earth, visible and invisible, whether thrones or dominions or principalities or powers. All things were created through Him and for Him. And He is before all things, and in Him all things consist."

Matthew, like John, doesn't begin his gospel account with the birth of Jesus; rather, he opens with the genealogy of Jesus Christ, reaching all the way back through the Old Testament to Abraham. In chapter 3 of his gospel, Luke goes back even further, tracing the story of Jesus all the way to Adam, the son of God. Paul too traces the story of Jesus back to Adam when he says, "And so it is written, 'The first man Adam became a living being.' The last Adam became a life-giving spirit" (1 Cor. 15:45). Even before the fall, the first man Adam pointed forward to the greater and final Adam, Jesus Christ. Luke closes his gospel with Jesus's own account of His story, so since we are learning about Him from Him, we should pay close attention as we read His words in Luke 24.

Two disciples were trying to put the story of Jesus together. They had been in Jerusalem and witnessed the events at the end of Jesus's life. They had seven long miles to try to figure it out as they journeyed from Jerusalem to Emmaus, but they couldn't understand. They were deeply distressed. Their hope had been deflated. They thought that He was the one to redeem Israel, but instead He was crucified and buried. Indeed, the tomb was empty, but Jesus was nowhere to be seen.

Note carefully what Jesus says to them: "'O foolish ones, and slow of heart to believe in all that the prophets have spoken! Ought not the Christ to have suffered these things and to enter into His glory?' And beginning at Moses and all the

Prophets, He expounded to them in all the Scriptures the things concerning Himself" (Luke 24:25–27).

Wouldn't you have liked to walk those seven miles with the three of them? It was the greatest walk those disciples would have in their entire lives as the Master Teacher told His own story, beginning in Genesis and moving all the way through the Prophets. It was the privilege of not only these two Emmaus disciples to hear Jesus tell His story but also the disciples who had been with Him during His earthly ministry. Luke tells us later in the same chapter that Jesus opened their minds to understand the Scriptures, everything written about Him in the Law of Moses and the Prophets and the Psalms. These things had to be fulfilled, and Jesus was telling them that He was the fulfillment (Luke 24:44–47).

He is the second Adam, who did not sin but was obedient to death on the cross. He is the Seed of the woman, who crushed the serpent's head (Gen. 3:15). He is the final Noah, who saved His people through the cross (Eph. 2:16). He is the final Abraham, in whom all the families of the earth are blessed (Acts 2:38–39; 3:25–26; Gal. 3:13–14, 29). He is the final Isaac, who was sacrificed for our sin. He is the final Passover Lamb (Ex. 12:13). He is the final sacrifice, whose blood atoned for our sins (Lev. 16:14–16). He is the final and perfect priest, who is greater than Aaron (Heb. 9:11–12). He is the true Israel, who was tested and tried in the wilderness and obeyed (Matt. 4:1–11). He is the one lifted up to deliver sinners from death (Num. 21:9). He is the Prophet greater than Moses (Deut. 18:15–22). He is the one who gives grace to covenant breakers (Deut. 27:1–26). He is the ark of the covenant and the blood on the mercy seat (Heb. 9:1–14). He is the true bread of life and the light of the world on the golden lampstand (John 6:48, 51; 8:12). He is the Commander of the army of the Lord (Josh. 5:14). He is the final Judge, who never fell into sin but delivered His people by taking their judgment for them (2 Cor. 5:21). He is the final kinsman-redeemer greater than Boaz (Ruth 3:12–13). He is the final Psalmist, who leads His people in praise to God (Heb. 2:12). He is the final Davidic King, who reigns in perfect justice and righteousness (John 18:37). He is the final Solomon, who not only is full of wisdom but is wisdom Himself (1 Cor. 1:30). He is the final Prophet, who suffered for His people and did so without opening His mouth in retaliation (Isaiah 53). And He is the Great Shepherd of the sheep (Ezek. 34:11–24).

Peter is proof that Jesus opened His disciples' minds to understand that day, for in Acts 2 we read his sermon, which he begins by citing David's words in Psalm 16:8–11 and ends by citing his words in Psalm 110:1. He speaks these words in between:

> Men and brethren, let me speak freely to you of the patriarch David, that he is both dead and buried, and his tomb is with us to this day. Therefore, being a prophet, and knowing that God had sworn with an oath to him that of the fruit of his body, according to the flesh, He would raise up the Christ to sit on his throne, he, foreseeing this, spoke concerning the resurrection of the Christ, that His soul was not left in

Hades, nor did His flesh see corruption. This Jesus God has raised up, of which we are all witnesses. Therefore being exalted to the right hand of God, and having received from the Father the promise of the Holy Spirit, He poured out this which you now see and hear. (Acts 2:29–33)

We cannot tell the story of Jesus in any way we please. We must learn from Jesus Himself and tell the story beginning with Genesis through Deuteronomy, moving through the Prophets and the Psalms, and then the New Testament Gospels and Letters, closing with Revelation, where the end of the story is told: "Now I saw a new heaven and a new earth, for the first heaven and the first earth had passed away" (Rev. 21:1). The end of the story isn't really the end, for we will spend an eternity worshiping Him "who is and who was and who is to come,… Jesus Christ, the faithful witness, the firstborn from the dead, and the ruler over the kings of the earth," the One who loves us and has freed us from our sins by His blood and "has made us kings and priests to His God and Father" (Rev. 1:4–6).

We have looked at some key texts, so now let's look at some key phrases for identifying the continuity between the Old and New Testaments. We might say that we go from Old Testament promise to New Testament fulfillment, or from Old Testament problem (sinners in need of a Savior) to New Testament solution (the Savior comes), or from Old Testament anticipation to New Testament realization, but not just a realization—a far-surpassing realization. For example, Jesus Christ is not just a greater Moses, Samson, prophet, priest, or king, but the greatest and final Moses, Samson, prophet, priest, and king. Furthermore, the Lord of history designs historical persons, offices, institutions, and events to foreshadow the full redemption to come. Thus, He foreshadows His great work of redemption in both words and works (events).[2]

The climax in all of Scripture is the gospel—the life, death, resurrection, and ascension of Jesus Christ. All the Old Testament writers look toward this climax. All the New Testament writers look both back to this climax and forward to the consummation of the kingdom, Christ's second coming, which was inaugurated at His first coming. There are really four main questions, then, when we are studying Scripture: (1) What is the original context of this passage? (2) Where are we in the history of redemption in this text? (3) How does this text relate to the gospel? (4) How do I apply this text to my life right now in light of where I am in redemptive history?

These questions keep us from a legalistic reading of the text ("Do this, and you will live"), a moralistic reading of the text ("Be a good person, and you will be saved"), a therapeutic reading of the text ("I'm good, you're good, God is good, everything is okay"), and an allegorical reading of the text ("I'm going to make this text refer to Christ no matter what interpretive principles I have to break!"). Instead, we will be women who glean a Christ-centered message.

---

2. Dennis Johnson, *Him We Proclaim: Preaching Christ from All the Scriptures* (Phillipsburg, N.J.: P&R, 2007), 225–26.

Introduction to Luke

If there is one thing people in our world today are desperately craving, continually seeking, and rarely finding, it is certainty. Most people wake up in the morning uncertain of who they are, where they stand in relation to this world and other people, and where they are going. The questions of who they are, whether they are loved, whether they have any purpose in life, and whether they have any future gnaws at their souls continually, leading many to despair and disillusionment.

Furthermore, the truthfulness and trustworthiness of Scripture are under attack in various spheres of influence, including many seminaries, Bible colleges, and churches all across our nation. It seems that we are in a "certainty crisis" that will be resolved only when we find truth or, more accurately, when Truth finds us. Jesus said, "I am the way, the truth, and the life. No one comes to the Father except through Me" (John 14:6). Luke wrote his gospel so that you and I might have certainty concerning the faith. He writes with passion and precision, giving an orderly account of Jesus's life, death, resurrection, and ascension.

The Author, Date, and Historical Background of Luke

The divine author of Scripture is God Himself: "All Scripture is given by inspiration of God, and is profitable for doctrine, for reproof, for correction, for instruction in righteousness, that the man of God may be complete, thoroughly equipped for every good work" (2 Tim. 3:16–17). But the Holy Spirit used human authors to speak and write the word of God (2 Peter 1:21).

There are several reasons that Luke, "the beloved physician" (Col. 4:14), is considered the author of the gospel that bears his name. First, the book tells us that the author was not an eyewitness but instead received facts handed down to him by eyewitnesses of the life and ministry of Jesus (Luke 1:1–4). Second, it is clear that the author has a great interest in the Gentiles, and Luke was most likely a Gentile. Third, the author of Luke is the same as the author of the book of Acts (Acts 1:1–5), and the "we" passages in the second half of Acts point to a companion of Paul, narrowing the choices down to a small handful of people, one of whom is Luke. Fourth, no one in the early church argued against Luke being the author. Since the early church tended to attribute the authorship of New Testament books to apostles, their acceptance of the authorship of Luke, who was not an eyewitness of Jesus's life and ministry, underscores the validity of ascribing the gospel to him.

There are strong arguments to date Luke in the early 60s AD. First, Acts (Luke's sequel) does not mention many key historical events from AD 65–70. Second, Acts ends with Paul's imprisonment in Rome instead of his death, around AD 62. Third, Luke makes no mention of Jesus's prophecy of the fall of Jerusalem being fulfilled in AD 70, certainly something he would have done if he were writing after that time.[1] So a date in the early 60s is most likely.

Luke was writing at a time when the Jews had rejected Jesus and an increasingly large number of Gentiles were turning to the faith. In the midst of such Jewish rejection, both Jews and Gentiles needed to be reminded to stay faithful, committed, and expectant of what the covenant God was doing in redemptive history.

The Purpose of Luke

Luke writes to encourage people who are questioning and doubting the truth to remain committed to following the God who has sovereignly ordained all things and in whom they can place their trust so that they may have certainty concerning the faith. He was aware that there were many compilations of the life and ministry of Jesus in his day, but he was compelled to write yet another one for several specific reasons. First, "it seemed good" to Luke, "having had perfect understanding of all things from the very first, to write" (Luke 1:3). Second, he wanted to write "an orderly account" (v. 3). Third, he was writing to a specific person, "most excellent Theophilus" (v. 3), whose name means "beloved of God."[2] Fourth, Luke was writing so that Theophilus (and all of God's children) may have "certainty of those things in which you were instructed" (v. 4).

Luke's gospel is the longest of the four Gospels in the New Testament, and he gives us much information that is not included in any of the others. The parables of the good Samaritan (10:25–37), the prodigal son (15:11–32), and the shrewd manager (16:1–9) are found only in Luke. Jesus's encounter with Zacchaeus (19:1–10), raising the widow's son at Nain (7:11–17), His words on the cross asking God to forgive His enemies (23:34), and His assuring word to the dying criminal that he would be with Him in paradise today (23:43) are found only in Luke. Only Luke begins his gospel

---

1. D. A. Carson and Douglas J. Moo, *An Introduction to the New Testament* (Grand Rapids: Zondervan, 2005), 207–8.

2. Philip Graham Ryken, *Luke*, vol. 2, *Chapters 13–24*, Reformed Expository Commentary (Phillipsburg, N.J.: P&R, 2009), 13.

with a formal prologue, in which he declares why he is writing, addresses his gospel to a particular person, and states his aim (1:1–4), and Luke alone writes a sequel to his gospel (the book of Acts).

Luke and Acts combine to show God bringing His promises in redemptive history to fulfillment in the life, death, resurrection, and ascension of Jesus Christ and in the renewal of the church, creating one new man in place of the two, uniting Jews and Gentiles through the reconciliation of the cross (Eph. 2:14–16). Luke emphasizes the movement toward Jerusalem, while Acts describes a movement away from Jerusalem.[3]

Luke quotes from the Pentateuch (the first five books of the Bible) ten times, from the Prophets seven times, and from the Psalms seven times.[4] Furthermore, there are about 439 Old Testament allusions in the book of Luke.[5] It is clear that Luke sees the promises of the Old Testament Scriptures fulfilled in the words and works of Jesus Christ, the Son of God.

The purpose of Luke becomes even clearer when we take a look at some key verses from the book:

- Inasmuch as many have taken in hand to set in order a narrative of those things which have been fulfilled among us, just as those who from the beginning were eyewitnesses and ministers of the word delivered them to us, it seemed good to me also, having had perfect understanding of all things from the very first, to write to you an orderly account, most excellent Theophilus, that you may know the certainty of those things in which you were instructed. (1:1–4)

- The Spirit of the LORD is upon Me,
  Because He has anointed Me
  To preach the gospel to the poor;
  He has sent Me to heal the brokenhearted,
  To proclaim liberty to the captives
  And recovery of sight to the blind,
  To set at liberty those who are oppressed;
  To proclaim the acceptable year of the LORD. (4:18–19)

- For the Son of Man has come to seek and to save that which was lost. (19:10)

- And beginning at Moses and all the Prophets, He expounded to them in all the Scriptures the things concerning Himself. (Luke 24:27; see also vv. 44–47)

---

3. Carson and Moo, *Introduction to the New Testament*, 202.

4. David W. Pao and Eckhard J. Schnabel, "Luke," in *Commentary on the New Testament Use of the Old Testament*, ed. G. K. Beale and D. A. Carson (Grand Rapids: Baker Academic, 2007), 251.

5. Pao and Schnabel, "Luke," 251.

An Outline of Luke

Different and detailed outlines of Luke can be found in commentaries, but for this Bible study, I suggest the following:

     I. Births of John and Jesus (1:1–2:52)
    II. Baptism and Temptation (3:1–4:13)
   III. Beginning of Jesus's Ministry in Galilee (4:14–9:50)
   IV. Befriending Sinners on the Way to Jerusalem (9:51–19:44)
    V. Betrayed in Jerusalem (19:45–24:53)

Each lesson will further divide this broad outline into smaller parts, but for now make note of these major divisions as you prepare to study Luke.

Perhaps you are feeling uncertain about your faith. Perhaps the storms of chronic illness, the death of a loved one, infertility, a financial crisis, or the like have washed over you like a flood and you feel like you are drowning in a sea of despair and disillusionment. Maybe the faith that you learned as a little girl seems a thing of the distant past, and you wonder if you can ever believe again as you did then. Perhaps a certain teacher, classmate, or friend has questioned your faith, and you are not sure why you believe what you believe or how to give a defense of your faith. Or maybe you know for sure what you believe, but you need your belief to be strengthened in the midst of a world hostile to the gospel, your own failures and sin, and Satan's temptations.

I invite you to open up the pages of Luke with me. There we will find exactly what the authors have promised. Our covenant God has promised to lead us into truth. Luke has promised to give us an orderly account so that we might have certainty regarding our faith. We will not be disappointed. The divine Author behind the human author has given us a book that we can cling to in the midst of seasons of doubt and in a world full of uncertainty—a book that exalts our Lord and Savior Jesus Christ, the One to whom all Scripture points.

Good News of Great Joy

Luke 1–2

Purpose...

Head. What do I need to know from this passage in Scripture?

- God calls Elizabeth and Mary to be the mothers of John the Baptist and Jesus, respectively, to fulfill His covenant and further the history of redemption.

Heart. How does what I learn from this passage affect my internal relationship with the Lord?

- I am a kingdom disciple who, by God's grace, has recognized Jesus Christ as both Savior and Lord of my life.

Hands. How does what I learn from this passage translate into action for God's kingdom?

- I will study Scripture so that I can have certainty regarding my faith and nurture others in the certainty of the faith.

- I will respond to God's plan for my life in submission, acceptance, and trust.

- I will magnify the Lord in my suffering and teach others to do the same.

- I will devote myself to worshiping the Lord and proclaiming His salvation.

- I will pray for those under my care, asking the Lord to increase their wisdom, stature, and favor with God and man.

Personal Study . . .

Pray. Ask that God will open up your heart and mind as you study His Word. This is His story of redemption that He has revealed to us, and the Holy Spirit is our teacher.

Ponder the Passage. Read Luke in its entirety. Then reread Luke 1–2.

- *Point:* What is the point of this passage? How does this relate to the point of the entire book?

- *Persons:* Who are the main people involved in this passage? What characterizes them?

- *Persons of the Trinity:* Where do you see God the Father, God the Son, and God the Holy Spirit in this passage?

- *Puzzling Parts:* Are there any parts of the passage that you don't quite understand or that seem interesting or confusing?

Put It in Perspective.

- *Place in Scripture:* What is the original context of this text? What is the redemptive-historical context—what has or hasn't happened in redemptive history at this point in Scripture? How does this text connect to Christ?

The following questions will help you if you got stuck on any of the previous questions, and they will help you dig a little deeper into the text, putting it all into perspective.

1. **1:1–4.** (a) In verse 1 why is the word "fulfilled" significant (see Luke 24:44–47 also)? What is Luke affirming from the very beginning of his gospel?

   (b) Why is Luke writing?

2. **1:5–7.** (a) Using a study Bible or another Bible resource, look up Herod, king of Judea. Also read Matthew's account of King Herod's actions in Matthew 2:1–18. What do you learn?

(b) What is Zacharias's (see 1 Chron. 24:1–19) and Elizabeth's lineage, and how does Luke characterize this couple?

(c) What did Elizabeth have in common with other important women in Scripture (see Gen. 18:11; Judg. 13:2; 1 Sam. 1:2)?

3. 1:8–17. (a) Read Proverbs 16:33. How does God use the lot to move forward His plan of redemption?

(b) What were the people doing while Zacharias was offering incense and praying, and who appears to Zacharias while he is serving in the Most Holy Place?

(c) In light of Exodus 30:1–10 and the angel's announcement, why is Zacharias's location significant?

(d) What is Zacharias's initial response, and what does the angel say to him?

(e) List the different points that the angel makes, looking up the following verses as you do so: Numbers 6:3 (v. 15); Judges 13:4, 7 (v. 15); 1 Kings 17 (v. 17); and Malachi 4:6 (v. 17).

4. 1:18–25. (a) What is Zacharias's second response to the angel? Compare this with Genesis 15:8; 17:17; and 18:9–15.

(b) How does the angel respond to Zacharias's question, and why is this significant (see Dan. 8:16–27; 9:20–27)?

(c) How did God discipline Zacharias?

(d) Contrast Elizabeth's response with Zacharias's, with Rachel's in Genesis 30:22–24, and with Hannah's in 1 Samuel 1:20, 27; 2:1–10.

5. **1:26–38.** (a) What do you learn about Joseph and Mary?

(b) How does Gabriel greet Mary, and why is this significant?

(c) Compare and contrast Mary's response to the angel with Zacharias's initial response in verse 12.

(d) What does Gabriel tell Mary (see also Gen. 49:8–12; 2 Sam. 7:11–13, 16; Isa. 7:14; 9:6; Dan. 2:44; Luke 24:44–47; 2 Cor. 1:20)?

(e) Contrast Mary's second response to the angel with Zacharias's second response in Luke 1:18, and Gabriel's answer to Mary's question with his response to Zacharias's question in Luke 1:19–20. How do we see God's grace displayed to Mary?

(f) Contrast Mary's third response with Sarah's (Gen. 18:9–15) and with Zacharias's (1:18–20).

6. 1:39–45. (a) How did Mary respond to the angel's message and God's sign to her (Elizabeth's conception and pregnancy)?

(b) What do we know about Judah from Genesis 49:8–12 that relates to the coming of John and Jesus?

(c) What did John do when Elizabeth heard the greeting of Mary (1:41a), and how does this relate to his calling (1:13–17)?

(d) How is Elizabeth being filled with the Holy Spirit a precursor of the fulfillment of Joel 2:28–29, which Luke records in Acts 2 (the day of Pentecost)? Of what does Elizabeth prophesy (1:42–45)?

(e) What are the reasons behind the blessings in verses 42–45 (see Deut. 28:4; Pss. 110:1; 127:3; Mark 8:29)?

7. 1:46–56. (a) How does Mary's song reflect Hannah's song in 1 Samuel 2:1–10? If you have time, compare verse 46 to Psalm 34:1–3; verse 47 to Isaiah 61:10–11 and Habakkuk 3:18; verse 48 to 1 Samuel 1:11 and Genesis 12:3; verse 49 to Isaiah 57:15; verse 50 to Deuteronomy 5:10 and 7:9; verse 51 to Isaiah 51:9 and Daniel 4:37; and verses 54–55 to Isaiah 41:8–10 and Genesis 17:19.

(b) How long did Mary remain with Elizabeth? In light of Luke 1:26, 39, at what point in Elizabeth's pregnancy would Mary have left? Where did Mary go? What risks were involved in this (see Matt. 1:18–19)?

8. 1:57–66. (a) How does verse 57 fulfill verse 13, and how does verse 58 fulfill verse 14?

(b) How did Elizabeth and Zacharias display their faith in God's promises by what they named their son?

(c) What happened immediately when Zacharias named his son, and how did this fulfill the angel's words in verse 20?

(d) What was the first thing Zacharias did when he was able to speak? How did the people respond, and why?

(e) Of what is Zacharias being filled with the Holy Spirit a precursor (see Joel 2:28–32; Acts 2)?

9. 1:67–80. (a) How does Zacharias view his son in light of God's Son? To answer this, compare the following verses:
- verse 68 with Pss. 106:48; 111:9
- verse 69 with 2 Sam. 22:3
- verse 71 with 2 Sam. 22:18
- verse 72 with Gen. 15:1–21; 26:1–5; 35:10–12; Ex. 2:24
- verse 73 with Gen. 22:16–17
- verses 74–75 with Ex. 7:16; 1 Kings 9:4–5
- verse 76 with Mal. 3:1
- verse 78 with Mal. 4:2
- verse 79 with Isa. 9:2; 42:6–7

(b) Compare Luke 1:80 with Genesis 21:8; Judges 13:24; 1 Samuel 2:21, 26; and Luke 2:40, 52. What do you learn?

10. 2:1–7.(a) What town did Joseph go to, and why?

(b) Look up 1 Samuel 20:6 and Micah 5:1–2. Why was it important that Joseph obey Caesar Augustus's decree? How did God use this power-hungry ruler to move forward His plan of redemption?

(c) Why is the term *betrothed* important even though Mary and Joseph were married at this point? What still has not occurred to ensure that Jesus has a virgin birth?

(d) How is Luke 2:6–7 a fulfillment of God's covenant with Abraham (Genesis 15) and with David (2 Samuel 7)? How is it a fulfillment of Micah 5:1–2?

(e) Consider Jesus's place of birth in light of Philippians 2:6–7. What do you learn?

11. 2:8–14. (a) In what country were the shepherds who were visited by the angels, and what were they doing when the angel of the Lord appeared to them? What do the people mentioned in Exodus 3:1–2; 1 Samuel 17:15; and Amos 1:1 have in common with them?

(b) To what does the "glory of the Lord" refer in the Old Testament (see Ex. 16:10; Lev. 9:6; Num. 14:10; 1 Kings 8:11; Ps. 138:5; Isa. 58:8; Ezek. 1:28)?

(c) What is the shepherds' response? Compare this with Zacharias's and Mary's response in Luke 1:12, 29.

(d) What three titles are used of Jesus by the angel in verse 11, and how do these anticipate Jesus's ministry?

(e) What is the sign that was given to the shepherds?

(f) What appeared with the angel, and why?

12. 2:15–20. (a) What was the shepherds' response to the angels' song and the angel of the Lord's message? Compare this with Mary's response to the sign in 1:39.

(b) What did the shepherds tell Mary and Joseph? How did this confirm the message that the angel had spoken to them?

(c) Compare the shepherds' response with the response of those who heard it and with Mary's response.

13. 2:21–35. (a) Why was it important that Jesus be circumcised (see Gen. 17:9–14; 21:4; Lev. 12:3; Matt. 1:1)?

(b) How did the name that Mary and Joseph gave to Jesus fulfill God's word through the angel and show their submission to God's will?

(c) Read Exodus 13:2, 12, 15 and Leviticus 12:8 as background for verses 22–24. What do you learn?

(d) What do you learn about Simeon in verses 25–28?

(e) How did Simeon recognize that Jesus was the fulfillment of God's promises (compare vv. 30–31 with Isa. 40:5; v. 32a with Isa. 49:6; 52:10; 56:1b; and v. 32b with Isa. 60:1–2; John 8:12; Rom. 9:4)?

(f) How did Mary and Joseph respond to Simeon's song?

(g) Compare Simeon's final words to Mary (vv. 34–35) with Isaiah 8:14–15 and 28:16. How is verse 35 ultimately fulfilled (see John 19:16–27)?

14. 2:36–40. (a) What do you learn about Anna?

(b) How does the phrase "redemption in Jerusalem" reflect Isaiah 52:8–10?

(c) Why was it important that Mary and Joseph perform everything according to the law?

(d) To what place did Mary and Joseph return to raise Jesus, and how does Luke summarize the first twelve years of Jesus's life (see also Matthew 2)?

15. 2:41–52. (a) How is verse 49 the climax of these verses?

(b) Compare Mary's focus and words to Jesus with Jesus's focus and words to Mary. In the end, what did Jesus do and why (see Ex. 20:12; Matt. 5:17)?

(c) How does Luke summarize the years of Jesus's life from the age of twelve to the time of Jesus's public ministry?

Principles and Points of Application

16. **1:1–56.** (a) Who do you need to pray for—that he or she will have certainty regarding the gospel message? Who do you need to proclaim the gospel to, and when will you do this?

(b) What are some steps you can take to increase your time studying Scripture so that you receive certainty of God's promises? What are you teaching those under your care about studying Scripture?

(c) How are you handling your present trials? When God answers your prayers, are you making sure you glorify and thank Him?

(d) What encourages or challenges you regarding Mary's response to God's plan as you think about how His plans are unfolding for you?

(e) How can we point to Christ in the midst of our own joyous blessings and exalt His name?

17. **1:57–2:20.** (a) Consider that your obedience to the Lord may encourage others to wonder at Him. Describe a time when someone else's obedience to the Lord made you wonder at Him.

(b) How are you training your children, or others in your sphere of influence, to glorify God with their lives?

18. 2:21–52. (a) How do you respond to your circumstances when they are inconvenient or undesirable?

(b) How have you responded to God's revelation in Scripture?

(c) How can parents be faithful to God's requirements for training their children? How can church members be faithful to assist parents in training their children according to Scripture?

Putting It All Together . . .

If there is one thing the world, our flesh, and Satan shout to us it is, "Glorify your own name!" Whether it's in marriage, parenting, ministry, the workplace, relationships, sports, or hobbies, we are told to make much of ourselves. But God's word sends a different message: "Whether you eat or drink, or whatever you do, do all to the glory of God" (1 Cor. 10:31).

In God's grace and mercy, He is sanctifying a people to glorify His name by pointing away from their own power, prestige, and position and to His Son, Jesus Christ. In this lesson we will learn about six such people—Elizabeth, Mary, Zacharias, John, Simeon, and Anna. These men and women, by God's grace, fulfilled humankind's greatest purpose—to glorify God and enjoy a relationship with Him forever.

I. Birth Announcement: John (1:1–25)

At the beginning of his gospel, Luke tells us his purpose in writing to Theophilus. Although we don't have any more information about Theophilus from Scripture or other resources, he was probably an actual person, most likely a high-ranking official of the Roman Empire since he is called "most excellent" (1:3). His name means "beloved of God" or "lover of God," and he represents all those who are God's chosen children.[1]

---

1. Philip Graham Ryken, *Luke*, vol. 1, *Chapters 1–12*, Reformed Expository Commentary (Phillipsburg, N.J.: P&R, 2009), 13.

Luke declares from the beginning what he will tell us again at the end (24:44–47). Jesus is the fulfillment of all that the Old Testament has promised. Luke wants Theophilus and all who read his gospel to have certainty concerning the faith. He was not the first person to write about the things Christ had accomplished. Many scholars believe that Luke used the Gospel of Mark as one of his sources. Nor was he an eyewitness or minister of the Word from the beginning. And yet, by God's grace, it seemed good to Luke, having followed things closely for some time past, to write an orderly account for Theophilus's certainty.

Luke was a traveling companion to the apostle Paul and had most likely interviewed many of the eyewitnesses of Christ's life during his travels and ministries. His name is Greek, so he was probably a Gentile. This sheds light on why he was so concerned to write a gospel that focused on Jesus as the fulfillment of the promise to Abraham to bless all the families of the earth through his seed (Gen. 12:3). Luke was not just a minister of the written Word though; he was also a minister of the living Word, Jesus Christ. His own certainty regarding Christ's life, death, resurrection, and ascension bound him to share it with those who had any doubts about the faith.

As a physician (Col. 4:14), Luke knew the gospel was the greatest medication to heal anyone's uncertain soul.[2] Certainly the beloved physician drew his strength from the greater Physician as he carefully recorded the healings Jesus performed for those who were ill, close to death, or already dead.

Luke begins his gospel by telling us the historical context. King Herod was king of Judea, a rule that lasted from 37 to 4 BC. Herod was famous for his architecture, building, and, most importantly, for rebuilding the temple in Jerusalem. Sadly, he was a cruel oppressor. Israel was oppressed almost as severely under King Herod as they were under Pharaoh during the time of the exodus (see Ex. 1:8–14, 22; 5:1–23).[3] So the time was ripe for a second exodus, which God would orchestrate through the death and resurrection of His Son.

When King Herod heard about Jesus's birth, he secretly summoned the wise men to search for the child so that when they found Him, he could also go and worship Him (Matt. 2:7–8). But King Herod had no intention of worshiping Jesus. Instead, he had every intention of putting the Christ child to death so that He would not grow up to be king. God warned the wise men not to return to Herod (v. 12). When Herod learned that the wise men had tricked him, he became furious and ordered that all the male children in Bethlehem and its districts who were two years old or younger be put to death, a fulfillment of Jeremiah 31:15 (vv. 16–18). But Herod could not stop God's plan. There was still a remnant who believed in the covenant promises that God had given to Abraham.

There was a couple who were part of this remnant, Zacharias and Elizabeth. From the beginning, Luke expresses how important this couple is to God's plan of

---

2. Ryken, *Luke*, 1:15.
3. R. C. Sproul, *A Walk with God: Luke* (Fearn, Ross-shire, Scotland: Christian Focus, 2011), 15.

redemption, as evidenced by the meaning of their names. Zacharias means "Yahweh has remembered again," and Elizabeth means "my God is the one by whom I swear" or "my God is fortune."[4]

It is important to note that Zacharias is a priest. Because there were so many priests at that time, serving in the temple to burn incense and pray on behalf of the nation of Israel was a once-in-a-lifetime opportunity. That Zacharias was chosen to do this was an immense privilege and would have been one of the greatest highlights of his life.

Zacharias was married to Elizabeth, who was descended from the priestly line of Aaron. Both righteous and obedient to the Lord, they were also barren (Luke 1:6–7). Barren women in that day were rejected by society and considered to be under God's judgment. But far from judging Zacharias and Elizabeth, the Lord had heard their pleas for a baby, which had seemingly gone unanswered, and was about to turn their barrenness to blessing. As He did with Abraham and Sarah (Genesis 18), Jacob and his wives (Genesis 29–30), and Elkanah and Hannah (1 Samuel 1), He was going to use Zacharias and Elizabeth to prepare the way for His Son. Be encouraged, dear believer—the providential hand of God has orchestrated your suffering for His purposes and your good.

Zacharias was inside the Most Holy Place praying while the people were praying outside the temple. It was at this time that an angel of the Lord, Gabriel (Luke 1:19), appeared to him, standing on the right side of the altar of incense. Zacharias, filled with fear, quickly received the angel's exhortation not to be afraid, for his prayer had been heard and Elizabeth would bear a son. He was to name him John, meaning "Yahweh has been gracious."[5]

Remarkably, John would be the one to prepare the way for the salvation of Israel in Jesus Christ. He would bring great joy and gladness to his parents and many others because he would be great before the Lord. He would be set apart from his mother's womb as one filled with the Holy Spirit who followed the rules of the Nazirite (Num. 6:3; Judg. 13:4, 7). He would turn many of the children of Israel to the Lord their God (see Mal. 2:6).[6] He would serve in the spirit and power of Elijah, who worked miracles and called others to repent. Although John didn't work miracles, he did call others to repent.[7] And he would "turn the hearts of the fathers to the children" (see Mal. 4:5–6) and the disobedient to the wisdom of the just.

By citing Malachi 4:6, Luke alerts the reader to the fact that after four hundred years of silence between the Old and New Testaments, God raised up one more prophet in order to prepare the people for His Son, the Prophet of all prophets. In

---

4. Darrell L. Bock, *Luke*, vol. 1, *1:1–9:50*, Baker Exegetical Commentary on the New Testament (Grand Rapids: Baker, 1994), 76.

5. Bock, *Luke*, 1:83.

6. Pao and Schnabel, "Luke," 258.

7. Bock, *Luke*, 1:88.

fulfillment of the Davidic covenant, God was bringing the final and greatest Davidic King, Jesus Christ, into the world and through John's ministry was preparing the way for His arrival (see 2 Sam. 7:12–16).

Because Zacharias responded in doubt, asking the angel for a sign instead of believing what God had said, the Lord disciplined him, making him mute until John's birth. But before the angel announced the consequence for Zacharias's doubt, he announced who he was: "I am Gabriel, who stands in the presence of God, and was sent to speak to you and bring you these glad tidings" (Luke 1:19).

Significantly, Gabriel was the angel who had told Daniel about the seventy weeks that were decreed for Israel and Jerusalem,

> To finish the transgression,
> To make an end of sins,
> To make reconciliation for iniquity,
> To bring in everlasting righteousness,
> To seal up vision and prophecy,
> And to anoint the Most Holy. (Dan. 9:24)

As one steeped in the Old Testament Scriptures, Zacharias would likely have wondered if the time had come for these words to be fulfilled.

Zacharias had just completed one of the most significant days of his life. He had heard one of the most incredible messages from an angel of God, receiving hope on behalf of all the people, and had gotten news that his old, barren wife would finally have a son. But sadly, he couldn't talk to anyone about it. Instead, he had to write his news on a tablet. Thankfully, the Lord disciplines His children in order to prune them so that good fruit can grow (Heb. 12:10), and this would certainly be true in Zacharias's life.

Some time after Zacharias and Elizabeth had returned home from Jerusalem, the Lord fulfilled His promise. For the first five months of pregnancy, Elizabeth did not go out in public. Remember, she had been ostracized as a barren woman. But now the Lord had taken away her reproach (see also Gen. 30:23). The next time she appeared in public, she would be visibly pregnant, and the entire world would see that she was, indeed, favored of the Lord. In the meantime, she responded to God's grace with words of adoration and praise. She believed what God had promised and gave Him the glory for what He had done in her life.

II. Birth Announcement: Jesus (1:26–38)

About six months after Gabriel appeared to Zacharias to tell him that Elizabeth would bear a son, he appeared to a young virgin named Mary to tell her that she also would have a son. To show that His kingdom is characterized by humility, God chose a humble young virgin and the small, unknown city of Nazareth in Galilee to bring His Son into the world.[8]

When Gabriel came to Mary, he greeted her in a marvelous and gracious way: "Rejoice, highly favored one, the Lord is with you; blessed are you among women!" (Luke 1:28). Mary was troubled because she did not understand this greeting, so Gabriel told her not to be afraid, for she had found favor (grace) with God. God had chosen Mary to bear His Son, Jesus, which means "the Lord is salvation." This would fulfill Isaiah's prophecy: "Therefore the Lord Himself will give you a sign: Behold, the virgin shall conceive and bear a Son, and shall call His name Immanuel" (Isa. 7:14).

Gabriel's words to Mary reveal five important things about Jesus. First, He would be great. In the Old Testament, every time the word *great* is used without qualification, it almost always refers to God.[9] So Gabriel saying that Jesus would be great affirms His deity. Second, He would be called "the Son of the Highest." This title is a pronouncement of the second person of the Trinity, the Son of God the Father. Third, Jesus would receive the throne of His father David in fulfillment of God's covenant with David (2 Sam. 7:1–17). Gabriel now announced the fulfillment of the promise for which Israel had been waiting and praying for hundreds of years. The kingdom of God was about to break into this world. Fourth, He would reign over the house of Jacob forever, a fulfillment of Genesis 49:8–12. Fifth, in fulfillment of the Davidic covenant, Daniel's prophecy of an everlasting kingdom (Dan. 2:44), and Isaiah's prophecy of a son given as the Prince of Peace and an everlasting ruler (Isa. 9:6–7), Jesus's kingdom would know no end.

In contrast to Zacharias, Mary responded to Gabriel's message with belief. She didn't doubt God's word but only wondered how He was going to accomplish it. How could a virgin have a baby? For the Lord, nothing is impossible (see Gen. 18:14). His ways are miraculous and mysterious. For Jesus to be 100 percent divine and 100 percent human, He had to be conceived by the Holy Spirit and born of the virgin Mary. The Holy Spirit would come upon Mary and the power of the Most High would overshadow her so that the child would be holy.

Unlike Zacharias, Mary did not ask for a sign, but the Lord, in His grace, gave her one. Gabriel told her that her relative Elizabeth was in her sixth month of pregnancy. He reminded Mary that Elizabeth had been barren. But barrenness has never been a barrier in the plan of God. You may be literally barren today, longing for a child. Or you might see no fertile ground in your life and ministry. You may be experiencing a barren period of financial loss or physical pain. Be encouraged, dear believer, by Mary's faith. She had every reason to fear, but she responded to God's word by faith. We too must place ourselves in God's hands, surrendering our desires and dreams to Him.

---

8. The region of Galilee was about forty-five to eighty-five miles north of Jerusalem and just north of Samaria, and about thirty miles wide. Bock, *Luke*, 1:106.

9. Ryken, *Luke*, 1:32.

III. Blessed among Women (1:39–45)

Mary didn't waste any time going to see Elizabeth. The trip to Zacharias and Elizabeth's hometown in the hill country of Judah was not an easy one. Mary would have traveled almost one hundred long, hard miles to get there through rugged wasteland.[10] Her journey would have given her plenty of time to ponder the angel's visit to her, the words Gabriel spoke, and her commitment to be the servant of the Lord. Did she recall the promises of the Old Testament and how the child within her womb would fulfill them? Did she identify with Sarah, Rachel, Leah, Ruth, and Hannah, chosen women to carry on the godly line? In the moments of solitary silence, she surely gave honor and praise to the Lord.

When Mary came to Zacharias's house and greeted Elizabeth, Elizabeth felt her child leap in her womb. The great prophet John and the greatest Prophet Jesus were "meeting" for the first time! God filled Elizabeth with His Spirit at that moment, revealing to her that salvation had come to her in Jesus Christ. Although Elizabeth's words are printed as prose in our Bible translations, they are actually a short poem.[11] Elizabeth recognized the unique role that God had given to Mary among women. She also recognized the blessedness of the fruit of Mary's womb. In addition, Elizabeth recognized, by God's grace, that Mary's child was her Lord, referring to Him as "my Lord" (Luke 1:43). Finally, Elizabeth recognized Mary's faith in the fulfillment of the promises of the Lord. How sweet the fellowship between these two women must have been!

Remarkably, Elizabeth, so close to giving birth after many long years of barrenness, placed all of her focus on the Christ child who was within Mary's womb. And she encouraged young Mary in her faith, commending her. Such spiritual mothering is a pattern that should be replicated in the church. Dear older woman, encourage the younger women in your church. Dear younger woman, seek the wise counsel of the older women in your congregation. We were not meant to be lone rangers. We need both mothers and daughters in the faith for our edification and encouragement.

IV. Blessed Be the Lord (1:46–56)

Mary responded to Elizabeth's blessings by magnifying the Lord. Echoing Hannah's prayer (1 Sam. 2:1–10), Mary magnified and rejoiced in God's salvation. Like Elizabeth, Mary made a profession of faith in the Christ child, "my Savior" (Luke 1:47). Mary recognized that the Lord had looked on her humble state by calling herself "His maidservant" (v. 48). She understood that all generations would call her blessed. God works through the generations of those whom He is calling out from the world to be His people in fulfillment of His promise to Abraham (Gen. 12:3). Mary recognized that God is mighty in His actions but that He is also holy in His name (see Isa. 57:15). She repeatedly recognized that the covenant mercy of God is only for those who fear

---

10. Ryken, *Luke*, 1:41.

11. Leon Morris, *Luke*, Tyndale New Testament Commentaries (Downers Grove, Ill.: IVP Academic, 1988), 91.

Him from generation to generation (see Deut. 5:10; 7:9). She proclaimed that God's kingdom is different from the kingdoms of this world. The proud and mighty are brought low while the humble are exalted. As she concluded, she recognized that Christ is the fulfillment of the promises made to Abraham (2 Cor. 1:20).

Significantly, Mary's song either quotes or alludes to verses from Genesis, Deuteronomy, 1 and 2 Samuel, Job, Psalms, Isaiah, Ezekiel, Micah, Habakkuk, and Zephaniah.[12] Her song proves what Jesus would later teach: "And beginning at Moses and all the Prophets, He expounded to them in all the Scriptures the things concerning Himself" (Luke 24:27).

Mary stayed with Elizabeth for three months, until the time Elizabeth was about to give birth, and then she returned home. At home she would face several obstacles. She was now three months pregnant, just about to start showing, but she was not married. She was only engaged to Joseph, and by her family and community standards, to be pregnant out of wedlock was shameful. But God was with Mary and was orchestrating every detail. An angel of the Lord appeared to Joseph in a dream, telling him not to fear taking Mary as his wife because she had conceived by the Holy Spirit and was carrying the Savior of the world (Matt. 1:18–25).

In every difficult circumstance, dear believer, God is with you. When you feel surrounded by darkness, magnify and rejoice in God your Savior. Recall His promises, His great acts of redemption, and His covenant mercy. Rest in His strength and power to accomplish His will.

V. Birth of John (1:57–66)

In demonstration of God's grace and in fulfillment of God's promise (see Luke 1:7, 14–17), Elizabeth gave birth to a son. True to the angel's message, Elizabeth's neighbors and relatives rejoiced with her and recognized that the Lord had shown great mercy to her. They arrived on the eighth day, the day of the child's circumcision, and, in this case, on the day he was named. Circumcision was the sign of the covenant that God had given to Abraham, so when the Jews circumcised their children, they were acknowledging their belief in God's covenant with Abraham (see Gen. 17:12–13).

All the people assumed the happy couple would follow the custom of their day and name their son after his father, Zacharias. But Elizabeth, who believed God's promises, knew that her son was not hers to name. God had already claimed him as His own. Since God had a special purpose for John in His plan of redemption, He gave him a special name meaning "the Lord is gracious."

The neighbors and relatives questioned her decision, so they went to Zacharias and asked him what the name of his son should be. Nine months earlier he had responded to God's promise in fear, doubt, and unbelief and had consequently endured the Lord's discipline, being unable to hear or speak. Now, by God's grace, that discipline

---

12. Ryken, *Luke*, 1:46.

bore the fruit of righteousness. Zacharias wrote, "His name is John" (Luke 1:63). By doing so he testified that God had named the child before his birth.

Immediately, Zacharias's mouth was opened and his tongue loosed so he could speak. Significantly, his first words praised God. Zacharias's obedience and God's mercy resulted in the people of the hill country of Judah talking about and hearing of these things and the fear of God coming upon them. Like Mary, the townspeople laid up these words in their hearts and pondered them, wondering who and what this child would be. John would not be the Redeemer, but the forerunner of the Redeemer. God's great act of redemption, the second exodus, was drawing near!

VI. Blessed Is the Lord (1:67–80)

While the neighbors, relatives, and all who heard about John's birth were asking, "What kind of child will this be?" (Luke 1:66), the Holy Spirit filled Zacharias so that he could tell them. Significantly, he did not begin with his son; instead, he began with the Son of God. First, he blessed the Lord God of Israel for His redemption and salvation that were soon to come in the life, death, resurrection, and ascension of Jesus. Jesus is the fulfillment of the Davidic covenant (2 Sam. 7:12–13), the One about whom the prophets spoke (Luke 24:27), the fulfillment of the Abrahamic covenant (Gen. 12:1–3; 15:1–21; 17:1–22; 22:1–18), and the greater Moses who leads His people in the second great exodus, delivering them from the power of Satan through His death so that they might serve Him in holiness and righteousness through the power of the Holy Spirit.

Second, Zacharias spoke of his own son, John, who would be called the prophet of the Highest. He would go before the Lord to prepare His way (see Mal. 3:1). John would speak of salvation, the forgiveness of sins, and the tender mercy of God. Zacharias said that in fulfillment of Old Testament prophecies (see Isa. 9:2; 42:6–7; Mal. 4:2), the Son would visit God's people from on high, bringing light, guidance, and peace (see Luke 24:36; John 8:12; 14:27; 16:33; 20:19, 21, 26).

Zacharias recognized the greatness of his son and the role he had been given in God's plan of salvation in relationship to the greatest Son, Jesus Christ, and God's greater work. Zacharias never saw his son apart from his relationship to the Son of God. From John's earliest days, Zacharias and Elizabeth pointed him to Jesus, connecting his life mission to the greater mission of Jesus Christ. Even though our children do not have the same unique role John had in redemptive history, we should help them connect their priorities in life to the person of Jesus Christ.

VII. Birth of Jesus (2:1–7)

Shortly after John's birth, Caesar Augustus pronounced a decree. Previously known as Octavian, he was the first emperor of the Roman Empire. It was under his rule that the phrase *Pax Romana* was coined because the entire empire was at peace. He was well known for his building initiatives, but he was a power-hungry man, and he wanted the entire world to be registered for the purpose of taxation. Sadly, for all of the peace that

Caesar Augustus seemed to bring to the Roman Empire, he led the people away from the true peace that only God could offer. He was the first of many emperors to take the title *dominus et deus*: lord and god.[13] He wanted people to see how great he was, not how great God is.

Caesar Augustus's registration was the first one when Quirinius was governor of Syria. By noting leaders like these, Luke reminds us that Jesus was born in real space-and-time history. Christianity is a religion based on historical fact. He also reminds us of God's sovereign rule over the affairs of this world. Although Caesar Augustus thought he was ordering a decree that would elevate his status as a king, he was really just an instrument in the hand of God to reveal the real King. Additionally, Luke wants us to see God's marvelous orchestration in preparing the world for the coming of His Son. This was the first time that the Roman Empire had been at peace under one ruler. What better time for the church to be able to take root in fertile soil than when God's people could go from town to town preaching the good news?[14] God had opened a small window of world peace to bring the King of peace into the world.

Through the prophet Micah, God had foretold that Jesus's birth would be in Bethlehem (Mic. 5:2). Through Caesar Augustus's decree that required all people to go to their own town, He was putting the right people in the right place at the right time to fulfill His word. It was important that to fulfill prophecy, then, Joseph, of the house and lineage of David, left Nazareth for Bethlehem, the city of David (2 Sam. 7:12–13).

Joseph and Mary had to travel about ninety miles to Bethlehem.[15] While they were there, the time came for Mary to give birth. Since the usual lodging place for travelers was full during the census, Mary and Joseph had to find lodging elsewhere. We don't know for sure where they were, but it was most likely either a stable for animals or a cave that was used as a stable for animals.[16]

There has never been a greater birth in a more humble place than Jesus's birth in Bethlehem. We sing about it as a silent and calm night, but it was anything but silent and calm. Think of Mary's cries of pain as she gave birth, her loneliness as she lay in an obscure place, and her fear as she, a young girl, gave birth for the first time with no other woman around. And yet there must have been cries of joy as she gave birth to the Christ child, her firstborn son. Consider Joseph's fear, as he was the only one to help his wife give birth, and his excitement as he watched God's Son and his son come into the world. Then think of Jesus's cries as a newborn child. They would reach their climax on the cross when Jesus cried out to His Father, who had forsaken Him so that you and I could be saved from sin, death, and Satan. Dear reader, have you cried out to Him, trusting in Him alone for your salvation?

---

13. Sproul, *Walk with God*, 29.

14. J. C. Ryle, *Luke*, Crossway Classic Commentaries (Wheaton, Ill.: Crossway, 1997), 35.

15. Bock, *Luke*, 1:204.

16. Bock, *Luke*, 1:208.

VIII. Birth of Jesus Announced to Shepherds (2:8–20)

There was another reason the night of Christ's birth was not silent. God chose to announce His Son's birth to shepherds in the same country who were out keeping watch over their flocks by night. If you know your Bible, this should not surprise you. God chose shepherds to accomplish His purposes: Jacob and his sons (Gen. 46:31–34); Moses (Ex. 3:1); David (1 Sam. 17:15); and Amos (Amos 1:1). Now he was choosing shepherds to be the first bearers of the gospel to the world. Furthermore, Jeremiah had prophesied that God would send the Messiah when shepherds were watching over their flocks in Jerusalem (see Jer. 33:13, 15–16).[17]

Shepherds were the outcasts of society. Since they tended the sheep that were most likely used as sacrificial animals in the temple, they were ceremonially unclean. So those Jews who were ceremonially clean rejected them. But God did not reject them. God has always had room in His plan for the outcasts, the widows, and the poor (see Isa. 61:1). In fact, while the ceremonially clean were sacrificing the sheep in the temple made with hands, God, the true temple, appeared to these shepherds with the news of the "Lamb of God who takes away the sin of the world" (John 1:29) and the "good shepherd" who "gives His life for the sheep" (10:11).

All of a sudden the hillside on which these shepherds were tending flocks became holy ground as the glory of the Lord shone around them, representing God's very presence (see Ex. 16:10; Lev. 9:6; Num. 14:10; 1 Kings 8:11; Ps. 138:5; Isa. 58:8; Ezek. 1:28).[18] Like Zacharias and Mary, the shepherds were filled with fear when they saw the angel of the Lord. But the angel quickly told them not to be afraid. Good news of great joy for all the people had come. The "Lamb of God" (John 1:36) and "great Shepherd of the sheep" (Heb. 13:20) had come to make complete and final atonement for God's people. The Savior, Christ the Lord, had been born. The greatest Prophet, Priest, and King had arrived!

Just as God had given Zacharias and Mary a sign, He also gave the shepherds a sign. They would find a baby wrapped in swaddling cloths and lying in a manger. Before they had time to ponder this, their quiet night on the hillside was interrupted again by a multitude of the heavenly host praising God and saying, "Glory to God in the highest, and on earth peace, goodwill toward men!" (Luke 2:14). As Philip Ryken so beautifully says, "It was not a hymn that rose up from the earth, but an anthem that came down from heaven."[19]

The multitude of voices must have deafened the shepherds' ears, and the brightness of God's glory must have blinded their eyes. It was a moment they would never forget and a message they could not hide. No wonder their response was one of haste to see the sign, and they were glorifying and praising God upon their return!

17. Ryken, *Luke*, 1:77.
18. Pao and Schnabel, "Luke," 267.
19. Ryken, *Luke*, 1:82.

Just as Mary hurried to see the sign of Elizabeth pregnant (Luke 1:39), the shepherds also hurried and found Mary and Joseph with baby Jesus lying in a manger (2:16). They told this young couple what the angels had revealed to them about their baby boy. How comforting this must have been to Mary and Joseph! God had not forgotten His word to them. What He had told them through the angel had come true. These humble beginnings were leading to something greater than anything anyone could ever imagine. God had come in the likeness of man to bring peace between God and man. Glory to God indeed!

IX. Blessings by Simeon and Anna (2:21–40)

Joseph and Mary were Jews who followed the law of Moses. They loved God and sought to follow Him with their lives. They were part of the remnant who were still waiting for the Messiah, even after four hundred years of silence between the Old and New Testaments. The first thing that they did in accordance with the law was to have Jesus circumcised. This was the sign of God's covenant with Abraham in which He had promised that Abraham would be the father of a multitude of nations. He would be "exceedingly fruitful," his descendants would be made into nations, kings would come from him, and his descendants would be given the land of Canaan as an "everlasting possession" (Gen. 17:4–8). Circumcision, which involved cutting off the male foreskin, was a visible sign in the flesh that Abraham's descendants would be set apart as God's chosen people. Jesus's circumcision, the first shedding of His blood, anticipated His blood being shed on the cross.[20] His circumcision displayed that He was a child of Abraham, the King of kings who had come through Abraham's descendants to be the Savior of the world.

In obedience to the purification laws (see Ex. 13:1–2; Lev. 12:3, 6–8), Joseph and Mary brought Jesus to Jerusalem to present Him to the Lord. Mary and Joseph were not wealthy enough to offer a lamb so they gave "a pair of turtledoves or two young pigeons" (Luke 2:24). This was another example of the Son of God's humble beginnings. Ironically, Mary and Joseph did offer a lamb, the Lamb of God who takes away the sin of the world (John 1:29).

Like Hannah, who presented Samuel to the Lord, Mary presented Jesus to the Lord so that He would be used for God's glory. When she presented her son, neither woman would have known what this would involve. Neither one of them could foresee the future and know what kind of pain such dedication would entail—or what joy. But they didn't have to know. Hannah and Mary walked by faith. They obeyed the law of the Lord and were spiritually blessed.

Although we no longer go to the temple, we are commanded to present our children to the Lord by way of infant baptism and by bringing them to church each week. We must instill in our children the importance of worshiping God and obeying His commandments. By doing so, we acknowledge that they are God's children first. We

---

20. Ryken, *Luke*, 1:89.

must pray for God's will to be done in their lives and instill in them the values of His kingdom. This is not the responsibility just of the parents but of the entire church family. We are to assist the parents in our congregation in raising their children in the ways of the Lord.

Mary and Joseph were not alone when they went to the temple. Luke singles out one man, Simeon (Luke 2:25–35), and one woman, Anna (vv. 36–38). Simeon was a righteous and devout man. He was part of the Jewish remnant who had not lost hope in God's promises of the Messiah during the four hundred long years of silence since God had spoken to His people. He daily followed the law of the Lord. Simeon's hope was in the Consolation of Israel, the arrival of the kingdom when God would fulfill His promises to Israel with the coming of Christ.[21] The Holy Spirit was upon Simeon in a special way: "he came by the Spirit into the temple" (v. 27). The Spirit had revealed to him that he would not see death before he saw the Lord's Christ. Now Christ had come to the temple. Simeon was able to take up the promise in his arms and bless God!

Simeon first recognized Jesus as God's salvation. He also recognized the fulfillment of the promise that God had made to him. Before his death, he had seen the Lord's Christ. Now he was ready to die. Finally, Simeon recognized that this was a light to bring revelation to the Gentiles (see Isa. 49:6; 52:10; 56:1) and the glory of God's people, Israel (see Isa. 60:1–2). Significantly, this is the first time Luke mentions the Gentiles as part of God's plan of redemption, the beginning of a thread that weaves its way throughout his gospel and Acts, emphasizing that God's salvation will reach every tribe, tongue, and nation.

Joseph and Mary marveled at what was said about Jesus. An angel had visited them each on separate occasions, together they had heard the shepherds speak of the angels, and now they were both hearing Simeon's words of blessing. Simeon also blessed Joseph and Mary. Then he told Mary, "Behold, this Child is destined for the fall and rising of many in Israel [see Isa. 8:14–15; 28:16], and for a sign which will be spoken against (yes, a sword will pierce through your own soul also), that the thoughts of many hearts may be revealed" (Luke 2:34–35). We don't know what Mary thought when she heard these words, but we do know what she was doing when the sword pierced her soul. She was standing by the cross on which Jesus hung, faithful to the very end, and ready to receive His instruction (John 19:25–27). And we know that after Jesus's ascension Mary was in the upper room with the rest of Jesus's followers, devoting herself to prayer (Acts 1:14). Mary didn't fully understand, but she believed. She wondered, but she never wavered. She never forsook her commitment to be the Lord's servant (Luke 1:38).

When the sword of the Lord comes to us through a bitter providence, whether it's the sword of a difficult marriage or singleness we didn't want, infertility or a rebellious child, cancer or chronic physical pain, our source of strength must be the Lord. We will find peace only when we turn to Him and submit to His lordship.

---

21. Pao and Schnabel, "Luke," 271.

Simeon was not the only one who met the Christ child at the temple that day. There was also a prophetess named Anna.[22] Anna was from the tribe of Asher, which was one of the tribes willing to participate in the feast of Passover in Jerusalem after the exile (see 2 Chron. 30:10–11).[23] In God's grace, He had preserved a remnant of believers from the Northern Kingdom of Israel. Anna had been married only seven years before she became a widow. It would have been very difficult to lose a husband so young, but Anna did not let her grief turn to bitterness and anger toward God. Instead, she spent every day at the temple, praying and fasting, waiting for the redemption of Jerusalem (see Isa. 52:8–10). The text does not make it clear whether Anna was eighty-four years old or had been a widow for eighty-four years when Christ was born, but she had faithfully worshiped God all those years, and when she saw the baby Jesus, she first gave thanks to God. Then she spoke of Him to all who were waiting for the redemption of Israel. Worship should precede witness, and worship is often our greatest witness.

After they had performed everything according to the law of the Lord, Joseph and Mary returned to their own town of Nazareth in Galilee. Luke does not record the wise men's visit, Mary and Joseph's flight to Egypt, Herod's command to kill all the male children two years old or younger in Bethlehem, and the angel of the Lord's message and warning in Joseph's dream that led them to Nazareth (see Matthew 2). Instead, Luke informs us that God placed Jesus in an earthly home where His parents loved the Lord and obeyed His word. God used them as instruments in His hand to instill strength and wisdom in His Son. Because He was sinless, His strength and wisdom could reach their full potential. And the favor of God could be fully on Him because there was no sin to separate Him from God. God was preparing Him for the ministry that would accomplish the redemption of His people. Like Joseph and Mary, we must help our children become strong and wise in the Lord, teaching them the Bible, praying for them and with them, and reflecting God's love to them. Dear mother, don't neglect this important responsibility. And if you are not a mother, don't minimize the influence you have on the children in your family and in your church family. Joyfully help their parents teach them the truths of Scripture and don't neglect praying for their salvation and growth in the grace and knowledge of Jesus Christ.

X. Boyhood of Jesus (2:41–52)

Luke records the only story about Jesus's boyhood in Scripture. When Jesus was twelve years old, Joseph and Mary went to Jerusalem to keep the feast of Passover, which they did annually. This would have been around an eighty-mile trip from Nazareth to Jerusalem.[24] About two thousand people would have crowded the city with about one thousand animals to be used for sacrifice.[25] But Luke's concern is not with the details

---

22. There were only seven prophetesses named in the Old Testament, according to the Jews—Sarah, Miriam, Deborah, Hannah, Abigail, Huldah, and Esther. Bock, *Luke*, 1:251.
23. Pao and Schnabel, "Luke," 274.
24. Bock, *Luke*, 1:264.
25. Ryken, *Luke*, 1:107.

of the Passover. Instead, he focuses on Jesus's reason for staying behind after the feast had ended and His parents had begun the trip home.

Jesus's decision to remain behind was the right one, but it caused much distress for His parents. Joseph and Mary were traveling back to Nazareth with a group of people, and they most likely assumed either that Jesus was with the other parent or that He was with another family member. So for an entire day of travel they did not realize He was gone. But at the end of the first day of travel, they couldn't find Him, so they had to return to Jerusalem.

After three days (one day toward Nazareth, one day back to Jerusalem, and one day searching for Jesus in Jerusalem) they found Jesus in the temple. He was sitting among the teachers, listening to them and asking them questions. His understanding and answers amazed those who heard Him, and when His parents observed what was going on, they were astonished. But instead of recognizing that this was exactly where He, as the Son of God, should be, Mary rebuked Him for staying behind and causing them so much distress.

Jesus responded with a mild rebuke of His own. He questioned why they were looking for Him and why they didn't understand that He must be in His Father's house. Significantly, this is the first time Luke records Jesus speaking, and He calls God "My Father" (Luke 2:49). No one had ever called God that before. The people had said "our Father" but never "my Father."[26] Jesus was revealing His unique relationship with God the Father, which is best understood in light of the doctrine of the Trinity. Furthermore, He declared His purpose. He had to be in His Father's house because His ultimate authority was God the Father. Yet He also submitted to the fifth commandment (Ex. 20:12) when he honored Mary and Joseph by returning with them to Nazareth, one example of how He fulfilled the law for us during His time on earth.

Mary and Joseph did not understand Jesus's words to them, but Mary did not disregard them. She treasured up His words and this incident in her heart. She continued to ponder the things of God, and by doing so her heart remained fertile for the gospel to take deep root so that when she stood by the cross and the sword pierced her own soul, she stood as a servant of the Lord who submitted to His will. God's plans for our children will likely be different from our expectations. It's important that we want what God wants for them and that we make this clear to them from their earliest age. "Jesus increased in wisdom and stature, and in favor with God and men" (Luke 2:52), and we should pray that this would be the case for our children and the covenant children in our churches.

What message is ringing in your ears today? Do you hear the deceptive, subtle whispers of the world, the flesh, and Satan telling you to glorify yourself? Or do you hear the

26. Ryken, *Luke*, 1:111.

word of God telling you to glorify God? By God's grace we can turn away from self-exaltation and exalt Him. We can turn away from worldly power, position, and prestige and magnify God's power, position, and prestige. We can turn away from Satan's lies that promise fulfillment but leave us empty and turn to Jesus, who declared, "I am the way, the truth, and the life. No one comes to the Father except through Me" (John 14:6).

Processing It Together...

1. What do we learn about God in Luke 1–2?

2. How does this reshape how we should view our present circumstances?

3. What do we learn about God's Son, Jesus Christ?

4. How should this impact our relationship with God and with others?

5. What do we learn about God's covenant with His people?

6. How are we to live in light of this?

7. How can we apply Luke 1–2 to our lives today and in the future?

8. How should we apply this passage in our churches?

9. Look back at "Put It in Perspective" in your personal study questions. What did you find challenging or encouraging about this lesson?

10. Look back at "Principles and Points of Application." How has this lesson impacted your life?

The Forerunner and the Fulfillment

Luke 3–4

Purpose...

Head. What do I need to know from this passage in Scripture?

- God prepares the world to receive His Son through the ministry of John the Baptist. Jesus proves that He is the second Adam and the true Israel who is obedient and faithful to the Father.

Heart. How does what I learn from this passage affect my internal relationship with the Lord?

- I am a kingdom disciple who has been given the Holy Spirit to strengthen me against the temptations of this world, my flesh, and the devil.

Hands. How does what I learn from this passage translate into action for God's kingdom?

- I will point others to Christ, not my accomplishments, and glorify God in my calling.
- I will pray for those who persecute me.
- I will teach the next generation to be faithful to the Lord.
- I will help others resist Satan's temptations by using the Bible.
- I will share the gospel with unbelievers.

Personal Study...

Pray. Ask that God will open up your heart and mind as you study His Word. This is His story of redemption that He has revealed to us, and the Holy Spirit is our teacher.

Ponder the Passage. Read Luke 3–4.

- *Point:* What is the point of this passage? How does this relate to the point of the entire book?

- *Persons:* Who are the main people involved in this passage? What characterizes them?

- *Persons of the Trinity:* Where do you see God the Father, God the Son, and God the Holy Spirit in this passage?

- *Puzzling Parts:* Are there any parts of the passage that you don't quite understand or that seem interesting or confusing?

Put It in Perspective.

- *Place in Scripture:* What is the original context of this text? What is the redemptive-historical context—what has or hasn't happened in redemptive history at this point in Scripture? How does this text connect to Christ?

The following questions will help you if you got stuck on any of the previous questions, and they will help you dig a little deeper into the text, putting it all into perspective.

1. 3:1–6. (a) Who was ruling at the time of John's and Jesus's ministries?

(b) Why is John greater than the other Old Testament prophets?

(c) How does his location fulfill Isaiah 40:3?

(d) How did John fulfill Isaiah 40:3–5, the angel's words in Luke 1:16–17, and Zacharias's prophecy in Luke 1:76–77?

(e) How does Luke use Isaiah 40:3–5 to (1) bridge the gap between the promises of the Old Testament and their fulfillment in the New Testament, (2) point to the second exodus, and (3) display that God is expanding His church?

2. 3:7–9. (a) What is John's main message?

(b) Why does John call the multitudes "you brood of vipers" (see Gen. 3:15; Ps. 140:1–3; Matt. 12:34), and what does the "wrath to come" refer to (see Mal. 3:2; 4:1)?

(c) How does a person prepare for the coming of the Messiah (see also John 8:39–40; Acts 26:20)?

(d) What does John warn the Jews from doing, and why was this a temptation for them (see Rom. 2:17–29; 3:1–2; 9:4–5)?

(e) How does John use Isaiah 10:33–34 in his message and the imagery from Isaiah 5:2; Jeremiah 2:21; Ezekiel 15:6; and Hosea 10:1?

3. 3:10–14. (a) How many groups of people respond to John's message?

(b) Who were they, and what question did they ask?

(c) How does John respond to each group?

4. **3:15–17.** (a) What was going on in the hearts and minds of the people who were hearing John's message, and how does John respond?

(b) Compare "One mightier than I is coming" with Isaiah 11:1–2; Malachi 3:1; and Psalm 118:26.

(c) What does it mean that Jesus will baptize with the Holy Spirit and with fire (see Isa. 30:27–28)?

(d) In verse 17, how does John use imagery from Psalm 83:13–14; Isaiah 29:5–6; 66:24b; Jeremiah 17:27; Obadiah 18; and Malachi 4:1a?

5. **3:18–20.** (a) What was John's interaction with Herod the tetrarch (see also Matt. 14:3–5; Mark 6:17)?

(b) What was Herod's response?

6. **3:21–22.** (a) How does Luke's focus here prepare for Luke 4:18 and Acts 2:17–21?

(b) What does the Spirit's descent signify (see Gen. 1:2; Isa. 11:1–9; 2 Cor. 5:17)?

(c) Of what is Jesus the fulfillment (see Gen. 22:2, 12, 16; Ps. 2:7; Isa. 42:1)?

7. 3:23–38. (a) About how old was Jesus when He began His ministry? Compare this with Genesis 41:46; Numbers 4:3; 2 Samuel 5:4; and Ezekiel 1:1. What do you discover?

(b) How do Luke's words "as was supposed" in verse 23 affirm the virgin birth?

(c) Compare Luke's genealogy of Jesus with Matthew's (Matt. 1:1–16). What similarities and differences do you find?

(d) With regard to 2 Corinthians 1:20, why is it important that Jesus has Adam, Noah, Abraham, and David in His line?

8. 4:1–4. (a) What had happened at the Jordan to cause Jesus to be full of the Holy Spirit (see Luke 3:21–22)?

(b) Who led Jesus into the wilderness, and for what purpose?

(c) What was Jesus's physical condition when the devil came to Him?

(d) What was the first thing the devil challenged about God, and how did Jesus respond?

(e) What is the original context of this citation?

9. 4:5–8. (a) What was the second thing the devil challenged about God, and how did Jesus respond?

(b) What is the original context of this citation?

10. 4:9–13. (a) How did the devil's approach change with the third temptation?

(b) How did Jesus respond, and what is the original context of this citation?

(c) Did the devil depart from Jesus for good, and why or why not?

(d) Compare Jesus's temptation and response with Adam's temptation and response in the garden of Eden. What does this tell us about Jesus?

(e) Compare Israel's response to the period of testing in the wilderness with Jesus's response to the devil. What does this tell us about Jesus?

11. 4:14–15. (a) How did Jesus return to Galilee?

(b) What kind of reports were the people in Galilee hearing about Jesus?

(c) Where was He teaching, and what was the people's response?

12. 4:16–19. (a) What passage of the Bible did Jesus read from in the Nazareth synagogue?

(b) How does Jesus fulfill both the Suffering Servant and the Messiah of whom Isaiah prophesied in Isaiah 40–66?

(c) What five things has Jesus been sent to proclaim?

(d) What is the year of Jubilee (see Lev. 25:8–22), and how does Jesus fulfill this?

13. 4:20–30. (a) How did the people initially respond to Jesus's words?

(b) How does Jesus reveal the people's motives?

(c) What examples did Jesus use to remind Israel that when they reject God's prophets, God takes His grace elsewhere?

(d) How do the widow of Zarephath and Naaman the Syrian foreshadow Acts 10:45–11:1?

(e) What does Jesus's departure in the midst of an angry mob reveal about Him?

14. 4:31–37. (a) How did those in the Capernaum synagogue respond to Jesus, and why?

(b) Besides teach, what did Jesus do in the synagogue?

(c) How did this display Jesus's power over the evil of this world, and how did the people respond?

15. 4:38–41. (a) What did Jesus do in Simon's house, and how did this display Jesus's power in this world?

(b) How do Jesus's healings foreshadow the consummation of the kingdom (see Rev. 21:3–4)?

(c) Who did the demons say that Jesus was, and why did He respond the way He did?

(d) What did Jesus do when He departed (see Mark 1:35)?

16. 38:42–44. (a) How did Jesus respond to the people of Capernaum who wanted Him to stay, and how does this fit with what He has already said (see Luke 4:18–19, 21)?

(b) What was Jesus preaching about, and where was He preaching?

(c) Using a Bible resource, look up "kingdom of God." What do you learn?

Principles and Points of Application

17. 3:1–22. (a) Have you recognized you are a sinner, repented of your sin, and trusted in Christ alone for your salvation?

(b) Ask God to give you the opportunity to share the gospel with someone this week and to open up the person's heart to respond favorably.

(c) What is the best way to respond when others recognize God's grace in you?

(d) In what ways do you need to change your attitude in the places God has placed you to serve?

(e) How do you respond when others seek to silence your witness through guilt, manipulation, threatening, persecution, or criticism? Pray that you will have the grace to stand firm, and ask God to save those who seek to silence you. Also, spend time in prayer for our persecuted brothers and sisters around the world.

(f) Why does it comfort you that your heavenly Father says that Jesus is His beloved Son in whom He is well pleased—and as a believer, you are united to His Son?

18. 3:23–38. (a) How are you teaching the truths of the faith to the next generation?

(b) Spend time in prayer thanking God for past generations who were faithful to the truth and asking Him to raise up future generations who will live for Christ.

19. 4:1–13. (a) How are you tempted to fulfill your desires in illegitimate ways, to worship and pursue the kingdoms of this world, or to test God's faithfulness to you in the wrong ways?

(b) How will you respond to these temptations?

20. 4:14–44. (a) Meditate on Isaiah 61:1–2, quoted in Luke 4:18–19. How have you received the gospel as one who is poor? How do you proclaim it to others? From what has Christ liberated you, and in what way were you blind? How are you proclaiming the year of the Lord's favor, which was inaugurated with Christ's first coming?

(b) Why does knowing that Jesus is the great healer who identifies with our suffering and pain bring you comfort?

(c) Pray for your pastors to remain faithful to preach the good news of the kingdom of God.

Putting It All Together...

Birthday parties, graduation open houses, weddings, and baby showers are celebratory events that fill us with anticipation and leave us with treasured memories. The attention, time, and money that go into preparing for these events varies, but no doubt those in charge of planning consider carefully how to make them meaningful. Balloons, cards, special food, gifts, and guests combine to make these occasions memorable for a lifetime. How much greater, then, was God the Father's planning and preparation for the beginning of His Son's ministry?

Before Jesus was born in Bethlehem, His heavenly Father appointed the governors and rulers He wanted in place. He raised up a prophet to prepare the way for His Son's words and works. He affirmed His blessing on His Son at His baptism. He orchestrated His Son's genealogy to fulfill His promises. And the Holy Spirit empowered His Son to triumph over the temptation of the devil and begin His ministry of teaching, healing, and preaching the good news.

I. Jesus's Forerunner (3:1–20)

In the Old Testament, God's calling of a prophet is often set in the context of the political ruler of the time (see, for example, Jer. 1:1–3). Not surprisingly then, Luke begins with a date and the names of seven rulers during the time of John's and Jesus's ministries, emphasizing John's and Jesus's prophetic roles. John was the precursor to the Prophet of all prophets.

The word of God came to John in the wilderness in the fifteenth year of Tiberius Caesar's reign, August AD 28 to August AD 29.[1] Pontius Pilate was governor of Judea at this time. Judea was part of a region that had originally been under the rule of Archelaus, but because he was a bad ruler, the people asked the Romans to remove him. The Romans granted the people's request, placing their own governor as ruler in AD 6, an office that Pontius Pilate held AD 26–36.[2] Herod, whose full name was Herod Antipas, was the son of Herod the Great and was tetrarch of Galilee from 4 BC to AD 39.[3] His brother Philip was tetrarch of the region of Ituraea and Trachonitis, which was northeast of the Sea of Galilee, from 4 BC to AD 33/34.[4] And Lysanias was tetrarch of Abilene. The religious leaders of John and Jesus's day were Annas and Caiaphas. Caiaphas (AD 18–36) was the high priest at the time, although his predecessor, Annas (AD 6–15), still wielded a great deal of influence. All of these secular and religious leaders, without exception, were known as evil rulers.[5] The stage was set in redemptive history for the appearance of the perfect ruler, Jesus Christ. In His grace and according to His promises in the Old Testament, God sent the forerunner, John the Baptist, to prepare the way for His Son.

By God's grace John heard the word of God when it came to him and acted on that word. It was his role to tell others that their hearts needed to be prepared for the Lord. Jesus was coming soon, but sadly the people were not ready. So in the entire region around the Jordan, John proclaimed a baptism of repentance for the forgiveness of sins. This call for baptism would have been offensive since the Jews regarded Gentiles as the only ones in need of baptism.[6] But John condemned this thinking, informing them of their desperate need of cleansing, despite their ancestry. John's proclamation fulfilled Isaiah's prophecy of a forerunner to prepare the way of the Lord (Isa. 40:3–5; Luke 3:4–6). God's salvation was about to appear in the flesh for all flesh to see.

In the ancient world it was customary for a herald to announce a king's arrival so that the people would be prepared to give the honor due him. How much more should

---

1. Morris, *Luke*, 110.
2. Morris, *Luke*, 111.
3. Morris, *Luke*, 111.
4. Morris, *Luke*, 111.
5. Ryle, *Luke*, 47.
6. Morris, *Luke*, 112.

a herald go before Jesus Christ, the King of kings and Lord of lords, to proclaim His arrival? This was especially true because the people were not prepared for the Lord. They needed Jesus to break into their lives and humble their pride, straighten their paths, level their hard hearts, and open their eyes so that they could see God's salvation in His Son. We need this too.

John's message was not popular, and his mannerisms were not preferred (see Matt. 3:4), but he did get people's attention. Entire crowds came to be baptized by him. Sadly, they were not truly repentant. They were looking for "fire insurance" in case John's message regarding God's judgment was true. But God gave John the discernment to see through the motives of these crowds. Using imagery from the Old Testament, John called them what they really were, a brood of vipers (see Gen. 3:1–15; Isa. 14:29; 59:5; Jer. 46:22). John discerned that these sons of the devil (see Rev. 12:9; 20:2) were not interested in repenting and bearing good fruits for the kingdom of God. Instead, they wanted to keep living as they were without the consequences of God's wrath.

John exhorted the crowds to bear fruit in keeping with repentance. Faith without works is dead (James 2:14–26). Our works do not save us, but they do prove our faith. The crowds, who were evidently mostly Jews, were resting on their genealogy, which included father Abraham, rather than making his faith their own (see Gen. 12:1–3; Isa. 51:1–2). Using imagery from the Old Testament (see Ps. 80:8; Isa. 5:2; 10:33–34; Jer. 2:21; Ezek. 15:6; Hos. 10:1; Mal. 3–4), John proclaimed that God chooses whomever He wills to be His children, and anyone who does not bear good fruit for the kingdom is cut down and judged.

Three groups of people came to John and asked him what they should do. It is the question that should be on all of our lips when we come face-to-face with the message of the gospel. You and I might have expected John to quote a tract and lead the people in a prayer of repentance. But instead, he gave very specific, practical, relevant advice to each of the groups.

John told them that they were to share their clothes and food with those who had none. Also, the tax collectors, who were notorious in the Roman Empire for overtaxing and pocketing the excess, were to collect only the amount authorized by the government. Notably, they were to remain in their profession, but they were to be honest and just in their dealings with others. The soldiers, who were not well paid and were tempted to get money by threatening or falsely accusing people of doing things and fining them, were to remain contentedly in their profession.

We need to hear John's message today. Christ does not remove us from the world but tells us to impact the world by His grace. Whether we are educators, politicians, social workers, or homemakers, we are called to proclaim and practice God's justice and righteousness.

The Jews had been expecting the Messiah, but after four hundred years of silence since the last prophet, Malachi, John was a new ray of hope that God had not forgotten His promises. Many people were even wondering whether John might be the Christ.

But while John had the perfect opportunity to make the most of his popularity, he instead pointed toward and exalted Christ. In language reminiscent of the Old Testament, John said that Jesus was mightier than he was (see Deut. 10:17; Isa. 11:2; 28:2). Jesus was the one who was coming in grace and yet also in judgment (see Ps. 118:26; Mal. 3:1). He was the one whose sandal John was not even worthy to untie; even Jewish slaves were not required to untie their masters' shoes because it was considered too much of a disgrace. Jesus would baptize with the Holy Spirit and fire.[7] And He would sift the people of this world into two groups: those who are His chosen people who walk by faith, and those whom He never knew because they never believed in Him (see Ps. 83:13–14; Isa. 29:5–6; Obad. 18; Mal. 4:1).

Proclamation of truth is often followed with persecution, and that was certainly true for John. Herod sought to silence him. This evil ruler had already wrecked two marriages, his own and his brother's, by taking his sister-in-law Herodias to be his wife. Worse than this, he imprisoned John. But John's imprisonment and later his beheading (see Matt. 14:10; Mark 6:27; Luke 9:9) could not impede God's plan of redemption.

True disciples of Jesus will always suffer for their faith and need not fear those who can imprison the body but cannot imprison the soul. Locked in the dark cell of a prison, many have seen the light of Christ shine brightest. In our darkest moments, the rays of light from the Son of God become brighter. He not only saves but He vindicates. And He gives us eternal life with Him.

II. Jesus's Family (3:21–38)

Not only were all the people baptized, but Jesus was baptized. John would have prevented Jesus from being baptized if it hadn't been for Jesus's insistence (Matt. 3:13–17). John felt like he needed to be baptized by Jesus, not the other way around. But Jesus was baptized so that He could identify with the sinners He had come to save. He was also endorsing John's ministry and identifying him as His forerunner. Most significantly, God the Father was endorsing His Son's ministry.

While He was baptized, Jesus was praying. We don't know what He said to His Father, but surely it had something to do with His ministry since the heavens were opened and the Holy Spirit descended on Him in bodily form, like a dove. Significantly, this literal, visible manifestation of the Spirit was inaugurating the time in redemptive history when the Spirit of God is with His people, a fulfillment of Old Testament prophecies (see Isa. 11:1–2; Joel 2:28–32; Acts 2:17–21). Just as the Spirit of God was involved in God's creation of the heavens and the earth (Gen. 1:2), so too He is present and active at the inauguration of God the Son's ministry, in which "old things have passed away; behold, all things have become new" (2 Cor. 5:17) for those who are in Christ Jesus.[8] Also, God the Father's affirmation of His Son shows that Jesus is the Son greater than

---

7. The imagery is found in Isaiah 30:27–28, where the context is also one of judgment. Pao and Schnabel, "Luke," 279.

8. Pao and Schnabel, "Luke," 280.

Isaac (see Gen. 22:12, 16), as well as the promised King (Ps. 2:6–8) and "[God's] Servant" in whom "[His] soul delights" (Isa. 42:1).

How precious is the truth that all of us who are robed in the righteousness of Christ hear the Father's voice ringing in our own ears—that we are His beloved daughters, and with us He is well pleased. Some of you have endured harsh, angry words of disapproval and abuse, rejection by parents, and the failure of dreams and shattered expectations. But we have a heavenly Father who approves of us in Christ. Indeed, He rejoices over us with His love (Zeph. 3:17).

Jesus was about thirty years old when He began His ministry. In the Old Testament, thirty was the age of Joseph when he began serving Pharaoh (Gen. 41:46), the age when men became eligible for the priesthood (Num. 4:3), the age of Ezekiel when he was called to minister (Ezek. 1:1), and the age of David when he became king (2 Sam. 5:4).[9] Luke records nothing about Jesus's life between the ages of twelve (Luke 2:41–52) and thirty. But we can assume that Jesus continued to grow in wisdom and stature and in favor with God and with man all those years. He continued to live each day in obedience to the law and to the glory of God. He continued to be faithful to the role of Messiah and Savior of the world. But the Father was ready to reveal His Son at the age of thirty to the world in a more profound way. The Son of God was ready to begin His ministry.

But before Luke tells us about Jesus's ministry, He records Jesus's family tree. This genealogy tells us five main things about Jesus and His family. First, Luke reminds us that Joseph was not Jesus's biological father (Luke 3:23). He is really the Son of God, born of the virgin Mary. Second, it tells us who Jesus is by tracing His line all the way back to Adam, the son of God. Jesus is the second Adam, who has come to succeed where the first Adam failed. Third, by going beyond Abraham to Adam, the genealogy confirms that Jesus did not come to save just Jews but also Gentiles. Fourth, Jesus's family tree shows us that He is the greater Adam, Noah, and Abraham, and the final and perfect Davidic King who fulfills all the promises of God (2 Cor. 1:20). Fifth, it shows us that God had been working out His plan of redemption over many generations through the lives of many individuals. Some of these individuals are familiar, like Zerubbabel, Nathan, David, Jesse, Obed, Boaz, Judah, Jacob, Isaac, Abraham, Noah, and Adam, but many are names that we have never heard of except in an Old Testament genealogy account. And almost half of them do not appear anywhere else in Scripture.[10] This list of names reminds us that God uses ordinary people to bring about His extraordinary plan. Many of the people in this list sinned grievously, yet God, in His mercy, forgave them and used them to bring the Savior into the world.

The Lord has always worked through covenant families (see Acts 2:39). Genealogies are testimonies of God's faithfulness to His promises. We should pray for our children and grandchildren and the covenant children in our churches to grow in

9. Bock, *Luke*, 1:351.
10. Ryken, *Luke*, 1:141.

their faith so that they can pass the faith to the next generation. We should thank God for those in our lineage who have taught the faith to us. We should give thanks for the Christians in our families and pray that God will grant repentance and salvation to those in our families who don't yet believe.

III. Jesus's Fast (4:1–13)

Jesus, full of the Holy Spirit, is now led by the Spirit into the wilderness to undergo temptation by the devil, over whom He would be victorious. For forty days Jesus fasted and was tempted by the devil, but at the end of the forty days, when Jesus was at His hungriest and weakest, the devil heightened his plan of attack. Three times he tried to destroy the Son's ministry.

First, the devil challenged His sonship (Luke 4:3). But Jesus knew who He was. There was not one moment of doubt for Jesus as there was for Adam and Eve when Satan came to them in the garden of Eden or as there was for Israel when they wandered in the wilderness for forty years, rebelling against God and questioning His love and provision for them. No, Jesus knew He was God's beloved Son. In our fight against the enemy, we too must know who we are. We must know and believe that we are the Father's daughter and act accordingly.

The devil also questioned God the Father's provision for His Son, challenging Jesus to make a stone become bread. But Jesus knew that His Father had placed Him in the desert for forty days without food to accomplish redemption. Significantly, Jesus responded by quoting Deuteronomy 8:3, which falls within the broader context of God's commands to the Israelites to love Him wholeheartedly (6:1–2, 4–5); to recognize that they were God's holy people (7:6); to know that the Lord is the faithful, covenant-keeping God (v. 9); and to remember the Lord by keeping His covenant (Deuteronomy 8). The Lord humbled the people with hunger in the wilderness and fed them with manna so that they would understand their sustenance was God's word, not bread (v. 3). Where Israel failed in the wilderness, murmuring against God and misunderstanding His love, Jesus, the true Israel, succeeded as the obedient Son of God.

The devil's second attack challenged Jesus's allegiance. He took Jesus up (most likely in a vision or a rapture[11]) and showed him all the kingdoms of the world in a moment, offering to give Him glory and authority if He would only worship him (Luke 4:6–7). Predictably, Satan tells half-truths. It is true that Satan is the ruler of this world, but he will be cast out (John 12:31). Since he does not have ultimate authority, he cannot give authority to whomever he chooses. God is sovereign over Satan and places kings and rulers where He wants to.

Satan offered Jesus a shortcut to attaining what had already been promised to Him by the Father (see Ps. 2:8; Dan. 7:14). He knew that He was to be King of kings, but the way of achieving this was not by a road of glory but by a cross of suffering. Significantly,

---

11. Bock, *Luke*, 1:374.

Jesus responded by quoting from the same context of Deuteronomy 6–8. Again, we see Jesus as the true Israel, responding in obedience and victory, citing Deuteronomy 6:13: "You shall worship the LORD your God, and Him only you shall serve" (Luke 4:8). Jesus knew Satan's offer was illegitimate. If He chose to worship Satan, He would not gain the kingdoms of this world at all. Instead, He would incur God's discipline, anger, and judgment (see Deut. 6:15).

Third, the devil challenged Jesus's faithfulness to Scripture by using Scripture. He took Jesus up to the pinnacle of the temple[12] and told Him to throw Himself down if He was God's Son. Then he quoted Psalm 91, which exalts the Lord's deliverance and protection for those who hold fast to Him in love.

Those who hold fast to the Lord in love do not put Him to the test. Instead, they wait for His deliverance. Jesus quoted again from the context of Deuteronomy 6–8, specifically 6:16: "You shall not tempt the LORD your God," which goes on to say, "*as you tempted Him in Massah*" (emphasis added). Again, where Israel failed, the true Israel, Jesus Christ, succeeded.

It is important to understand that at the beginning of His ministry, Jesus declared in this small victory over Satan that He would win the large victory as well. He would use divine power, but He would not use it in illegitimate ways. The kingdoms of this world would become His, but the cross of suffering had to come first. In fulfillment of Scripture, Jesus would strike His foot against a stone, even with God's protection over Him, but He would win the victory through His death and resurrection (Gen. 3:15). Jesus, the perfect God-man, came to do His Father's will, and His gaze was fixed on His Father's plan.

We should note that Satan did not depart from Jesus forever but only "until an opportune time" (Luke 4:13). Christ's ministry and cross were still ahead. It's a good reminder that after winning the victory over one temptation in our lives, another one is sure to follow. Satan will tempt us to question God's authority and goodness. We must stand firm by putting on the full armor of God (see Eph. 6:10–20).

IV. Jesus's Fulfillment (4:14–44)

It was only by the power of the Spirit that Jesus returned to Galilee after forty days of fasting and temptation in the wilderness. A report about Him went throughout all the surrounding country of Galilee, and evidently it was a positive one because as He was teaching in the Galilean synagogues, all were glorifying Him. Sadly, there was an exception. Those in His hometown of Nazareth would reject Him.

Jesus in the Synagogue in Nazareth (4:16–30)

When Jesus came to His hometown of Nazareth, He went to the synagogue on the Sabbath. Significantly, this was His habit (Luke 4:16). When Jesus stood up to read in

---

12. Philip Ryken explains that this was "either the roof over the sanctuary or the royal portico that soared five hundred feet above the Kidron Valley." *Luke*, 1:160.

the synagogue, the attendant gave the scroll of the prophet Isaiah to Him. Jesus took the scroll, unrolled it, and found the specific place that prophesied of His coming and ministry, Isaiah 61:1–2. Isaiah 61 recalls the servant and the prophet figure of chapters 40–55 and restates His specific mission described in those chapters, all of which Jesus fulfills. This passage also follows the call to repentance and the promise of God's salvation in Isaiah 58–60. Isaiah 61:1–2 tells us that the One who has received the special anointing of the Spirit of the Lord God will proclaim good news to the poor, liberty to the captives, sight to the blind, liberty to the oppressed, and the year of the Lord's favor.

The last is a reference to the year of Jubilee, when slaves were released from servitude and debtors from debt, and landowners received back their property (Lev. 25:8–22). Jesus had come to fulfill the purpose of the year of Jubilee by setting slaves to sin free, releasing sinners from their debt of sin, and restoring the promise of the land to its rightful owners, the elect of God, which would ultimately be fulfilled in the new heaven and new earth.

Even though the people spoke well of Jesus and marveled at His gracious words, their hearts were hard. Ironically, while they marveled at His words, He marveled at their unbelief (see Mark 6:5–6). He used a proverb (Luke 4:23) and the ministries of Elijah and Elisha to reveal their unbelief. First, He referred to 1 Kings 17:8–24. God had sent Elijah to Zarephath after he warned wicked King Ahab of God's judgment. The Lord told Elijah that He had commanded a widow in Zarephath to feed him while he was there, but this widow did not have the resources to do so. She had to act on God's command in faith, and when she did, the Lord provided ingredients for bread in abundance. This widow was not just a blessing for Elijah. He was also a blessing to this woman. He brought the word of the Lord to her home, and she believed it herself (v. 24).

Don't miss the impact of the story. Elijah, the great prophet of God, was rejected by Israel's king, and because of this rejection he was sent to a Gentile widow who embraced the word of the Lord. In the same way, Jesus would be rejected by the Jews, which would mean open doors for the Gentiles (see Acts 10:44–48; Rom. 11:11–24; Eph. 2:14–16). Additionally, the people in Nazareth wanted Jesus to perform miracles before they would believe that He was who He claimed to be, but Jesus wanted them to believe first. The story of the Zarephath widow shows that she believed the Lord's word before Elijah performed the miracle of giving her never-ending supplies of bread.[13]

The second story that Jesus uses comes from 2 Kings 5:1–19, where Naaman, commander of the army of the king of Syria and a leper, is sent to the king of Israel to be cured. Naaman had heard of Elisha, the great prophet, from his wife's little servant girl from Israel who had been carried off by the Syrians. Naaman's visit was to show hardened Israel that there was a prophet (Elisha) among them (v. 8). In the end, Naaman embraced the God of Israel.

---

13. Ryken, *Luke*, 1:185.

Likewise, the Jews in the Nazareth synagogue needed to recognize that there was a true Prophet among them and that God had a plan for the Gentiles. Furthermore, the Jews needed to believe before they could be healed, just as Naaman had to believe that God would heal him before he got in the Jordan River. Sadly, the Jews failed to see their need for healing because they were blind to their condition of spiritual leprosy.

The people in the Nazareth synagogue responded to these two stories about Elijah and Elisha with anger. Not only was Jesus professing to be the fulfillment of Isaiah 61:1–2 but He was also pronouncing judgment on them by revealing their hearts. In response they drove Him out of town and attempted to throw Him off a cliff. But Jesus passed through their midst and went away. Not even an angry mob could deter God's plan of redemption. Jesus's time to die would come, and it would be at the hands of angry people, but it would not be at that time. Jesus still had work to do.

Sometimes we can do what is right in God's eyes and still be rejected by family and friends, coworkers and neighbors. Don't let them deter you. Keep your eyes on Jesus and go your way. Sometimes we can't get away, though. A husband, a parent, an in-law, or a teenage or adult child may ridicule us for our faith. If that is the case, we must stay and pray. We must continue to serve them with the love of Jesus and pray that the Lord will open up their blind eyes. By His grace we will endure even the most painful ridicule, recognizing that Jesus endured much more.

There is another lesson from this incident at Nazareth. Some of us are acting like the people in Nazareth. Jesus is familiar to us. We have grown up hearing about Him in Sunday school and family devotions. We have heard His name from our parents or siblings all our lives, but we do not believe that He is the Son of God. We want Him to prove Himself by doing mighty things for us, and when He doesn't, we get angry and want to throw Him out of our lives. Or we might be willing to keep Him in our lives, but it will be on our terms, not His. Dear reader, what have you done with Jesus? Have you embraced Him or rejected Him?

Jesus in the Synagogue in Capernaum (4:31–37)

Jesus was not deterred from His Father's plan and purpose for His life, not even by an angry mob in His hometown. He kept His eyes fixed on His Father and went down to Capernaum in Galilee. Capernaum was located on the northwest shore of the Sea of Galilee and was a major town for the Jews that had an important trade economy focused on agriculture and fishing.[14] Jesus went there to continue to proclaim good news to the poor, liberty to the captives, recovery of sight to the blind, liberty to the oppressed, and the year of the Lord's favor (see Luke 4:18–19). Jesus kept His custom of going to the synagogue on the Sabbath, displaying for us the importance of this means of grace (corporate worship) in our own lives. Jesus taught in the synagogue, and the people were astonished at His authority. He also displayed His power and authority over unclean spirits.

---

14. Bock, *Luke*, 1:428.

In the synagogue there was a man who had the spirit of an unclean demon. We don't know exactly how this unclean demon manifested itself in his life, but part of the manifestation was verbal because he cried out to Jesus with a loud voice. Even though the man was crying out with a loud voice, Jesus addressed the demon. Therefore, it was the demon who was behind the man's words: "Let us [demons] alone! What have we [demons] to do with You, Jesus of Nazareth? Did You come to destroy us [demons]? I [a demon] know who You are—the Holy One of God!" (Luke 4:34).

Notably, this demon knew that Jesus was the enemy. Also, he suspected that Jesus had come to destroy demons. He knew the battle between good and evil and that Jesus is more powerful than evil. In addition, he associated Jesus with His hometown, emphasizing His humanity, but he also called Him the Holy One of God, emphasizing His divinity. Finally, he knew who Jesus is, the Holy One of God.

Jesus responded to the demon with a rebuke: "Be quiet, and come out of him!" (Luke 4:35). The demon threw the man down in the midst of the crowd in the synagogue and came out of him, having done the man no harm. The people were amazed at Jesus's authority and power, and the report about Him continued to circulate throughout the entire region (see v. 14).

Jesus in Simon's House (4:38–41)

Jesus did not minister in only public places like the synagogue; He also ministered in private places like Simon Peter's home. Simon Peter's mother-in-law was ill with a high fever and close to death. Her family cried out to the Lord on her behalf. Jesus, displaying His power and authority over the evil of physical suffering, rebuked the fever and it left her. As a testimony of God's power, the Lord enabled her to have the strength to immediately arise and begin serving them. Jesus also healed many other sick people that day.

These healings are a foretaste of what life will be like in the New Jerusalem when there will be no more suffering and death (Rev. 21:4). While it is not wrong for us to pray that the Lord will heal us (see James 5:14), we must expect suffering in this life and learn to be content in the midst of it as we rely on the sufficiency of God's grace (2 Cor. 12:9).

Before the passage ends, Luke adds another note about demons. They came out of many people, professing Jesus to be who He is, "the Son of God," but they professed with the wrong motives, so He silenced them. Proclaiming who Jesus is with hatred toward Him does not please Him. That's why proclaiming Christ is the duty of believers who can say with love in their heart, "He is the Son of God!"

Jesus in Seclusion (4:42–44)

When it was day, Jesus departed and went to a solitary place to pray (see Mark 1:35). Although we don't know what Jesus prayed, certainly these hours of prayer were the strength behind His ministry. Significantly, it was after He prayed that He was able to say no to the crowds who wanted Him to stay in Capernaum and yes to His Father's plan, which involved preaching the good news of the kingdom of God in other towns.[15]

Jesus set the example that ministry should begin with prayer. We must take our plans and purposes to our Father so that He can make them conform to His plans and purposes. By putting prayer first, we will, by God's grace, fulfill the purpose He has for our lives.

◆ ◆ ◆ ◆

Christ's ministry, far superior to any ministry ever known, is an event still worthy of celebration. And indeed, this is what we do each time we come together as believers for corporate worship. As we listen to the preaching of the word and engage in the sacraments on the Lord's Day, we celebrate that Christ came to preach the good news of the kingdom of God. Just as John the Baptist prepared the way for Christ's ministry during His first coming, so too the church of God prepares the way for His second coming by proclaiming the gospel to every tribe, tongue, and nation. As worthy of celebration as His baptism and beginning ministry were, though, how much greater will the celebration be at "the marriage of the Lamb," when believers, the bride of Christ, will behold their beloved Bridegroom and "inherit all things" (Rev. 19:7; 21:7).

---

15. The *kingdom of God* does not refer to a physical, political kingdom for God's people but a spiritual one. It was inaugurated at Christ's first coming and will be consummated when He returns. This kingdom is a direct attack on the kingdom of this world that is ruled by Satan. As believers await its consummation, they are to proclaim the kingdom of God and teach others about the Lord Jesus Christ.

Processing It Together...

1. What do we learn about God in Luke 3–4?

2. How does this reshape how we should view our present circumstances?

3. What do we learn about God's Son, Jesus Christ?

4. How should this impact our relationship with God and with others?

5. What do we learn about God's covenant with His people?

6. How are we to live in light of this?

7. How can we apply Luke 3–4 to our lives today and in the future?

8. How should we apply this passage in our churches?

9. Look back at "Put It in Perspective" in your personal study questions. What did you find challenging or encouraging about this lesson?

10. Look back at "Principles and Points of Application." How has this lesson impacted your life?

The Master Fisherman and Teacher

Luke 5–6

Purpose . . .

Head. What do I need to know from this passage in Scripture?

- Christ, the Master Fisherman and Teacher, calls others to follow Him by loving their enemies, bearing good fruit, and building on the foundation of the word of God.

Heart. How does what I learn from this passage affect my internal relationship with the Lord?

- I am a kingdom disciple who has received God's call to follow Him.

Hands. How does what I learn from this passage translate into action for God's kingdom?

- I will love my neighbors by praying for them and proclaiming the gospel to them.
- I will worship God on the Lord's Day in a local church and engage in acts of mercy.
- I will seek the Lord's will in making decisions.
- I will embrace suffering and live with an eternal perspective.
- I will pray for my enemies and show them mercy.
- I will stop judging others and instead repent of my sins.
- I will, by God's grace, bear the fruit of righteousness in my life and ministry.
- I will build my life on the word of God and teach others to do the same.

Personal Study...

Pray. Ask that God will open up your heart and mind as you study His Word. This is His story of redemption that He has revealed to us, and the Holy Spirit is our teacher.

Ponder the Passage. Read Luke 5–6.

- *Point*: What is the point of this passage? How does this relate to the point of the entire book?

- *Persons*: Who are the main people involved in this passage? What characterizes them?

- *Persons of the Trinity*: Where do you see God the Father, God the Son, and God the Holy Spirit in this passage?

- *Puzzling Parts*: Are there any parts of the passage that you don't quite understand or that seem interesting or confusing?

Put It in Perspective.

- *Place in Scripture*: What is the original context of this text? What is the redemptive-historical context—what has or hasn't happened in redemptive history at this point in Scripture? How does this text connect to Christ?

The following questions will help you if you got stuck on any of the previous questions, and they will help you dig a little deeper into the text, putting it all into perspective.

1. **5:1–11.** (a) Where was Jesus, and what is another name for this place in Scripture (see John 6:1)?

   (b) What was the crowd doing, and how did Jesus respond?

   (c) What miracle did Jesus perform after He had finished speaking, and for whom?

(d) What do Peter's two responses to Jesus reveal about the tension within him?

(e) What did the miracle display about Jesus, and what did it reveal about Simon Peter?

(f) Who were the others with Simon Peter, and what was their response to Jesus and His miracle?

(g) How does Jesus's call of the first disciples reflect the calls of Elisha (1 Kings 19:19–21) and Isaiah (Isa. 6:8–13)?

2. 5:12–16. (a) What do you learn about leprosy from Leviticus 13:1–14:32, and in light of this, why is it significant that Jesus touched the leprous man?

(b) What did Jesus tell the leprous man to do and not do, and why (see Lev. 14:2–32)?

(c) What is the leprous man's response to Jesus's command in verse 14, and how does this help explain verse 15 (see Mark 1:45)?

(d) What was Jesus's response, and why is this significant?

3. 5:17–26. (a) Who had come to hear Jesus, from where had they come, and what does this tell us about Jesus's ministry?

(b) How does verse 17 relate to Luke 3:21–22; and 4:1, 14?

(c) What was the response of the scribes and Pharisees to Jesus healing the paralytic, and why (see Ex. 29:46; Ps. 130:4; Isa. 43:25; Mic. 7:18)?

(d) What did Jesus call Himself (v. 24), and what was Jesus claiming by using this title for Himself (see Dan. 7:13–14)?

(e) How were the paralytic man's response and the crowd's response to Jesus alike?

4. 5:27–32. (a) What is Levi's other name (see Matt. 9:9), and why would his occupation pose a challenge to following Jesus?

(b) What did Levi do for Jesus, and who was there?

(c) Compare the Pharisees' and their scribes' response to the disciples with Exodus 15:24; 16:7–12; 17:3; Numbers 11:1; 14:2, 27–29, 36; 16:11, 41; 17:5, 10; Psalms 59:15; 106:25; and 1 Corinthians 10:10. In whose footsteps do they follow?

(d) What is Jesus's response to the scribes and Pharisees, and how does this relate to Luke 4:18–19, 21, 43?

5. 5:33–39. (a) What charge against the disciples did the Pharisees and scribes bring to Jesus?

(b) What is the background of fasting in the Old Testament (see Lev. 16:29, 31; 23:26–32; Num. 29:7–11, where the phrase "afflict your souls" refers to fasting)?

(c) What is Jesus's first response to the scribes and Pharisees, and what does this mean?

(d) What is Jesus's second response to the scribes and Pharisees, and what are His two main points?

6. **6:1–5.** (a) Was the disciples' action on the Sabbath lawful (see Lev. 19:9–10)? If it was, what was the problem (see Ex. 20:8–11; 34:21; Deut. 5:12–15)?

(b) What does Jesus proclaim about Himself using 1 Samuel 21:1–6?

7. **6:6–11.** (a) Who is watching Jesus closely, and why?

(b) What is Jesus's response to the scribes and Pharisees?

(c) What was the response of the scribes and Pharisees to Jesus healing the man?

(d) Who is Jesus again revealing Himself to be (see 6:5)?

8. **6:12–16.** (a) Where is Jesus "in these days" (see 4:14)?

(b) How did Jesus prepare to choose the twelve apostles?

(c) From what group did Jesus choose the twelve apostles, and what are their names (see also Matt. 10:2–4; Mark 3:16–19; Acts 1:13)?

(d) How do the twelve apostles relate to the twelve tribes of Israel (see Ex. 24:4; Luke 22:28–30; Rev. 21:12–14)?

(e) What do you learn about Judas Iscariot, and how is this fulfilled (see Luke 22:3–6, 21–23, 47–48)?

9. **6:17–19.** (a) What was the first thing that the newly chosen apostles did with Jesus?

(b) Why did the people come to Jesus, and what was His response?

(c) By whose power did He do this (see Luke 3:22; 4:1, 14, 18)?

10. **6:20–26.** (a) Whom does Jesus address in His sermon?

(b) How do the four blessings relate to the four woes?

(c) How do Jesus's words in verses 20–24 reflect the promises given in Isaiah 61:1–2, which are fulfilled in Jesus's ministry (see Luke 4:18–19)?

(d) How does verse 21 reflect the prophecy in Isaiah 25:6–9?

11. 6:27–31. (a) How were Israel's enemies defined in the Old Testament (see Ex. 23:22–33; Deut. 28:7), and how do Jesus's exhortations in verses 27–28 define *enemies?*

(b) What are the four exhortations and the four examples that Jesus gives of loving one's enemy?

(c) How does verse 31 reflect Leviticus 19:18?

12. 6:32–36. (a) How do Jesus's questions in verses 32–34 contrast the love of an unbeliever with the love of a believer?

(b) What is the background of "sons of the Most High" (see Deut. 14:1; Hos. 1:10; 11:1)?

(c) Why are God's children to love their enemies (see also Lev. 19:2; Ps. 25:6; Isa. 63:15–16; Dan. 9:9, 18; Hos. 2:19)?

13. 6:37–42. (a) What four exhortations does Jesus give, and how does He illustrate His point in verses 37–38?

(b) There are three parts to Jesus's parable (vv. 39, 40, 41–42). What is the point of each one?

14. 6:43–45. What is Jesus teaching through this parable (see also Matt. 7:15–20; 12:33–37)?

15. 6:46–49. (a) What kind of people is Jesus targeting in this parable?

(b) Contrast the two builders.

Principles and Points of Application

16. 5:1–11. (a) Describe your earliest memory of understanding what it means to follow Jesus.

(b) In your present circumstances, what do you need to give up in order to follow Him wholeheartedly?

17. 5:12–26. (a) For what do you need to pray "Lord, if you will, you can…"?

(b) How can you make prayer a daily priority, especially before making decisions?

(c) How do you respond to God's physical healing and forgiveness of your sins, and how are you teaching others to do the same?

18. 5:27–32. How are you showing the marginalized in your town or city the love of Jesus? How can you invest in their lives?

19. 6:1–11. (a) How do your attitude and actions on Sunday reflect (or not reflect) that Jesus is Lord of the Sabbath?

(b) Do you know an elderly person or someone who is chronically ill who would appreciate a visit? Could you show hospitality to someone who is lonely or new to your church? Is there a homeless shelter where you could serve? How can you display mercy to others on the Lord's Day?

20. 6:20–26. (a) How do the four beatitudes encourage you to persevere and endure in the Christian life?

(b) In what ways do the four woes convict you? Repent of specific sins.

21. 6:27–42. (a) How are you showing Christ's love to your enemies?

(b) Who do you need to stop judging? Instead, which of your own sins should you turn your attention to, asking the Lord to change you before you gently approach someone else who needs to change?

22. 6:43–49. (a) What kind of fruit does your life display, and in what areas do you need to grow (see Gal. 5:22–23)?

(b) Using Luke 6:48–49 and Psalm 127:1–2, pray and ask the Lord to help you and your family build your house on the rock.

Putting It All Together...

When hopelessness overwhelms us, it can be easy to quit. Whether we are in a relationship, a ministry position, or a career, there are times we feel that we can't persevere. But oftentimes during these moments, the Lord reveals things about our hearts that we never would have seen apart from the adversity.

When guilt overwhelms us, it can be easy to feel unworthy to continue serving the Lord. We feel unclean. But often it's during those times that the Lord reveals His grace to us. We learn the truth that we can be clean again because Christ's blood washes us.

When suffering overwhelms us, we often feel that we won't make it through the pain. But many times this is when we learn that the greatest healing has already occurred in our life. God has forgiven us of our sins. We can continue to suffer while glorifying God.

In hopelessness, guilt, and suffering, we can trust in the Fisher of men, the Son of Man, the Bridegroom, and the Great Physician. He gives more grace, abundant mercy, cleansing power, and forgiveness of sins. In light of such grace and mercy, He calls us to an entirely different kind of life. A life built on the foundation of Jesus Christ produces the fruit of love, especially for our enemies.

I. Christ Calls by the Lake (5:1–11)

As Jesus stood by the lake of Gennesaret (also called the Sea of Galilee in Matt. 4:18) with the multitude eager to hear the word of God, He seized the opportunity to make Peter's boat a pulpit. Although we don't know what He said, it was certainly gospel-centered preaching (Luke 4:18–19). Jesus did not just teach the people; He displayed the power and authority of God's word by a miracle.

He moved from addressing the crowd to addressing an individual. Simon Peter was a fisherman who knew his occupation well. He was convinced that after a night of fruitless toil, there were no fish in the sea to catch. But Jesus wanted to test Peter's faith. He knew that Peter would be one of His apostles, so He was preparing him to trust in His word.

Jesus told Peter to put his nets into the water to catch fish. By faith, Peter did so. And when he did, he experienced the grace, mercy, power, and authority of Christ. Peter and the other fishermen were overwhelmed with the amount of fish in their nets. There were so many that the nets were breaking and they had to ask their partners in another boat to help. But both boats became so full that they started sinking. Seeing the miracle, Peter fell down before Jesus and said, "Depart from me, for I am a sinful man, O Lord!" (Luke 5:8).

This is the response of everyone to whom God reveals His grace. When we come face-to-face with the power and authority of God's word, we also come face-to-face with the reality of our own sin. When Isaiah saw his sin in light of the holy King, he was prepared to answer God's call to speak His word in Israel (Isa. 6:5, 8). Similarly, Jesus was preparing Peter to follow His call by revealing His grace, power, and authority. Jesus continues to do this for those He calls. He reveals His grace to us by opening up our blind eyes to see His power and authority. Only then can we respond to His call, believe in His name, and become His disciple.

Peter was not the only one called that day by the Fisher of men to be a fisher of men. Simon's fishing partners saw Jesus's power and believed in Him. James and John, sons of Zebedee, and Andrew (Matt. 4:18–22) also left everything behind and followed Jesus. By God's grace they saw that catching men was more important than catching fish. Because they heard and believed the word of God, they gave up their livelihood to live for Jesus.

Have you, dear friend, heard and believed the word of God, forsaking all else and following Jesus? If so, how are you making disciples (Matt. 28:18–20)? One of the ways we make disciples is to teach them God's word. But we must know God's word ourselves so that we can explain it to our children and grandchildren, family and friends, neighbors and coworkers.

II. Christ Cleanses a Leper (5:12–26)
While Jesus was in a Galilean city, a man full of leprosy came to Him. Leprosy was a disease on the skin. Anyone with leprosy was pronounced unclean by the priest and sent outside the camp of the covenant community (Lev. 13:45–46). So this man was going against the rules and regulations for a leprous person. Remarkably, instead of seeing his limitations, this leper saw his liberty. The person on whom he had placed all his hope, the One he believed could heal him from his disease, and the One who did the miraculous stood before him.

When the leper saw Jesus, he fell on his face and begged Him, "Lord, if You are willing, You can make me clean" (Luke 5:12). Strikingly, this man who belonged outside the city was in the city, facedown, begging. Without doubting God's authority or presuming on His grace, this leprous man cried out to Jesus. Significantly, Jesus stretched out His hand and touched him. According to the law, Jews were not supposed to touch a leprous person. Leprosy was highly contagious. The leprous person was unclean. This man had been ostracized from society and was forced to live alone without the touch of another person. But Jesus reached out His hand of compassion and touched him.

I used to take my children to volunteer each week at a dementia unit in one of our local retirement communities. A man who was always sitting in the hallway constantly groaned. Several of the ladies with unkempt hair were curled up in recliners trying to get comfortable. The hallways were filled with the smell of suffering and death. Sometimes it was hard for my children and me to reach out our hands and touch them. But when we did, they responded! They felt the love in our touch, and they came alive for a moment. You could see it in their eyes. And how they loved my children! They loved to hear the chatter and laughter of little ones and see the stature of a growing boy and girl. While many in society had tucked them out of sight and mind, they recognized that we had voluntarily come to touch them.

Although we try to deny it, all of us are untouchable, unlovely, and unclean. Because of our sin, we have all fallen short of God's glory (Rom. 3:23). And except for God's grace, we would remain unclean. Thankfully, we have a High Priest who has gone outside the camp to cleanse us with His blood. He has brought us before the Father's throne so that we may be pronounced clean.

Jesus did not just give this leprous man compassion; He also gave him a new way of life. He cleansed this man of his leprosy. Since Jesus adhered to the Mosaic law, He told the man to tell no one, but to go and show himself to the priest and make an offering for his cleansing as proof to the priests that he was healed (see Lev. 14:1–32). Most likely Jesus didn't want the man to tell anyone for two reasons. First, there were enough reports about Jesus and crowds following Him, so He didn't need any more publicity surrounding His ministry. Second, the healed man needed to be pronounced clean by the priests so that he could be welcomed back into society. But the formerly leprous man "went out and began to proclaim it freely, and to spread the matter, so that Jesus could no longer openly enter the city, but was outside in deserted places; and they came to Him from every direction" (Mark 1:45).

In response, Jesus withdrew to pray. He knew the power source behind His ministry was prayer to His Father. He knew that as busyness in ministry increased, so must prayer. Do you believe prayer is that important? Dear believer, we must pray. Your marriage, parenting, career, and ministry are too dependent on God's power to not pray. Whatever it takes, make time to pray.

On one of the days that Jesus was teaching in Capernaum in Galilee (see Mark 2:1), the power of the Lord was with Him to heal (see Luke 3:22; 4:1, 14). His critics, the Pharisees and teachers of the law, had come from every village of Galilee and Judea and from Jerusalem. Others specifically sought Jesus to heal a paralytic, coming to Jesus in faith. Although there was no easy way to get to Him because of the crowd, they were not deterred. They went up on the roof, removed some of the tiles, and let the paralytic down before Jesus. Instead of reprimanding the men for interrupting Him, He commended them for their faith.

Significantly, the first thing Jesus did was forgive the paralytic man of his sins. His paralysis was not his greatest problem; sin was. This upset the scribes and the Pharisees, who believed there was only one God and He alone could forgive sins. For Jesus to forgive this man's sins was to put Himself on the same level of authority as God. Indeed, He was claiming to be God.

Jesus knew their hearts and dealt with their questioning. It was easier to tell the paralytic that his sins were forgiven than to command him to get up and walk. No one could see whether his sins were forgiven. But everyone would be able to see whether he could walk. So Jesus revealed His authority on earth to forgive sins by enabling this man to walk.

Notably, Jesus calls Himself the Son of Man, claiming to fulfill Daniel 7:13–14, which tells about the Ancient of Days (God the Father) giving the Son of Man (God the Son) an everlasting kingdom in which people from every nation would serve Him. In other words, Jesus was proclaiming Himself to be the promised Messiah.

When Jesus commanded the paralytic to get up, pick up his bed, and go home, He proved to the crowd that He had power over both physical and spiritual paralysis. Happily, the man believed, obeyed Jesus, and glorified God. The crowd also glorified God and professed that they had seen extraordinary things that day. Sadly, the Pharisees persisted in criticizing Jesus, as they will do throughout the rest of the gospel.

If we reject Jesus's claim to be King and persist in unbelief, we will find salvation in no other person and in no other place. When the Son of Man returns, we will face eternal judgment. But if we believe in Jesus, trusting Him to save us, we have the joy of an eternity with Jesus before us.

III. Christ Converts Levi (5:27–32)

While Jesus was still in Capernaum, He saw a tax collector named Levi, also known as Matthew (see Matt. 9:9), sitting at the tax booth. Tax collectors were one of the most detested classes in Israel because they collected taxes for the Romans from their own countrymen.[1] But Jesus told this tax collector to follow Him. This is always the way of Christ. He is the great Fisher of men. We do not seek Him; He seeks us. What a glorious truth! Not one of us deserves to be chosen. There was nothing in us that was righteous when God chose us to be His daughters. Yet He comes to us and calls us to follow Him.

When Levi heard Jesus's call, he left everything behind and followed Him. The first thing he did was to prepare a great feast in his house for his new Master. Levi, having been a tax collector, was probably one of the wealthiest of the twelve apostles and could have afforded to throw an elaborate feast. In his joy and excitement about his new profession as a fisher of men, he invited his old friends from the tax-collecting business to recline at the table with him and Jesus. This was the source of the Pharisees' grumbling against Jesus, the same sin Israel was guilty of in the desert (see, for example, Ex. 15:24; 16:7–12; 17:3). They complained that He was eating and drinking with the wrong crowd.

But Jesus knew His calling and answered their grumbling in light of it. Those who are well do not need a physician; only the sick do. He had not come to call the righteous (that is, the self-righteous), but sinners to repentance. This was an indictment against the Pharisees and scribes, who were so self-righteous that they were hardened to their need for Jesus and unresponsive to His call.

As Philip Ryken reminds us, "The story of Levi's conversion is really the story of every believer in Christ. This is how God saves sinners. First he chooses us by grace (*election*) and calls us to follow Christ (*effectual calling*). By the word of the Holy Spirit,

---

1. Sproul, *Walk with God*, 88.

he enables us to turn away from sin (*repentance unto life*) and follow Jesus (*saving faith*). And as we follow Jesus, we glorify God (*worship*) and proclaim his gospel (*witness*)."[2] Is this your story, dear reader? And if so, how are you investing in the lives of those who feel unworthy to even step foot inside a church building? Are you praying for them and sharing the hope of the gospel with them?

IV. Christ Claims Lordship (5:33–6:11)

The scribes and Pharisees weren't done interrogating Jesus and His disciples. They went on to question the difference in fasting and prayers between Jesus's disciples and the disciples of John the Baptist and the disciples of the Pharisees. In the Old Testament, fasting was required only on the Day of Atonement, but by the time of Jesus, fasting had become a regular discipline among the Jews.[3] Since Jesus's disciples were eating and drinking instead of fasting and offering prayers, the Pharisees felt superior to them.

By using the illustration of a wedding to explain why His disciples were not fasting, Jesus reprimanded the Pharisees for their self-righteousness. He compared Himself to a bridegroom, a concept God used in the Old Testament to illustrate His relationship with Israel (see Isa. 54:5–8; 62:4–5; Jer. 2:2; Ezek. 16; Hos. 2:16–23). By demonstrating Himself to be the Bridegroom, Jesus proclaimed that He is God. One day the Bridegroom would be taken away from His church, and Jesus saying this foreshadowed His death, resurrection, and ascension. Only then would His people have a reason to fast until His return. But believers don't just fast during the Interadvent age; they also feast at the Lord's Table. This feast confirms our union and communion with Christ and testifies to and renews our thankfulness to and engagement with God, as well as our mutual love and fellowship with our brothers and sisters in Christ.[4]

Jesus also told the scribes and Pharisees a parable to correct their thinking. We don't tear a new garment in order to patch an old one. Think of when someone gets a hole in their pants. You do not rip a new pair of pants to fix the holey ones; you buy a patch to match the old ones. To rip a new pair of pants would ruin a good garment that wouldn't even match the old one. Also, if someone puts wine in an old wineskin,[5] they waste the new wine because the old wineskin would be too brittle to hold the weight of the new wine. Likewise, Jesus had not brought a patch to Judaism or new wine to be dumped into the old way of religion.[6] He had inaugurated the new covenant and had come to make all things new.

To make another point, Jesus told the Pharisees and scribes that those who drink the old wine become content with its taste and don't desire the new wine. Similarly,

---

2. Ryken, *Luke*, 1:231.

3. Pao and Schnabel, "Luke," 293.

4. Westminster Larger Catechism 168.

5. "Wineskins were usually made from sheepskin or goatskin, and the neck area of the animal became the neck of the container. The body portion was skinned, the hair was removed, and the hide was treated to prevent the skin from changing the taste of the contents. Finally, it was sewn together." Bock, *Luke*, 1:520.

6. Morris, *Luke*, 141–42.

there would be many in Judaism who would remain content with the old-time religion rather than embrace the new covenant that Jesus had inaugurated. This is a danger for us. Sometimes it's more comfortable living with religious tradition than it is to fully embrace Christ.

Still in Galilee, Jesus was walking through the grain fields with His disciples one Sabbath. Undoubtedly, they were busy doing ministry and were getting something to eat along the way. Plucking, rubbing, and eating the grain were not against the law. The leftover harvest gleanings and the grain on the edges of the fields were to be left for the poor and the sojourner (see Lev. 19:9–10). But the Pharisees were upset that this was being done on the Sabbath, which was against their law. They had added their own rules and regulations to the law of the Lord and stood in judgment over those who broke them. They began in the right place, observing the Sabbath (see Ex. 20:8–11; 34:21), but they ended wrongly, putting religious rules above people's basic need for food.

In response Jesus reminded them of a story in the Old Testament that occurs very soon after Jonathan warned David to flee from Saul (see 1 Sam. 21:1–6). The first place that David went was to Nob, to Ahimelech the priest. Tired and hungry from the journey, he asked for bread for himself and for his men. The only bread that Ahimelech had was the holy bread, which only priests were allowed to eat (see Ex. 25:30), but Ahimelech, unlike the Pharisees, put mercy ahead of ceremonial law. By referring to this story, Jesus connected Himself with David (see also Luke 1:32–33, 68–79; 2:11; 3:22, 31), emphasizing that He is the final and Davidic King.

Second, Jesus declared that as the Son of Man (see Dan. 7:13), He is Lord of the Sabbath. As the one who is greater than David, He could certainly choose to put mercy over ceremonial law on the Sabbath by allowing His disciples to eat grain from the fields.

On another Sabbath in Galilee, Jesus entered the synagogue to teach. There was a man whose right hand was withered, most likely a form of muscular atrophy.[7] The scribes and Pharisees were watching Him so that they could accuse Him of wrongdoing if He healed on the Sabbath. Jesus, aware of their hard hearts, told the man to come and stand in front of Him. Then He asked him, "Is it lawful on the Sabbath to do good or to do evil, to save life or to destroy?" (Luke 6:9). This question was not intended for the man but for the scribes and Pharisees. Jesus looked at them with authority and "anger, being grieved by the hardness of their hearts" (Mark 3:5). Then Jesus told the man to stretch out his hand. He restored the man's hand, putting mercy over the laws of the Pharisees. Sadly, although Jesus had done nothing wrong, the scribes and Pharisees furiously discussed what they might do to Him, a foreshadowing of Jesus's coming death at the hands of hardened men.

The Westminster Confession of Faith reminds us that the Lord's Day is to be "taken up, the whole time, in the public and private exercises of his worship, *and in the duties*

---

7. Morris, *Luke*, 143.

of necessity and mercy" (21.8; emphasis added). Getting up early to feed the homeless before corporate worship, visiting residents at the local nursing home, taking a meal to someone who is suffering, and praying with the discouraged are a few ways we can extend mercy on the Lord's Day. How will you and your family engage in such acts?

V. Christ Chooses Leaders (6:12–16)

Still in Galilee, Jesus went out to the mountain to pray to His heavenly Father for an entire night because He had a very important decision to make the next day. He was about to choose the men who would be closest to Him in His earthly ministry, the twelve apostles (see also Matt. 10:2–4; Mark 3:16–19; Acts 1:13). Although there were many disciples of Jesus, there were only twelve apostles. A disciple is "a learner or student"; an apostle is "one who is sent."[8] These apostles were not the religious elite in town; rather, they were ordinary men, and when Jesus called them, they followed Him. Sadly, one of them, Judas Iscariot, would later betray Jesus (see Luke 22:3–6, 21–22, 47–48).

If the Son of God needed to spend all night in prayer to God the Father before making an important decision, we need to do so all the more. Before we choose Bible study leaders and teachers, volunteers for children's and youth ministry, a spouse, a career change, a change in location, or anything of importance, we should pray. Prayer displays a dependent and humble attitude before our heavenly Father as we seek His will for our lives and ministries.

VI. Christ Challenges Lawlessness (6:17–49)

Jesus came down from the mountain with His twelve apostles in order to preach the good news of the kingdom of God (see Luke 4:43). Multitudes of people from different places came to hear Him and be healed of their diseases. Those who were troubled with unclean spirits were cured. By the power of the Holy Spirit (see 3:22; 4:1, 14, 18), He graciously healed them all. By displaying His power over the prince of this world and his demons, Jesus gave the people a foretaste of what was to come when He defeated Satan on the cross and what will ultimately come when He returns to bring in the new heaven and the new earth, where there will be no more evil.

Importantly, the context of Jesus's sermon on the plain is teaching His disciples (Luke 6:20). Also, while there are some similarities between this sermon and the Sermon on the Mount, which Matthew records in chapters 5–7, there are also many differences. It is probably best to understand these as similar sermons that Jesus preached on two different occasions.[9]

Jesus began His sermon with four blessings and four woes that parallel each other in significant ways. The first blessing is for the poor, for theirs is the kingdom of heaven. While Jesus is speaking of the materially poor, He is more focused on addressing the

---

8. Sproul, *Walk with God*, 98–99.
9. Ryken, *Luke*, 1:258.

spiritually poor. These are the people who have given up everything for His name's sake and are poor for the sake of the kingdom.

In contrast, He warned the rich, who have already received their consolation (Luke 6:24). Wealth in and of itself is not wrong. It is what people do with their wealth or how they depend on it that matters. Do we keep it to ourselves, or do we give it away in the name of Jesus? Do we depend on it for our security, or do we trust the Lord to provide for our needs?

The second beatitude addresses those who are hungry; in the future they will be satisfied. This relates to the first beatitude because those who are poor are often hungry. Jesus promises that the day is coming when believers will be invited to the marriage supper of the Lamb (Rev. 19:9). That will be a wonderful feast that satisfies the deepest hunger!

In contrast, Jesus warns those who are full now that they will be hungry later (Luke 6:25a). Those who have everything that they want by the world's standards but are poor spiritually will be hungry when the day of the Lord comes. Those who are invited to the marriage supper of the Lamb (a supper of salvation) will experience great joy, but those who are invited to the great supper of God (a supper of judgment) will experience great suffering (Rev. 19:17–18).

The third beatitude consoles those who weep now because of suffering for the sake of the kingdom. One day there will be no more pain, tears, or sorrow, and they will laugh (Rev. 21:4). In contrast, Jesus warns those who laugh now because they will weep later (Luke 6:25b). Those who are never serious about spiritual things, think that life is a party, and fail to understand that their lives are the Lord's and are to be lived for His glory will in the end mourn and weep because it will be too late to place their trust in God and walk in His ways.

The fourth beatitude concerns those who are hated, excluded, reviled, and spurned on account of the Son of Man. They are to rejoice and leap for joy because their reward is great in heaven. Although the prophets of the Old Testament endured such persecution, they looked by faith to the heavenly city.

In contrast, Jesus warned those who are flattered by men, such as the false prophets (Luke 6:26). While it is important for believers to have a good reputation (see Titus 2:8), something is usually wrong when everyone speaks well of us. This reveals that we are putting on different faces for different folks in order to find favor with people instead of fearing God.

Remember, Jesus was poor, hungry, sad, hated, excluded, reviled, and spurned (see Isa. 53:3–6). He calls His people to give up the satisfaction, security, and significance of this world to follow Him. He asks us to suffer for His name's sake, knowing the cross comes before the consummation of His kingdom. The kingdom of God has already been inaugurated through the incarnate Son of God, Jesus Christ. Rejoice in suffering and tribulation, dear believer, knowing that one day you will be rewarded in heaven, along with all those who have gone before you, not least of which are the prophets of old.

Next, Jesus exhorted His disciples to love, the characteristic trait of believers (Luke 6:27–38). He began with four exhortations: "Love your enemies, do good to those who hate you, bless those who curse you, and pray for those who spitefully use you" (vv. 27–28). Unbelievers may do all of these things for those who love them, but Jesus calls the believer to go beyond loving the loveable and express love to their enemies. This kind of love reflects God's electing love of us while we were still His enemies (see Eph. 2:1–10).

In the Old Testament, Israel's enemies were from different nations and followed different religions. But in the New Testament, the idea of an enemy takes on a far broader meaning. It is anybody who hates us, curses us, or abuses us. When we bless our enemies and pray for them, love will follow, by God's grace. I have seen this in my own life. When I have consistently prayed for someone who has been unkind to me, I have, by God's grace, grown in love for him or her. As we bring our enemies before our heavenly Father, we realize that except for the grace of God, we would be like them. We begin to see them through Christ's eyes, as sinners in need of a Savior, and our hearts are warmed with compassion as the Spirit works within us.

Jesus gave illustrations for His exhortations. If someone slaps your cheek, you should offer your other cheek too (Luke 6:29a). In other words, don't fight back. If someone takes away your cloak, you should also give them your tunic (v. 29b). In other words, for the sake of the kingdom of God, give up your comfort. If someone asks you for something, give it (v. 30a). Generosity must characterize the disciple of Jesus Christ. If someone takes away your goods, don't demand that they give them back (v. 30b). We are to overcome evil with good (see Rom. 12:19–21). Finally, if you desire that someone treat you in a certain way, treat her that way (Luke 6:31). In other words, be the first to take godly action. If I want a particular person to be kind to me, I should show kindness to her first.

Jesus continued to illustrate Christlike love (Luke 6:32–34). He explained that it doesn't take supernatural power to love those who love us. Worldly love, with its selfish motives, returns love for love. But godly love, with its selfless motives, is to return love even to those who do not love us.

Also, Jesus said that it doesn't take supernatural power to do good to those who do good to us. Worldly love returns good for good, but godly love does good even to those who treat you badly.

Finally, He noted that it doesn't take supernatural love to lend to others who will return what is borrowed in full. Worldly love motivates people to lend to others if they know they will receive back the same amount. Notably, the Old Testament civil law allowed Israel to charge their enemies with interest (see Deut. 23:19–20). But Jesus calls His disciples to go beyond this. Disciples of Jesus are not simply to look out for their own interests but for the interests of others.

Jesus summarized His teaching by ending where He began: "Love your enemies, do good, and lend, hoping for nothing in return." But this time He included a blessing: "Your reward will be great, and you will be sons of the Most High" (Luke 6:35). God the Father will recognize and bless the faithful disciple who has gone beyond the worldly way of love to display the love of God. Those who live this way reflect that they are daughters of the Most High (see Gen. 14:18; Luke 1:32). Jesus is the Son of the Most High first and foremost, but all those who are in Christ Jesus have the privilege of being sons and daughters of the Most High because of Christ's atoning work on the cross.

Because God is kind to the ungrateful and evil, His children must be as well: "Therefore be merciful, just as your Father also is merciful" (Luke 6:36; see also Neh. 9:19, 27–31; Ps. 25:6; Dan. 9:9, 18–19; Hos. 2:19). We must display God's lovingkindness to our enemies, praying for them, doing them good, and showing them mercy.

Jesus continued His call to love by giving four exhortations concerning judgment followed by an illustration and a promise. First, "judge not, and you shall not be judged" (Luke 6:37a). In other words, don't have an attitude toward others that never forgives, seeks to shame, and never encourages them to seek the love and mercy of God.[10] Second, "condemn not, and you shall not be condemned" (v. 37b). We must look at what Christ has done for us and forgive others, offering grace to them instead of condemnation (Rom. 8:1). Third, "forgive, and you will be forgiven" (Luke 6:37c). If we do not grasp the truth that God in Christ has forgiven us, we will not be able to forgive those who have wronged us (Eph. 4:32). But once we understand the gracious love of the Father and the forgiveness that we have in Christ, we will extend forgiveness to others who have wronged us, knowing that even while we were yet sinners, God the Father was reconciling us to Himself through Christ (2 Cor. 5:19). Fourth, "give, and it will be given to you" (Luke 6:38). Our love is to go beyond our heart and our words to our actions. We are to be gracious to others, helping them in their needs.

The promise for such love is beautifully illustrated by the imagery of counting grain. When measuring corn, the seller fills the measure three-quarters full and gives it a good shake to make the grains settle, then fills the measure to the top and gives it another shake before pressing the corn together with both hands and heaping it into a cone until there is no more room for a single grain.[11] What measure of blessings comes to the one who is extravagant in grace! It is a reflection of God's grace to us. But the promise also serves as a warning: "For with the same measure that you use, it will be measured back to you" (Luke 6:38).

Jesus closed His sermon with three parables. The first parable (Luke 6:39–42) uses three illustrations. First, a blind man cannot lead a blind man because they will both fall into a pit (see Isa. 24:17–18; Jer. 48:43–44). In other words, we must choose our leaders carefully, following those who faithfully seek the Lord.

---

10. Bock, *Luke*, 1:605.

11. Jeremias, as quoted in Bock, *Luke*, 1:607–8.

Second, since we will become like our teachers, we must choose our teachers carefully (Luke 6:40). They should be trained in the truths of God's word, give godly counsel, rightly divide the word of God, and love mercy. Jesus surely had Himself in view here as the teacher whom they should choose to follow first and foremost.[12]

Third, we must take the log out of our own eye before we take the speck out of our brother's eye (Luke 6:41). We must be slow to correct others and gentle when we do, examining ourselves before gently exhorting another.

The second parable is about a good tree that bears good fruit and a bad tree that bears bad fruit (Luke 6:43–45). This is not a parable that focuses on judging the fruit of others but on examining the fruit in our own lives. It is only by the Holy Spirit that we are changed into a good tree that produces the good fruit of love, joy, peace, patience, kindness, goodness, faithfulness, gentleness, and self-control (see Gal. 5:22–23).

The third parable is about a man who built his house on the foundation of a rock and a man who built his house without a foundation (Luke 6:46–49). Those who build their lives on the Rock will withstand the trials of this world, but those who build their lives on the ideologies of this world will ultimately be destroyed.

◆ ◆ ◆ ◆

If you are crying out to the Lord, "I can't do this anymore," be comforted that Jesus is with you. If you are crying out, "I am unclean," be assured that Jesus's blood is sufficient to cover your sin. If you are crying out, "I can't continue to suffer like this," be encouraged that even if you physically suffer for a lifetime, Jesus has taken away your spiritual suffering by dying on the cross for your sin and extending forgiveness to you.

Glorify God today for His grace and mercy, then extend grace and mercy to those who are hard to love. Except for the power of the Holy Spirit, this is impossible to do. But by God's grace, we too can love even our enemies, resting in the truth that vengeance is the Lord's and our future is securely grounded in Jesus Christ.

---

12. Ryken, *Luke*, 1:288.

Processing It Together...

1. What do we learn about God in Luke 5–6?

2. How does this reshape how we should view our present circumstances?

3. What do we learn about God's Son, Jesus Christ?

4. How should this impact our relationship with God and with others?

5. What do we learn about God's covenant with His people?

6. How are we to live in light of this?

7. How can we apply Luke 5–6 to our lives today and in the future?

8. How should we apply this passage in our churches?

9. Look back at "Put It in Perspective" in your personal study questions. What did you find challenging or encouraging about this lesson?

10. Look back at "Principles and Points of Application." How has this lesson impacted your life?

Jesus Displays His Authority

Luke 7–8

Purpose...

Head. What do I need to know from this passage in Scripture?

- Jesus reveals His authority over death, the kingdom, sin, revelation, creation, and demons.

Heart. How does what I learn from this passage affect my internal relationship with the Lord?

- I am a kingdom disciple who accepts God's purposes for my life by faith and responds by glorifying and loving Him.

Hands. How does what I learn from this passage translate into action for God's kingdom?

- I will teach others that our salvation is not based on our worthiness but on Christ's.
- I will display compassion to the hurting.
- I will help others grow in wisdom by studying the Bible.
- I will support those in ministry with prayer and other resources.
- I will recognize the importance of the covenant community.
- I will entrust both the physical and spiritual healing of my loved ones to the Lord.

Personal Study...

Pray. Ask that God will open up your heart and mind as you study His Word. This is His story of redemption that He has revealed to us, and the Holy Spirit is our teacher.

Ponder the Passage. Read Luke 7–8.

- *Point:* What is the point of this passage? How does this relate to the point of the entire book?

- *Persons:* Who are the main people involved in this passage? What characterizes them?

- *Persons of the Trinity:* Where do you see God the Father, God the Son, and God the Holy Spirit in this passage?

- *Puzzling Parts:* Are there any parts of the passage that you don't quite understand or that seem interesting or confusing?

Put It in Perspective.

- *Place in Scripture:* What is the original context of this text? What is the redemptive-historical context—what has or hasn't happened in redemptive history at this point in Scripture? How does this text connect to Christ?

The following questions will help you if you got stuck on any of the previous questions, and they will help you dig a little deeper into the text, putting it all into perspective.

1. 7:1–10. (a) Did the centurion go to Jesus to ask for help? If not, whom did he send?

(b) What are the two reasons the elders gave Jesus to show that the centurion was worthy of Jesus healing his servant, and what does this reveal about the centurion?

(c) In what did the centurion place his hope, and why?

(d) There is only one other time that Jesus is said to have marveled at someone. Compare Mark 6:6 with Luke 7:9. What is different?

(e) Compare 2 Kings 5:1–16 with Luke 7:1–10. How are Jesus's word and work superior to Elisha's?

2. 7:11–17. (a) With what emotion, words, and action did Jesus respond to the situation in Nain, and why is this significant (see also Num. 19:11)?

(b) How is the crowd's description of Jesus true but not thorough enough?

(c) How does the phrase "God has visited His people" reflect the covenant of grace (see, for example, Lev. 26:12)?

(d) Compare 1 Kings 17:17–24 with Luke 7:11–17. How are Jesus's word and work superior to Elijah's?

3. 7:18–23. (a) Where was John receiving reports (see Luke 3:20), and what was his response?

(b) What did John mean by "the Coming One" (see Ps. 118:26; Mal. 3:1; Luke 3:16)?

(c) How did Jesus respond to John's question (see also Luke 4:18–19; 1 Kings 17:17–24; 2 Kings 5:1–16; Isa. 26:19; 29:18–19; 35:3–4; 42:7; 61:1–2)?

(d) How is Jesus's beatitude in verse 23 a blessing and a warning?

4. 7:24–35. (a) How was John a prophet and more than a prophet (see Ex. 23:20; Isa. 40:3; Mal. 3:1; Luke 1:17, 76)?

(b) In verse 28, what does Jesus mean that the one who is least in the kingdom of God is greater than John the Baptist?

(c) How does Jesus's description of the Pharisees in verses 30–31 connect them to the wilderness generation (see Deut. 32:4b–5, 20; Jer. 7:29)?

(d) How are the Pharisees and lawyers described in verses 31–34?

(e) How are those who declared God just described in verse 35?

5. 7:36–50. (a) How did the woman of the city behave toward Jesus while He was dining at the Pharisee's house?

(b) What does Jesus's response to the Pharisee reveal?

(c) How does Simon respond to Jesus's question, and was he right?

(d) Contrast how Simon treated Jesus with how the woman treated Him.

(e) What does Jesus reveal Himself to be when He forgives the woman's sins (see Luke 1:69; 2:30; 4:18–19)?

6. **8:1–3.** (a) How was Jesus fulfilling His purpose (Luke 4:18–19, 43)?

(b) Who accompanied Him?

7. **8:4–15.** (a) What two groups is Jesus addressing in this parable, and what are four different ways that people might respond to God's word?

(b) What makes the difference between those who respond by God's grace and those who do not respond?

(c) How do the following passages provide background for this parable (Isa. 55:10–11; Jer. 4:3; 31:27; Ezek. 36:9; Dan. 2:18–19, 27–30, 47; Hos. 2:23)?

(d) How does Luke use Isaiah 6:9–10 in verse 10?

8. **8:16–18.** (a) How does Luke 8:8, 15 provide the context for these verses?

(b) What future event of redemptive history is ultimately in view in these verses, and how does it also apply to the present?

9. 8:19–21. (a) How has Jesus's mother heard the word of God and done it (see Luke 1:26–38)?

(b) What is Jesus's point in these verses then?

10. 8:22–25. (a) What does this event reveal about Jesus's humanity? His deity?

(b) In light of the following Old Testament passages, what does Jesus's calming the storm reveal (Ex. 14; Pss. 24:1–2; 29:3–4; 32:6–7; 33:6–7; 46:1–3; 65:5–8; 69:13–15; 77:16–20; 93:3–4; 104:7–9; 107:23–32; 124:1–5)?

11. 8:26–33. (a) What did the man with a demon cry out when he saw Jesus, and who was really speaking?

(b) What did the demons beg Jesus not to do, and what is "the abyss" (see Rev. 9:1–2, 11; 11:7; 17:8; 20:1, 3)?

(c) What did the demons ask Jesus to do instead, and what was the outcome?

12. 8:34–39. (a) What are the different responses of individuals and groups to Jesus's miracle?

(b) How does the story of the man possessed by demons in the region of the Gadarenes (or Gerasenes) display issues of purity and impurity for the Jews (see Lev. 11:24–28; Num. 19:11, 14–16)?

(c) How does Jesus once again put the need of a human over and above the ceremonial law?

13. **8:40–48.** (a) What kind of man came to see Jesus, and why?

(b) What stopped Jesus as He was on His way to Jairus's house?

(c) In light of Leviticus 15:19–30, what kind of life did this woman have?

(d) What did Jesus do for this woman, and how does this compare to Luke 7:44–50?

14. **8:49–56.** (a) How did Jesus encourage Jairus in a perilous moment?

(b) In front of whom did Jesus perform the resurrection miracle?

(c) What did Jesus say to those who were weeping and mourning, and how did they respond?

(d) Contrast Jesus's instruction to the healed demoniac (Luke 8:39) with His instruction to the girl's parents. Why do you think they are different?

Principles and Points of Application
15. **7:1–10.** How are you displaying humility and faith in God's word in your present circumstances?

16. **7:11–17.** Meditate on verse 13, recognizing that no matter the outcome of your circumstances, God is compassionate toward you in the midst of them and is the one who will one day usher in the new heaven and new earth, where there will be no more tears (Rev. 21:4).

17. **7:18–35.** (a) Have you believed in Jesus alone for salvation, or do His word and works offend you?

(b) If you are a believer, you are a child of wisdom. How are you growing in wisdom by studying the Bible, and how are you teaching others to do the same?

18. **7:36–50.** How have you poured out your best acts of service and worship for the Lord while loving Him much, rejoicing in His mercy, and receiving His forgiveness and peace?

19. **8:1–3.** What are some ways you can help your pastors and elders? Make a point of implementing these things.

20. **8:4–18.** Which kind of soil characterizes you, and why? Which kinds of soil characterize your loved ones? Give thanks and pray according to your specific answers.

21. **8:19–21.** (a) How can you grow in seeing the covenant community as your family?

(b) How are you serving as part of the covenant family by using your gifts for the other members' edification and encouragement?

22. **8:22–25.** In your present distress, how are you accusing God of being asleep and not caring, or fretting that you are perishing, or trusting in His authority over your circumstances?

23. **8:26–39.** (a) When you meet someone who has been rejected or scorned by society, how do you respond to him or her? How should you respond to him or her?

(b) How will you respond to God's grace in your life?

24. **8:40–56.** (a) How are you displaying faith in Jesus's power to heal in your present circumstances?

(b) How should you respond to a friend who tells you that she has prayed for God to heal her from a physical condition for years, but there's been no improvement?

Putting It All Together . . .

We all have had the experience (many times for most of us) of rebelling against authority. Probably our earliest memories of this are when we didn't want to do something our mother or father told us to do. But if we're honest, we have wanted at times to disregard the instructions of bosses, coaches, teachers, pastors, elders, and governing authorities. Certainly those in authority can abuse their power, but exercised in a God-honoring way, authority is for the good of humankind. The authority that godly husbands exercise over their wives, godly pastors and elders exercise over their flocks, and government authorities exercise over the people is a gift to those under their leadership. How much greater is the gift of God's authority over all things.

The risen Christ commissioned His disciples to go and make disciples of all nations with the assurance that "all authority has been given to Me in heaven and on earth" (Matt. 28:18). This absolute authority is anticipated in the life of Christ, a truth we especially see in Luke 7–8, which records Jesus displaying His authority over death, the kingdom, sin, revelation, creation, and demons. This should comfort us as we face suffering and sin and fight against it. Since Jesus has authority over such things, believers have every reason to hope that He will help them in their time of need.

I. Jesus Displays His Authority over Death (7:1–17)

Following His sermon on the plain, Jesus entered Capernaum, a city located on the Sea of Galilee that served as His home base for ministry. A Roman centurion had a highly valued servant who was sick and at the point of death. Presumably, the centurion heard about Jesus from all the reports that were circulating around the region and sent Jewish leaders to Him to request He come and heal his servant.

Interestingly, these Jews pleaded with Jesus to respond favorably to the centurion's request for two reasons. First, the Gentile centurion loved the Jewish nation. In other words, he loved God's people, and God had promised Abraham that He would bless those who blessed His people (Gen. 12:3). Second, he built a synagogue for the Jews so that they could worship God. In other words, the Gentile centurion enabled the worship of God through his building efforts. Again, in light of Genesis 12:3, it is no surprise that Jesus went with the Jews.

Before Jesus reached the house, the Roman centurion was overwhelmed by his unworthiness for Jesus to come and heal his servant. This Gentile realized that he was a sinner unworthy to stand in the presence of grace. So the centurion sent friends to Jesus, telling Him he wasn't worthy of His presence but still requesting that He would heal his servant by speaking a word. The centurion believed in the power of God's word. Just as he had the command of soldiers by the power of his word, he believed, by God's grace, that Jesus had even greater power. The Jewish leaders also saw the power of God's word, for at their return, they found the servant well.

There are only two times that Scripture says Jesus marveled at others, once for unbelief and once for belief. First, He marveled at the people's unbelief in His hometown of Nazareth (Mark 6:6). Second, He marveled because of the centurion's belief (Luke 7:9). Jesus told the crowd that He had not found such faith even in Israel. Significantly, God was opening the door of salvation to the Gentiles, as had been His plan all along (Gen. 12:3). We saw this with Rahab, Ruth, and Naaman in the Old Testament (see Josh. 2:8–14; Ruth 1:16; 2 Kings 5:1–16), and we see it again in the New Testament in the life of Cornelius (Acts 10) and in references to a people from every nation, tribe, people, and tongue (Acts 2; Rev. 7:9; 14:6).

Jesus healing the centurion's servant teaches us three important truths. First, no one is beyond the reach of God's grace. There are probably people in your family or circle of friends who you are tempted to believe are beyond the reach of God's grace, but they are not. Don't stop praying for the Lord to save them. Second, no one is worthy to receive God's grace. All of us have sinned and fall short of God's glory (Rom. 3:23). Don't try to attain salvation by works. Cast yourself on Christ and His work on your behalf. The Lord saves and sanctifies us by His grace alone. Third, God's word is powerful. It convicts and converts, calms and comforts, pierces and penetrates, discerns and delights (see Ps. 119; Heb. 4:12). Don't neglect reading it, studying it, meditating on it, and sharing it with others.

Soon after Jesus displayed His authority over death in Capernaum, He did the same in the town of Nain. Nain was a small town in Galilee that was twenty miles southwest of Capernaum and six miles southeast of Nazareth.[1] Jesus was traveling from Capernaum to Nain with His disciples, and a great crowd followed Him. As He drew near the gate, there was another crowd in mourning approaching. A man, the only son of his mother, had died and was being carried outside the town for a proper burial. Already a widow, this mother was now childless. Obviously she had drawn compassion from the town, but now she received compassion from the Lord.

Notably, the Lord saw her first and had compassion on her. Then He told her not to weep. Jesus approached the bier and touched it, an unclean action for a Jew (see Num. 19:11). But Jesus repeatedly put people's needs before the ceremonial law. No wonder the bearers of the bier stood still! When Jesus told the young man to arise, the dead man sat up and began to speak. By the power of His word and His authority over death, Jesus raised this man from the dead (see also Luke 8:40–56; John 11:38–44). Then He gave him back to his mother. By raising this widow's son from the dead, Jesus gave her a foretaste of what heaven will be like. No wonder He told her not to weep. She had her beloved son back in her arms (see also 1 Kings 17:17–24).

In response, reverent fear seized the crowd, and they glorified God. They recognized Jesus as a great prophet and that God had visited His people. It's not surprising that reports of Jesus's words and works spread throughout the region of Judea and Galilee. But the crowd didn't go far enough. Jesus is not just a great prophet; He is the greatest and final Prophet, Priest, and King; the Messiah; the promised One who came to fulfill all the promises of God (2 Cor. 1:20).

Jesus's compassion is as real today as it was in Nain. Regardless of the outcome of our distressing circumstances, God is compassionate toward us in the midst of them. All things are not yet made new. But His presence is with us. And we live with the hope that one day we will be with Christ in the new heaven and the new earth, where there will be no more tears and no more sorrow (Rev. 21:4).

II. Jesus Displays His Authority over the Kingdom (7:18–35)

Hearing the reports of Jesus that were spreading all around Judea and Galilee, John the Baptist's disciples reported everything to John, who was in prison (Luke 3:20). Upon hearing these reports, John sent two of his disciples to the Lord to ask Him if He was the Promised One (see Ps. 118:26; Mal. 3:1), or if they should keep looking (Luke 7:20). Luke does not tell us whether John asked this question for his own sake or if he just wanted his disciples to learn the answer, but it is an important question, one with which we all must grapple. Remember, Luke is writing so that we might have certainty of our faith (1:4).

---

1. Bock, *Luke*, 1:649.

Like all of Jesus's disciples, John's two disciples are to testify of Jesus's words and work. Jesus cites the same text from Isaiah that he had quoted in the Nazarene synagogue (Isa. 61:1–2; Luke 4:18–19) and also refers to several other passages in Isaiah (see Isa. 26:19; 29:18–19; 35:3–4; 42:7, 18). Jesus is fulfilling what Isaiah and Malachi had promised. The person who believes in Jesus and accepts Him as the Messiah will be saved, but the one who rejects Him as the Messiah will be judged.

After John's disciples left, Jesus addressed the crowds concerning John. Three different times Jesus asked the multitudes what they had gone out into the wilderness to see (Luke 7:24–26). The first time He responded with a rhetorical question: "A reed shaken by the wind?" John was definitely not a reed shaken by the wind. The angel had told Zacharias that John would go before Jesus in the spirit and power of Elijah (1:16).

The second time Jesus answered with another question—"A man clothed in soft garments?"—and an answer (Luke 7:25). He reminded the crowds that those who are dressed in luxurious clothing are found in king's courts. John was obviously not in king's courts; he was in the wilderness, and he wore camel's hair and ate wild locusts.

The third time that Jesus asked the question, He also answered with another question and then answered it: "A prophet? Yes, I say to you, and more than a prophet." Then He explained how John was more than a prophet by using two Old Testament references. Exodus 23:20 places John's and Jesus's ministries in the context of a second exodus, in which they would lead the new Israel, the New Testament church, into the promised land of glory. Malachi 3:1 pronounces John's role as one who prepared the way for the climactic moment of salvation history—the life, death, resurrection, and ascension of Christ. John is not more than a prophet because of his greatness but because he rolls out the carpet for the King of kings.

To clarify John's role, Jesus told the crowds that among those born of women none are greater than John, but among those born again in the kingdom of God, all are greater than John. The era of the kingdom, the time of the New Testament church, far surpassed the greatest of the Old Testament times because greater revelation was given. New Testament saints look back to what Jesus did on the cross to atone for the sin of God's people. The Old Testament saints looked forward. Since John was executed by Herod before Jesus died on the cross, he was considered a part of the old era. In response to Jesus's words, those in the crowd who had been baptized by John declared God just, but the Pharisees and lawyers rejected God's purpose.

Jesus closed with a question that compares the Pharisees and scribes who had rejected God's purpose with the rebellious wilderness generation (Luke 7:31; see Deut. 32:5, 20). To explain further, He used a childhood chant that was part of the popular culture. Children played a game in the marketplace that mimicked weddings or funerals, two things they saw a lot of, but some children did not want to play. So the children who were playing gave those who didn't want to play a choice between a wedding or a funeral. They played the flute so that they could act out a wedding, but they did not dance. So they sang a dirge to get them to act out a funeral, but they didn't want to do that either.[2]

On the one hand, John the Baptist came singing a dirge, without eating and drinking in celebration. But instead of heeding his message, the Pharisees and scribes accused him of having a demon. On the other hand, Jesus came eating and drinking, but they accused Him of being a glutton and drunkard, a friend of tax collectors and sinners. In the end, it didn't matter what the Pharisees and scribes thought, for "wisdom is justified by all her children" (Luke 7:35). The children of wisdom are Jesus and John the Baptist and all of those who believe in Jesus's name.

Dear reader, are you a child of wisdom? Jesus "became for us wisdom from God" (1 Cor. 1:30). All those who trust in Christ alone for salvation will be saved. If you are already a child of wisdom, you grow in wisdom through the study of the Bible. Are you teaching your children, grandchildren, or those under your care to do the same?

III. Jesus Displays His Authority over Sin (7:36–50)

After comparing the Pharisees with the rebellious wilderness generation, Luke records a story that further reveals their rebellion and shows that Jesus is a friend of sinners. Jesus did not totally reject the Pharisees; He agreed to have dinner with Simon. But Simon represents all those who reject God's purposes, while the woman of the city, a sinner, represents all those who accept God's purposes (see Luke 7:29–30).

There was a woman of the city of Capernaum who was a sinner. At some point she had learned about Jesus's love and forgiveness, and she responded in love. When she learned that Jesus was at Simon's house, she went to Him. In her day the house would have been open for guests to come in from the streets and join the dinner. Jesus would have been reclining at the table, and when the woman approached Him, she was standing behind Him at His feet. She had brought an alabaster flask of ointment (oil) in order to anoint His feet. The oil would have been costly for her to pour out, but she loved Jesus and wanted to thank Him for being her Savior.

She must have begun weeping in remorse for her sins, but surely her weeping turned to tears of joy. As she wept, her tears fell and made Jesus's feet wet, so she needed to wipe them. She took her hair down, a disgraceful thing for women to do in public in that day, and began wiping His feet with her hair. Then she began kissing His feet and anointing them with oil.

Simon the Pharisee was probably embarrassed for her and that this was happening in his home. But more than that, he was using this event to suggest that Jesus was not a prophet. While he was not saying this out loud, he was thinking it. So Jesus, knowing Simon's heart and thoughts, told him a parable.

Two people were indebted to a moneylender. One owed him five hundred denarii (about twenty months' wages), and the other fifty denarii (about two months' wages). Neither could pay their debts, so the moneylender canceled them. Jesus asked Simon

---

2. Ryken, *Luke*, 1:336.

which one of the debtors would love the moneylender more. Simon rightly judged that the one with the larger debt would love him more.

Still speaking to Simon, Jesus turned toward the woman and contrasted her actions with Simon's. Simon had failed to give Jesus a basin of water to wash His dirty feet when He entered his home, as was the custom in that day. In contrast, at a home that was not hers, the woman cleansed Jesus's feet with her tears and dried them with her hair. Also, Simon gave Jesus no kiss of greeting, but the woman never ceased kissing Jesus's feet from the time she came in. Simon had not anointed Jesus's head with oil, but the woman anointed Jesus's feet, the part of His body that usually only a servant would touch. Finally, Simon loved little, but the woman, who saw and understood the grace of God and the forgiveness of sins, loved much.

Jesus told the woman, "Your sins are forgiven." Then He said, "Your faith has saved you. Go in peace" (Luke 7:48, 50). The power of Jesus's word prevailed over Simon's words of doubt and disbelief. The dinner party guests asked the question that Luke wants every reader to ask and answer: "Who is this who even forgives sins?" (v. 49).

I'm glad that Luke doesn't tell us the woman's name or her sins. It makes it easier for us to hear our own name and see our own sin in this story. Every one of us is a "woman in the city who was a sinner" (Luke 7:37). But we are also Pharisees. In our self-righteousness, we often seek to disqualify others from God's grace.

Thankfully, our moneylender is more than willing to cancel our debt of sin. He invites us to weep in His presence, confess our sins, and receive His grace and forgiveness. He accepts our love shown through acts of service and worship. And He willingly extends peace to us. Dear sinner, you will never have a more merciful moneylender. Don't run from Him in shame. Run to Him in repentance. Cast yourself on Christ. Your sins are great, to be sure, but His grace is greater and His mercy is more.

IV. Jesus Displays His Authority over Revelation (Luke 8:1–21)

Jesus continued proclaiming the kingdom of God in cities and villages, fulfilling His purpose (see Luke 4:18–19). His twelve apostles and some women accompanied Him. These women had experienced the power of Jesus firsthand, being healed of evil spirits and infirmities. Luke names only three of the women who accompanied Jesus, but from these we learn several important lessons.

First, Jesus considered women an important part of His ministry. In those days women were not allowed to follow Jewish teachers and learn from them, so it is noteworthy that Jesus welcomed women who had the desire to learn from Him. Second, Jesus did not define these women by their pasts. Once afflicted by evil spirits and infirmities, they were now welcomed into Jesus's presence to serve and minister alongside Him. Third, He did not discriminate between classes. The wife of Herod's household manager and the wealthy women who provided for Jesus out of their own means did not fit the description of the poor for whom Jesus had come, but He welcomed them.

It didn't take long before a great crowd of people from many different towns had gathered around Jesus. He used this opportunity to teach a lesson about the kingdom of God with a parable. Jesus used an illustration from agriculture, something the people of that day would have easily understood. A sower would sow his seed before he plowed the ground.[3] His seed would fall in four different places. Some fell on the path and never germinated. Some fell on rock and died. Some fell among thorns and were choked in the end. And some fell into good soil and produced a good crop.

Although any farmer would have been able to relate to this story and everyone would have easily understood it, not everyone could understand how this illustration related to the kingdom of God. Only Jesus's true disciples, whose eyes and ears had been opened by God's grace, could understand the connection.

Significantly, Luke refers to Isaiah 6:9–10, one of the most quoted Old Testament passages in the New Testament (see Matt. 13:14–15; Mark 4:12; Luke 8:10; John 12:40; Acts 28:26; Rom. 11:8). It always refers to the Jews' hardened and unbelieving hearts.[4] Just as the prophet Isaiah was called to proclaim the gospel even though many rejected it, so too Jesus, as the greatest and final Prophet, was called to proclaim the gospel even though many rejected it. Israel's failure to heed God's call to repentance in Isaiah's day would be repeated in Jesus's day. But this was part of God's plan. Israel's rejection of the gospel led to the Gentiles' engrafting, so that the fullness of both Jews and Gentiles might be saved (see Romans 9–11).

Although not all parables should be treated as an allegory, Jesus treats this one as such and defines it clearly. The sower is God, and the seed is the word of God. Those along the path are like people who have heard the gospel, but before they place their faith in Jesus, the devil comes and takes away the word from their hearts so that they are never saved.

Those on the rock hear the word of God and even get excited about it for a time. But they never really have true faith because their roots are not good. In times of testing, when life gets tough, they fall away (see Heb. 6:4–8). These are people who have been in church and have listened to the preaching of the word, yet they remain hardened toward the gospel, turning away from the only One who can save them.

Those that fell on the thorns hear the word of God, but they hear the call to pleasure, power, prestige, and position more. They turn away from God's word to the things of this world and pursue those things instead.

There is only one of the four that describes God's elect. By the grace of God, God's children are those who hear the word of God, hold fast to His words, and bear fruit for God's glory. If we are honest, we must confess that as believers, we are tempted daily by the other three soils. Who hasn't felt the intense warfare of the battle with Satan as we walk along our pilgrim way? Who hasn't fallen away from fervent love of the Lord at one time or another? Who hasn't been tempted to focus more on the pleasures of

---

3. Morris, *Luke*, 170.
4. Ryle, *Luke*, 104.

this world than on God's word? We are in constant need of God's grace to hold fast to the word of God and bear the fruit of righteousness.

Jesus continued to reinforce the lesson of this parable by telling another one (Luke 8:16–18). A lamp is lit so that someone can see. We don't turn on a light and then cover it; that would defeat the purpose of turning it on. So too, we are not to hear God's word and then hide it. When the fire is lit within our ears, we are not to put it out with our hearts. We should not hide our faith from others. Our light should shine for all to see.

It was a joy for me to sing "This Little Light of Mine" when I was a girl, but it has been more fun to teach it to my children, watch them sing it, and then watch them teach it to younger children in our church so that the truth continues to be passed from one generation to another. We must not hide our lights or let Satan blow them out. There is coming a final day of judgment when the secrets of people's hearts will be revealed. Dear sinner, let the light of God's word shine on your sin now and expose it for what it is. Don't hide it until the day of judgment; then it will be too late to repent. Instead, be one who listens to God's word and applies it to your life (see Prov. 1:2–6; 9:9).

Jesus again addressed hearing and doing the word of God (Luke 8:19–21). In the midst of a large crowd, Jesus's mother, Mary, and his brothers came to see Him, but they could not reach Him. Some of the crowd saw them and told Jesus that they were trying to get to Him, but Jesus, while not disregarding the importance of family, seized the moment to teach a greater lesson. The family of God consists not of physical bonds, but of spiritual bonds. The Christian's family is made up of those who both hear the word of God and do it. As important as it is to respect our physical families, it is of greater importance for us to understand what it means to be a part of the covenant community. When we became a Christian, we became part of the family of God. We are to gather with this family every Lord's Day to worship together, hear the word of God, and engage in the sacraments. And we are to use our spiritual gifts to edify and encourage one another to the glory of God.

V. Jesus Displays His Authority over Creation (Luke 8:22–25)

Have you ever been caught off guard by a storm? You were out on the lake enjoying a day of boating and waterskiing when a big storm came up, and you headed quickly to the marina to dock the boat and get home. You were out walking when a big storm swept through your area, and you barely made it to safety. Or you were sailing through life when you found yourself suddenly in the storm of financial disaster, unemployment, chronic illness, death of a loved one, infertility, or infant loss. Regardless, when the storms of life come, we want to know that God is not sleeping.

The evening of the day Jesus taught the parables, He got into a boat with His disciples to sail to the other side of the lake (Mark 4:35; Luke 8:22). Though He is God, Jesus subjected Himself to the frailty of humanity, including the need for sleep. Since His ministry was extremely demanding, it's not surprising that He was tired. The disciples, seasoned fishermen that they were, likely didn't mind that Jesus was asleep until a storm arose. As the Sea of Galilee was surrounded by mountains, winds came up quickly and created chaos for those on it.[5] The waves brought water crashing into the boat, and the disciples feared for their lives. Rightly, they called on their Master, who was still sleeping. Jesus got up and commanded the wind and raging waves to stop. Significantly, He spoke and they obeyed, just as God spoke creation into existence and it came to be (Genesis 1–2). Creation has always been under the authority of the mighty God, and Jesus's command of creation revealed that He is God. He will once again exert His power over creation when He returns and ushers in the new heaven and the new earth.

In response to His disciples' frantic plea, Jesus questioned their faith. Faith accepts that our circumstances are under God's control, but the disciples felt out of control. Faith trusts God to do the impossible and hopes in God's deliverance, but the disciples thought they were going to die.

In response to Jesus's authority over creation, the disciples were afraid and marveled because they had witnessed God's power. They had seen the winds and water obey Jesus. They had seen God in the flesh. Their question strikes at the heart of Luke's gospel: "Who can this be? For He commands even the winds and water, and they obey Him!" (Luke 8:25). Is Jesus just a good teacher, miracle worker, and prophet, or is He Lord and Savior?

Dear reader, where is your faith right now? In the midst of stormy seas, do you wonder if God is asleep and fear you are going to die in your relational troubles, physical pain, depression, and disillusionment? Or do you trust in His authority over your circumstances and follow Him? Do not fear, dear believer. He is with you in the raging waters and the fiery trials. Crises will not consume you. Your Redeemer will rescue you (see Isa. 43:1–2).

VI. Jesus Displays His Authority over Demons (Luke 8:26–39)

Since His time of testing in the wilderness, Jesus had been ministering in the region of Galilee (Luke 4:14). He now sailed to a place that is opposite of Galilee, the country of the Gadarenes (or Gerasenes in some Bible translations). Going to a country where He was much less known in order to display His authority over demons was part of His mission to proclaim the kingdom of God in cities and villages (8:1).

When Jesus stepped onto land, a demon-possessed man from the city met Him. Sadly, this man had been demon possessed and had worn no clothes for a long time, and he did not live in a house, but among the tombs. For the Jews, a naked man living among the dead would have cried out impurity (see Num. 19:11, 14, 16). This man had been seized by the unclean spirit many times and was kept under guard, bound with chains and shackles, although he would break the bonds and be driven by the demon into the desert.

---

5. Morris, *Luke*, 174.

If this man were walking around our city today, he would quickly be locked up and shut away from society. But when Jesus saw him, He had compassion on him and commanded the unclean spirit to come out. The unclean spirit replied, "What have I to do with You, Jesus, Son of the Most High God? I beg You, do not torment me!" (Luke 8:28). It is important to note that even the demons recognize Jesus's authority, deity, and power over them. They are fighting a losing battle that will end when Jesus Christ returns and Satan and the demons are thrown into the abyss (Rev. 20:10).

Jesus responded to the unclean spirit by asking his name. The man answered, "'Legion,' because many demons had entered him" (Luke 8:30). The demons begged Jesus not to command them to depart into the abyss and suggested another plan. Because it was not yet time to throw Satan and his demons into the abyss (see Rev. 20:10), Jesus agreed to their request, and they entered into a large herd of pigs, which then rushed down the steep bank into the lake and drowned.

In response, the herdsmen fled and proclaimed what had happened in the city and in the country. The people who heard their report went to see what had occurred. When they came to Jesus, they found the once demon-possessed man sitting at Jesus's feet, clothed and in his right mind. Those who had seen the miracle told the people how the man had been healed. The people of the region, seized with great fear, asked Jesus to leave. The healed man begged Jesus to let him go with Him, but Jesus told the man to return to his home and declare how much God had done for him, a command he obeyed. Jesus got into the boat and returned to Galilee, just as the people had asked Him. Sadly, because of their fear, they missed the opportunity to hear from Jesus.

You and I are like the naked, demon-possessed man walking among the tombs. All humankind is dead in their trespasses and sins, naked and exposed before the Creator and worthy of condemnation. But when God saves us, we are no longer dead but alive in Christ. We are no longer naked but clothed in Christ's righteousness. We are no longer worthy of condemnation but pardoned by the blood of Christ. If you, dear reader, prefer Jesus to leave your presence, hear the warning in this story. Jesus listened to the people's request and got in the boat and went away. There comes a time when it is too late to turn to Jesus. Don't push Him away. Call on His name. There is no other way to be saved.

VII. Jesus Displays His Authority over Disease and Death (Luke 8:40–56)

In the country of the Gadarenes, the people asked Jesus to depart from them, but in Galilee the crowd was waiting for Jesus's return and welcomed Him. Jairus, a ruler of the synagogue, needed Him to come to his house and heal his daughter. Knowing Jesus was his only hope, he fell down before Him, imploring Him to come to his house. His daughter, who was about twelve years old, was dying. Jairus must have been relieved when Jesus went with him, but it was difficult to fight through the pressing crowds, especially since Jesus was on a different schedule from his. Jesus was kingdom-minded. He knew that His purpose was not just to heal one girl but many people. Not surprisingly then, He stopped along the way to Jairus's house to see who had touched Him and been healed by His power.

Among the crowd, there was a woman who had had a discharge of blood for twelve years, the same number of years that Jairus's daughter had been alive. This discharge rendered her unclean (see Lev. 15:25–27). Her only hope of being clean again was to be healed of her discharge. Sadly, she had spent all she had on physicians, but not one could heal her.

Jesus felt the power go out from Him when she touched Him and was healed. He asked in the midst of the pressing crowd, "Who touched Me?" (Luke 8:45). To Peter, the question was ridiculous. He was thinking, *How could Jesus not be touched in the midst of such a pressing crowd?* But Jesus knew that this touch had been different. He knows the touch of faith.

The woman, who wanted to remain anonymous, realized she couldn't. Trembling, she fell down before Him, declaring in the presence of the people why she had touched Him and the result—immediate healing. What a testimony of bold and gracious faith! Jesus gave this woman an opportunity to share her faith, testify of His goodness, and bring Him glory, and she did not falter. Though she started out trembling, she finished by making a bold proclamation of Jesus's healing power.

In response, Jesus tenderly addressed her with a term of endearment, "daughter" (Luke 8:48). Then He told her that her faith in Him had made her well. Finally, He told her to go in peace (see also 7:50). If you are a child of the covenant, you too are a daughter of God the Father (see 2 Cor. 6:18). Filled with impurity and uncleanness, with no cure for your disease, you can be healed, cleansed, and made pure because Jesus took your infirmities on Himself. Have you, dear believer, fallen down at the feet of Jesus and worshiped Him? Have you declared to others that Jesus has cleansed you from your sin and made you pure?

While this daughter of the King was being healed and testifying of God's goodness, Jairus received news that his daughter was dead and he didn't need to trouble the Teacher anymore. Mercifully, upon hearing this man's words, Jesus told Jairus, "Do not be afraid; only believe, and she will be made well" (Luke 8:50). Jesus's words and the miraculous healing He had just accomplished must have greatly encouraged Jairus, who continued on with Jesus to his house.

On their arrival, Jesus took Peter, James, and John and Jairus and his wife into the room where their daughter had died. Jesus told the weepers and mourners to stop, for she was only sleeping. They laughed at Him because they were sure she was dead. Indeed, the girl had died, but for the Lord over death, it was as if the girl were only sleeping. He took her by the hand and said, "Little girl, arise" (Luke 8:54). Immediately her spirit returned, and she got up. To prove further that she was alive, Jesus directed them to give her something to eat.

The girls' parents were amazed, but Jesus told them not to tell anyone. Unlike in the country of the Gadarenes, here in Galilee, where Jesus was popular, it was dangerous to keep spreading reports of healing. If people focused only on Jesus's ability to heal and bring them immediate comfort, they would miss the point of His ministry. Following Jesus means that suffering comes before glory. The Bible does not promise that we will be healed of our emotional, physical, and spiritual pain in this world, but we know that we will be healed in glory. Let us not grow weary but look to the One who is to come and to the Holy City, where there will be no more death, mourning, crying, or pain (Rev. 21:4).

Perhaps you need to be reminded today that God has authority over all things. Whether find yourself in a season of suffering or in a time of battling a habitual sin, be encouraged that Jesus, to whom "all authority has been given" (Matt. 28:18) is able and ready to help you. He has authority over death, the kingdom, sin, revelation, creation, demons, and disease. How comforting that "we do not have a High Priest who cannot sympathize with our weaknesses, but was in all points tempted as we are, yet without sin." Believing this, we "come boldly to the throne of grace, that we may obtain mercy and find grace to help in time of need" (Heb. 4:15–16).

Processing It Together...

1. What do we learn about God in Luke 7–8?

2. How does this reshape how we should view our present circumstances?

3. What do we learn about God's Son, Jesus Christ?

4. How should this impact our relationship with God and with others?

5. What do we learn about God's covenant with His people?

6. How are we to live in light of this?

7. How can we apply Luke 7–8 to our lives today and in the future?

8. How should we apply this passage in our churches?

9. Look back at "Put It in Perspective" in your personal study questions. What did you find challenging or encouraging about this lesson?

10. Look back at "Principles and Points of Application." How has this lesson impacted your life?

The Kingdom of God Has Come Near

Luke 9–10

Purpose . . .

Head. What do I need to know from this passage in Scripture?

- Christ reveals the values of the kingdom of God and calls His followers to display them.

Heart. How does what I learn from this passage affect my internal relationship with the Lord?

- I am a kingdom disciple who enjoys listening to Jesus's teaching through the Scriptures.

Hands. How does what I learn from this passage translate into action for God's kingdom?

- I will proclaim the gospel in whatever spheres of influence the Lord has placed me.
- I will pray and study the Bible each day.
- I will wholeheartedly follow Jesus.
- I will pray for the Lord of the harvest to send out laborers into His harvest.
- I will show mercy to those around me.

Personal Study . . .

Pray. Ask that God will open up your heart and mind as you study His Word. This is His story of redemption that He has revealed to us, and the Holy Spirit is our teacher.

Ponder the Passage. Read Luke 9–10.

- *Point:* What is the point of this passage? How does this relate to the point of the entire book?

- *Persons:* Who are the main people involved in this passage? What characterizes them?

- *Persons of the Trinity:* Where do you see God the Father, God the Son, and God the Holy Spirit in this passage?

- *Puzzling Parts:* Are there any parts of the passage that you don't quite understand or that seem interesting or confusing?

Put It in Perspective.

- *Place in Scripture:* What is the original context of this text? What is the redemptive-historical context—what has or hasn't happened in redemptive history at this point in Scripture? How does this text connect to Christ?

The following questions will help you if you got stuck on any of the previous questions, and they will help you dig a little deeper into the text, putting it all into perspective.

1. 9:1–6. (a) What did Jesus give the twelve apostles when He called them together?

(b) What did He send them out to do, and how does this reflect Jesus's own purpose (see Luke 4:18–19, 43)?

(c) What weren't the apostles to take on their journey, and what was Jesus teaching them?

(d) How many houses were they to enter in each city, and how does this imply the importance of moving along from city to city to proclaim the kingdom of God?

(e) What were the apostles to do when people did not receive them, what did this signify, and how does this reflect Jesus's rejection in Nazareth (see Luke 4:22–30)?

2. 9:7–9. (a) What was Herod's response to the reports he was hearing about Jesus?

(b) Who were people saying Jesus was, and what do you learn about this prophet from 2 Kings 2:1–2 and Malachi 4:5?

3. 9:10–17. (a) How did Jesus respond to the crowds following Him after He had sought to get away with His apostles, and how does this relate to Luke 9:2?

(b) Contrast the apostles' response to the crowd with Jesus's response.

(c) What was the first thing Jesus did with the five loaves and two fish, and what was the outcome of this miracle?

(d) How does Jesus's miracle recall Exodus 16:1–17:7 and 2 Kings 4:42–44, and how is it superior?

4. 9:18–20. (a) What was Jesus doing while His disciples were not with Him?

(b) Who were the crowds saying that Jesus was (see also Luke 9:7–8)?

(c) How did Peter answer Jesus's question (see also Matt. 16:17–19)?

(d) How does the title Christ, or Messiah, relate to the Davidic covenant (see 2 Sam. 7:1–17; Luke 2:11; 20:41–44)?

5. 9:21–22. (a) Why did Jesus not want His apostles to tell anyone who He was?

(b) The Jews expected the Messiah to be a mighty and strong political leader. What is the true Messiah like (see also Ps. 118:22; Isa. 53; Dan. 7:13–14)?

6. 9:23–27. (a) Contrast pursuing Jesus with pursuing the world.

(b) What warning does Jesus give to those who are ashamed of Him?

(c) What do you learn about the title Son of Man in Daniel 7:13–14?

(d) To what event(s) does Jesus refer in verse 27?

7. 9:28–36. (a) Who did Jesus take up on the mountain?

(b) Briefly summarize the events of the transfiguration.

(c) How does this event reflect Exodus 24:9–18; 34:29–35; Deuteronomy 18:15; Psalm 2:7; Isaiah 42:1; Malachi 3–4; and Luke 3:22?

(d) How does Jesus speaking with Moses (representing the Law) and Elijah (representing the Prophets) relate to Matthew 5:17 and 2 Corinthians 1:20?

8. 9:37–45. (a) Briefly describe the events of this miracle.

(b) Compare Deuteronomy 32:5 with Luke's phrase in verse 41, "O faithless and perverse generation." With whom is Luke comparing the generation of Jesus's day?

(c) Why will Jesus be delivered into the hands of lawless men (see Isa. 53:6b)?

(d) Why didn't the disciples understand what Jesus said or ask Him to explain?

9. 9:46–48. (a) What disagreement arose among Jesus's disciples, and how did Jesus respond?

(b) Read Matthew 18:1–6 and Mark 9:33–37. What else do you learn about this event?

10. 9:49–50. (a) What did John and the other apostles try to do, and how did Jesus respond?

(b) Compare these verses with Numbers 11:24–30. What do both accounts teach?

11. 9:51–56. (a) How does verse 51 signal a transition from Jesus's Galilean ministry (Luke 4:14–9:50)?

(b) What does "to be received up" refer to (see Acts 1:11, 22), and what does "He steadfastly set His face" convey (see Isa. 50:7; Jer. 21:10; 42:15–17; Ezek. 21:2–6)?

(c) What is significant about where Jesus sent messengers to make preparations for Him?

(d) What do you learn about the Samaritans from Luke 10:33–35; 17:11–19; and Acts 8:14?

(e) Did the people of Samaria accept Jesus, and why?

(f) Contrast the response of James and John to the Samaritans (see also 2 Kings 1:1–17) with Jesus's response.

12. 9:57–62. (a) What is the main principle of each interaction that occurred between Jesus and the three potential disciples?

(b) How do verses 61–62 echo 1 Kings 19:19–21?

(c) How does verse 62 allude to Genesis 19:26?

13. 10:1–12. (a) What should be the first response to knowing the harvest is plentiful but the workers are few?

(b) According to verse 3, what will characterize the disciples' journey (see also Isa. 40:11; 53:7; Jer. 50:6–7; Ezek. 34; Mic. 2:12)?

(c) How did the kingdom of God come with Jesus's incarnation, and how will it be consummated at His second coming (see 1 Cor. 15:24–28; 2 Tim. 4:1, 18; Heb. 12:28; 2 Peter 1:10–11; Rev. 11:15)?

(d) What do you learn about Sodom from Genesis 19; Deuteronomy 29:23; 32:32; Isaiah 1:9–10; 3:9; Jeremiah 23:14; and Ezekiel 16:43–58? In light of your findings, what does Jesus's statement in verse 12 mean?

14. 10:13–16. (a) Use a concordance to look up *Bethsaida* and *Capernaum* to discover what works Jesus did in those places.

(b) What were Tyre and Sidon condemned for in the Old Testament (see Isa. 23; Ezek. 26–28; Joel 3:4–8; Amos 1:9–10)?

(c) How is God's judgment against Israel's enemies now applied to Israel (see Isa. 14:13–15; Ezek. 28:2–10)?

(d) What is the relationship between Jesus and His disciples?

15. 10:17–20. (a) In what state of mind did the seventy-two return, and what did they say to Jesus?

(b) How did Jesus respond to them (see also Gen. 3:15; Deut. 8:15; Ps. 91:13; Isa. 14:12–15)?

16. 10:21–24. (a) How do these verses display the triune God?

(b) Name some of the prophets and kings from the Old Testament who would have loved to have seen and heard what the disciples saw and heard.

17. 10:25–37. (a) How does verse 27 reflect Deuteronomy 6:5 and Leviticus 19:18?

(b) What kind of heart did the lawyer have?

(c) How does Jesus's mercy extend beyond the Samaritan's?

(d) What must the lawyer do with his correct answers?

18. 10:38–42. (a) "As they went" where (see Luke 9:51)? What village did they enter (see John 11:1)?

(b) What woman welcomed Jesus into her house, and who was her sister?

(c) How did Mary and Martha respond differently to Jesus's presence, and how did the Lord respond to each of them?

(d) What is the "good part" (or portion) that Mary chose (see Pss. 16:5; 73:26; 119:57; 142:5)?

Principles and Points of Application

19. 9:1–9. (a) How are you proclaiming the kingdom of God to others by the Holy Spirit's power, and how are you teaching those under your care to do the same?

(b) Who do you believe that Jesus is, and how do you seek to see and hear Him?

20. 9:10–17. (a) How do you withdraw from the busyness of life to spend time with the Lord?

(b) Jesus thanks the Father for His provision of food. What implications does this have for you and your family? How are you teaching your children to do the same?

21. 9:18–27. (a) Spend time in prayer today, beginning by adoring who God is, then confessing your sins and thanking God for all He has done, and ending with prayer for yourself, family, and friends.

(b) In what ways are you involved in proclaiming the gospel to the nations?

(c) How does your life reflect that you have followed Jesus and are not ashamed of the gospel?

22. **9:28–50.** How do you respond to people who do service in the name of Christ but don't agree with your doctrines or don't belong to your denomination? Pray for the church's unity.

23. **9:51–62.** (a) Who are you tempted to judge? Repent and leave judgment to the Lord. Begin praying for the person or people you are tempted to judge, asking God to save them from their sin.

(b) In what ways do you devote more time to comfort, convenience, family, friends, and commitments than you do to the King of the kingdom?

24. **10:1–24.** (a) Spend time in prayer asking the Lord to send out laborers into His harvest. Also, pray for those ministering on the mission field and for those who are considering going, asking the Lord to provide them with encouragement and edification, resources, financial support, friendships, and perseverance.

(b) If you are a believer, rejoice that your name is written in heaven. Teach those believers under your care to regularly rejoice in this as well.

25. **10:25–37.** (a) How does your life reflect love for the Lord and for your neighbor?

(b) Who are you most like—the priest, the Levite, or the Samaritan? How do you need to grow in showing mercy to others?

26. 10:38–42. (a) How is your home centered on Christ?

(b) What is the importance of family devotions? How can you be more consistent in this practice?

(c) What do you need to put aside so that you have time to study Scripture?

Putting It All Together...

We live in a culture where being dependent on someone or something is seen mostly as a weakness instead of a strength. We are told that we can save ourselves from hardship by working hard, satisfy our desires through our own means, work in our chosen field by depending on our knowledge and education, and obtain future financial security by wise investments. Even in the church, believers have a tendency to isolate themselves instead of depending on others. But such independence is antithetical to the gospel of Jesus Christ.

Throughout His ministry, Jesus repeatedly displayed our desperate need for Him. He revealed that we need Him to save us from our sin. He showed that we need Him to be truly satisfied. He demonstrated that we need His power for ministry. He manifested that we need His grace to extend mercy to others. And He makes it clear that we need Him to be our teacher as we study Scripture.

As believers learn to depend on Christ for everything, they will also learn to depend on one another. Of course there is only one Savior. But believers are to be interdependent as they minister in Christ's name, do the work of evangelism and engage in mercy ministries, and as they seek to know God more and make Him known through the proclamation of the word of God. Luke 9–10 reminds us that because Jesus sends out disciples, satisfies our deepest longings, suffers to atone for our sins, shines as the true light, shows mercy to God's people, and shows disciples the ways of the Lord, believers are utterly dependent on His strength and salvation.

I. Jesus Sends (Luke 9:1–9)

By giving His apostles power and authority over demons and diseases and sending them out to proclaim the kingdom of God, Jesus was extending His ministry (see Luke 4:18–19, 43). Before He sent them, He instructed them. They were not to take anything for the journey. Instead, they were to depend on Jesus alone. They were to stay at only one house in each town. Jesus had given them a mission to proclaim the kingdom of God, so they were to keep moving until many towns had heard the message. When people rejected them, as His hometown had rejected Him (see vv. 22–30), they were to shake the town's dust from their feet. This action reflected the belief of the Jewish rabbis, who thought the dust of Gentile lands was defiled. Strict Jews would remove the dust from their shoes when they returned from any Gentile town. So when the apostles shook the dust off their feet, they were declaring that the Israelites who rejected the kingdom of God were no better than the Gentiles whom they despised; whether Jew or Gentile, neither belonged to the kingdom if they rejected it.[1]

The apostles obeyed Jesus's commission. They went through the villages, preaching the gospel and healing. Although the authority the apostles were given as eyewitnesses of Jesus Christ was unique, by the Holy Spirit within us we have also been given Jesus's power and authority. We have been given the Great Commission and are to depend on Him as we proclaim the gospel to the nations (Matt. 28:18–20).

Not surprisingly, Herod the tetrarch (Herod Antipas), the political ruler of Galilee from 4 BC to AD 39[2] and the son of Herod the Great, who had tried to kill baby Jesus (Matt. 2:13), heard about Jesus's ministry in Galilee. He was perplexed by the people's conclusions about Jesus. Some people were saying that John the Baptist had been raised from the dead, but Herod had beheaded John, so he didn't think it could be him. Others were saying that Elijah had appeared (see 2 Kings 2:1–2; Mal. 4:5), but Herod wasn't convinced. Some thought that Jesus was one of the Old Testament prophets raised from the dead, but Herod wasn't content with that either. He still asked, "But who is this of whom I hear such things?" (Luke 9:9). It is the question that Luke has been putting before us from the beginning of the book so that we may be certain about the faith. The only way we can see Jesus is by grace. God alone opens blind eyes to see, deaf ears to hear, and hard hearts to receive the gospel of Jesus Christ.

Dear reader, who do you believe that Jesus is? If you are a Christian, you have a mission. Jesus sends His people to carry the gospel to all people. Some will serve as missionaries overseas. Others will serve refugees in their hometown. Still others will share the gospel with their next-door neighbors. All of us should pray for and support the mission work being done around the world.

II. Jesus Satisfies (9:10–17)
Upon their return the apostles gave Jesus a missions report. Recognizing that they had poured themselves out in ministry and were in need of rest, Jesus took them away from the crowds to Bethsaida, a town on the northeast corner of the Sea of Galilee. But again the crowds appeared. In keeping with His purpose (Luke 4:43) and in setting an example for His apostles, Jesus welcomed the crowds, told them about the kingdom of God, and cured those who had need of healing.

---

1. Morris, *Luke*, 183.
2. Bock, *Luke*, 1:822.

When evening came the apostles told Jesus to send the crowd away to the city, but He had other plans. To teach His apostles a lesson of dependence, He displayed His power and authority over food and miraculously provided for the needs of the people. Significantly, Jesus does not tell the apostles that He will give them something to eat. Instead, He tells the apostles to give the crowds something to eat. Doubting their five loaves and two fish would be enough to feed the nearly five thousand men, they mentioned the idea of buying food for everyone. But around two hundred denarii would be needed to buy enough food (Mark 6:37; John 6:5–7), more than seven months of basic earnings (one denarius was a day's basic wage).[3]

Jesus had a better plan. He told the apostles to have the crowd sit in groups of about fifty. Then He took the five loaves and two fish and said a blessing, displaying His dependence on His heavenly Father and recognizing that He had given all authority and power to Him. Then He broke the loaves[4] and gave them to the apostles to feed the crowd, teaching them that they had work to do in His name. Interestingly, after all the people ate to their satisfaction, there were twelve baskets of leftovers. Jesus had done what only God can do; He multiplied a person's resources in order to provide for the needs of the people. The crowd responded, "This is truly the Prophet who is to come into the world" (John 6:14).

Just as the Lord sent bread from heaven for the Israelites in the wilderness and provided water from the rock at Horeb (Ex. 16:1–17:7), and just as Elisha provided for a hundred men in need of food with one man's twenty loaves of barley and fresh ears of grain (2 Kings 4:42–44), so too Jesus, the final Prophet, miraculously provided enough food for the five thousand.

This Prophet is worthy of our time. We should withdraw from the busyness of ministry and life to spend time with Him alone and with His people. He is also worthy of our thanksgiving. We should take time to thank Him for providing our daily bread. In addition, He is worthy of our trust. Jesus is the bread of God who has come down from heaven and gives life to the world (John 6:33). Only those who look to Jesus by faith have their deepest hunger, eternal life with God, truly satisfied.

III. Jesus Suffers (9:18–27)

Jesus had been praying alone, but His disciples were with him in Caesarea Philippi (Matt. 16:13). Notably, this was a pagan place in which the worship of the great god Pan was prominent.[5] Jesus asked His disciples a question that has been asked several times in Luke's gospel, but this time the question was being asked *by* Jesus: "Who do the crowds say that I am?" (Luke 9:18). Like Herod, the disciples knew that some said He was John the Baptist, others Elijah, and still others a risen prophet from the past

---

3. Bock, *Luke*, 1:831.

4. The tense of the verb in the Greek implies that Jesus kept breaking the loaves continuously. Ryken, *Luke*, 1:437.

5. Morris, *Luke*, 187.

(vv. 7–9). Most importantly, Jesus asked, "But who do you say that I am?" and Peter, on behalf of the twelve, answered correctly, "the Christ of God" (v. 20).

Significantly, the word for Christ in the Greek is the same word that the Hebrew uses for Messiah, the Anointed One. Throughout the Old Testament, different prophets, priests, and kings were anointed (see Ex. 29:7; 1 Sam. 16:1–13; 1 Kings 1:39; 2 Kings 9:1–6), but God promised that one day He would send the greatest and final Prophet, Priest, and King (see Gen. 3:15; Deut. 18:18; 2 Sam. 7:12–16; Ps. 89:4; Isa. 9:7; Mic. 5:2).[6] Also, at the beginning of Jesus's birth narrative, the title Christ is connected with the promise of the Davidic covenant (Luke 2:11). The next time Luke will use this title is when Jesus is addressing the Sadducees. Again, the connection with the Davidic King is made: "How can they say that the Christ is the Son of David…. David calls Him 'Lord'; how is He then his Son" (20:41, 44)? Jesus Christ is the final and perfect Davidic King who will reign forever on the throne in fulfillment of God's covenant with David (see 2 Samuel 7). Additionally, Peter's confession reminds us that God sent Jesus. He is the fulfillment of all God's promises throughout the Old Testament (2 Cor. 1:20).

Jesus strictly warned and commanded His apostles not to tell anyone that He was the Christ of God. This was because He still had many works to do to testify of who He was before He suffered at the hands of sinful men in Jerusalem. Those who would speak of Jesus as the Christ first had to understand what this means. The disciples did not yet understand. Only after the resurrection would the disciples be ready to proclaim what they knew and understood to be true.[7]

Although Luke has given hints of Jesus's suffering (Luke 2:35; 5:35), Jesus now tells His disciples that He would suffer many things, including rejection and death.[8] Importantly, Jesus uses the title Son of Man in anticipation of His death (Luke 9:22; see Dan. 7:13–14). His prediction alludes to both Isaiah 53 and Psalm 118:22, the former giving great detail as to what Jesus's suffering will entail, and the latter speaking of the rejected stone becoming the cornerstone. The Lamb of God had come to atone for the sins of God's people, and God's justice had to be satisfied by the perfect Son of Man.

Turning His attention to all His disciples, Jesus taught what discipleship means (Luke 9:23–27). First, disciples must deny themselves. They must look to Jesus alone as King. Second, disciples must take up their cross daily. They must suffer for the name of Jesus, whether that involves rejection or ridicule, loss of power or position, unemployment or unkindness. Third, disciples must follow Jesus hoping that one day they too will be resurrected and live forever with Him in glory.

When we deny ourselves, we lose our lives in this world for the sake of God's kingdom, letting Christ determine how and when He is going to use us. When we take up our cross, we recognize there is no profit in gaining the world if we lose eternal

---

6. Ryken, *Luke*, 1:450.
7. Bock, *Luke*, 1:846.
8. Bock, *Luke*, 1:847.

life. And when we follow Jesus, we agree to be unashamed of Him so that He will be unashamed of us when He returns in glory. Dear friend, do not delay in deciding to follow Jesus. One day it will be too late.

Jesus closed with this statement: "There are some standing here who shall not taste death till they see the kingdom of God" (Luke 9:27). Some see this as a reference to the resurrection and ascension of Jesus. Others believe Jesus is speaking about the day of Pentecost, when He sent His Spirit to renew His church. Still others say that this refers to the destruction of the Jewish temple in AD 70. And some say that Jesus is speaking of His transfiguration, which is recorded in the following verses.[9] Regardless which view you hold, what is most important is that you not taste death until you have trusted in the King alone for your salvation.

IV. Jesus Shines (9:28–36)

About eight days after Jesus taught His disciples about the meaning of discipleship, He took Peter, John, and James up on the mountain to pray.[10] As Jesus was praying, "the appearance of His face was altered, and His robe became white and glistening" (Luke 9:29). Two men, Moses and Elijah, who appeared in glory, were standing and talking with Him. They were speaking of Jesus's departure (literally, His "exodus"), which He would accomplish in Jerusalem.

During this time the disciples were very drowsy, but they became fully awake and saw Jesus's glory, as well as Moses and Elijah. Peter, impressed with Jesus's glory, wanted to linger in the moment. He suggested to Jesus that the three of them (Peter, John, and James) make three tents, one for Jesus, one for Moses, and one for Elijah. But Peter did not understand the supremacy of Christ. While he was speaking, a cloud came and overshadowed Peter, John, and James. The Father will not share His glory with anyone else, including Moses and Elijah. These prophets pointed toward the greatest and final Prophet, Jesus Christ. Peter, John, and James must listen to Him.

The account of the transfiguration must be understood in light of the Old Testament. Of particular importance is the book of Exodus. Both the confirmation of God's covenant with Israel (Exodus 24) and the transfiguration account occur on mountains. The presence of the cloud in the transfiguration account recalls God's guidance of His covenant people by way of the cloud (Ex. 13:21–22; 14:19–20, 24; 16:10; 19:9, 16) and Moses entering the cloud and speaking with God (24:15–18). The alteration of Jesus's face is similar to Moses's shining face (34:29). The word translated "departure" in Luke 9:31 (ESV) recalls the exodus event, implying that Jesus's death, resurrection, and ascension is the second great exodus. The Father's command to listen to His Son (v. 35) recalls His command for Israel to listen to the prophet Moses (Deut. 18:15).

---

9. Ryken, *Luke*, 1:466–67.

10. There have been three proposed locations for this mountain: Mount Hermon, near Caesarea Philippi; Mount Tabor in southern Galilee, six miles from Nazareth; and Mount Meron, northwest of the Sea of Galilee. Bock, *Luke*, 1:866.

Finally, the mention of "tabernacles" (Luke 9:33) alludes to the tabernacle (Exodus 25–28) or the Feast of Tabernacles (Lev. 23:43).[11]

Besides the book of Exodus, there are other important Old Testament connections. First, Elijah's presence at the transfiguration recalls Luke 4:25–26 and 9:18–19, both of which relate to the prophecies in Malachi 3–4. John the Baptist fulfills the role of Elijah as the one who prepares the way of the Lord, and Jesus fulfills the hope of the Messiah.

Second, the appearance of Moses and Elijah together recalls a number of parallels between these Old Testament men of God. There were unusual circumstances surrounding the end of their lives on earth (Deut. 34:5–6; 2 Kings 2:11); both men experienced God's glory (Ex. 33:18–23; 34:5–8; 1 Kings 19:8–18); and both were pivotal prophets in the history of Israel. Together, they represent the Law and the Prophets, which Jesus Christ came to fulfill (Matt. 5:17).[12] I love how Philip Ryken puts it: "When Moses and Elijah appeared with Jesus on the mountain, it was as if the whole Old Testament was standing up to say that everything was coming together in Christ."[13] Remember, two witnesses were needed for verification according to Old Testament law (see Deut. 17:6). Moses and Elijah were the two.

Third, God the Father addressing Jesus as "My beloved Son" (Luke 9:35) most likely alludes to Isaiah 42:1, which is the beginning of the first of the four Servant Songs: "Behold! My Servant whom I uphold, My Elect One in whom My soul delights." Verse 35 also points back to Jesus's baptism, when God the Father spoke from heaven, saying, "You are My beloved Son; in You I am well pleased" (3:22). This is a reference to Psalm 2, a royal Davidic psalm, which is again alluded to here (see especially v. 7).[14] The Old Testament truly sings of Christ as the greatest and final Prophet, Priest, and King.

Jesus shines His light in our hearts to save us from the darkness of sin. The world, the flesh, and the devil want to put out our light, but with the strength of the Holy Spirit, it can shine brightly in our homes and churches, in neighborhoods and offices, and at parks and poolside. How are you letting your light shine for all to see, beginning with your own family?

V. Jesus Surprises (9:37–50)

The day after the transfiguration, the crowds found Jesus. Within the crowd was a father of an only child who was afflicted with an unclean spirit that hardly left him. He had already begged Jesus's disciples to cast out the unclean spirit, but they were unable to because they did not pray (see Mark 9:29). Jesus rebuked the crowd: "O faithless and perverse generation, how long shall I be with you and bear with you?"

---

11. Pao and Schnabel, "Luke," 311–12.
12. Pao and Schnabel, "Luke," 312.
13. Ryken, *Luke*, 1:473.
14. Pao and Schnabel, "Luke," 312.

(Luke 9:41), another allusion to the rebellious wilderness generation (see Deut. 32:5, 20; Luke 7:31–35).[15]

When the boy was brought to Jesus, He observed the convulsions and asked the father questions about the duration of this problem. In almost a desperate final attempt, the father asked Jesus if He could do anything to help his son. Jesus revealed that His power to heal was not a possibility but rather a certainty for the one who believes, to which the father responded with a cry: "Lord, I believe; help my unbelief!" (Mark 9:24). With authority, Jesus rebuked the unclean spirit and healed the boy, giving him back to his father. And all who witnessed such miraculous power were surprised at the majesty of God.

Jesus frequently turned His disciples' attention away from His miraculous works of healing to His greater purpose of suffering. He took the opportunity on their journey through Galilee to teach His disciples that "the Son of Man is about to be betrayed into the hands of men" (Luke 9:44; see also Isa. 53:6b). The greatest event in redemptive history was about to take place, but the disciples did not understand Jesus's words. God continued concealing the fullness of Jesus's upcoming suffering from them, and they were afraid to ask Jesus what He meant.

This misunderstanding of Jesus's suffering also led to a misunderstanding of God's kingdom. Sadly, the disciples were arguing about which one of them was the greatest. Jesus, who could read right through the reasoning of their hearts, seized the moment to teach them a lesson. He took a child and put him by His side, an uncommon action for teachers of that day. But Jesus said to His disciples, "Whoever receives this little child in My name receives Me; and whoever receives Me receives Him who sent Me. For he who is least among you all will be great" (Luke 9:48). In other words, we must exercise humility to meaningfully interact with children, and this is the same humility we must have to commune with the triune God.[16] When we take the time to care for the weak and the helpless of our world in a posture of humility and in the name of Jesus, we are closest to understanding greatness in the kingdom of God.

Jesus closed His ministry in Galilee by answering one of the apostle John's questions. Speaking on behalf of the apostles, John told Jesus that they had seen someone casting out demons in His name, and they tried to stop him because he was not one of His disciples. Strikingly, Jesus told John not to stop this person's ministry, reminding him that the one who is not against Him is really for Him. Similarly, when Joshua pleaded with Moses to forbid two men from prophesying in the camp, Moses replied, "Are you zealous for my sake? Oh, that all the LORD's people were prophets and that the LORD would put His Spirit upon them!" (Num. 11:29).

Our greatest enemies are not those of other denominations, but the world, our own flesh, and the devil. Sound doctrine is important, but the Lord uses many Christians who believe differently than we do to further His kingdom. We must seek unity

---

15. Pao and Schnabel, "Luke," 312.
16. Ryken, *Luke*, 1:490.

among the body of Christ, serving together where we can without compromising our convictions that are grounded in the Bible.

VI. Jesus Sets His Face toward Jerusalem (9:51–62)

When the days grew near for His death, Jesus set His focus on going to Jerusalem, where He would face trials leading to crucifixion. Jerusalem was known as the city where prophets had lost their lives (Matt. 23:37), so to set His face toward Jerusalem was to set His face to die (see Isa. 50:7). But after death would come resurrection and then ascension. Committed to His Father's will, He began His journey to Jerusalem, continuing to minister along the way.

Significantly, He sent messengers ahead to make preparations in a Samaritan village. There had been a long history of hatred between Jews and Samaritans. The latter were a mixed race of Israelite and non-Israelite blood that recognized only the Pentateuch, the first five books of the Old Testament, and worshiped on Mount Gerizim instead of in Jerusalem (see John 4:20). The last thing the Samaritans wanted to do was help a Jew get to Jerusalem by the easiest and fastest route. The Jews also hated the Samaritans and preferred to avoid Samaria on their way to Jerusalem.

But Jesus was different. He wanted to go through Samaria to extend His mission to the Gentile world (see Luke 10:33; 17:16; Acts 8). Sadly, the Samaritans did not receive Jesus. This angered James and John, the "Sons of Thunder" (Mark 3:17). They wanted to call down fire from heaven and consume those who had rejected their Lord. But Jesus knew that the time of judgment had not yet come. He was still extending mercy, hoping that some of the Samaritans would believe. So He rebuked James and John for their desire to judge the Samaritans. Even so, Jesus did not remain in the village but went to another one.

It is easy to relate to James and John, isn't it? Someone rejects Jesus or the Holy Scriptures, and you want to judge instead of showing mercy and leaving judgment to the Lord. But the Bible says that judgment is the Lord's, and He will repay (Rom. 12:19). By God's grace, John learned to stop judging. After Jesus's ascension and the day of Pentecost, John took the gospel to many Samaritan villages (Acts 8:25), perhaps even to the one he had wanted to burn with heaven's fire. By God's grace, John went from a judger to a lover, faithfully proclaiming the gospel to the Samaritans.

On the way to Jerusalem, Jesus encountered three potential disciples. The first one said, "Lord, I will follow You wherever You go" (Luke 9:57), but this person had not thought about the difficulty of discipleship. If Jesus, the Son of Man, had become homeless for our sake and had nowhere to lay His head, a luxury even foxes and birds have, His disciples must be willing to do the same. We must count the cost of discipleship before making rash commitments and be willing to give up everything for Him.

The second person responded to Jesus's call by saying, "Lord, let me first go and bury my father" (Luke 9:59). But Jesus told him to let the spiritually dead[17] bury their

---

17. Ryle, *Luke*, 135.

physically dead since they have no business to do for the kingdom of God. If this man wanted to follow Jesus, he must go and proclaim the kingdom of God immediately. The King had come! In other words, we must keep our priorities in perspective, especially with family responsibilities.

The third person Jesus encountered also committed to following Him as long as he could first say farewell to those at his home. Jesus responded by alluding to Lot's wife: "No one, having put his hand to the plow, and looking back, is fit for the kingdom of God" (Luke 9:62; see also Gen. 19:26). In Jesus's day, a farmer had to plow with his eyes directly ahead in order to make a straight trench in rocky soil.[18] We too must set our eyes on Christ and serve as His ambassadors.

VII. Jesus Sends Again (10:1–24)
After sending His twelve apostles out to heal and proclaim the kingdom of God (Luke 9:1–2), the Lord now expands His ministry by sending out seventy[19] others in pairs of two to heal the sick and proclaim that the kingdom of God had come near to them (10:9). The Lord sent them to places that He was going in order to prepare the way for His coming. Significantly, the first thing He tells them to do is pray. Since the harvest is plentiful but the workers are few, they must earnestly pray that the Lord of the harvest would send out laborers into His harvest.

That the harvest is plentiful should encourage us. There are many people who are going to respond to the gospel. That the laborers are few should convict and challenge us. We should be willing to be involved in missions by either sending or going and always praying. That Jesus is the Lord of the harvest should instill confidence in us. We proclaim; He saves. The outcome of our evangelism does not depend on us but on the Lord. Jesus's instruction to pray that the Lord would send out laborers into His harvest reminds us that He needs laborers. Pray that the Lord will raise up more and more men, women, and children to have hearts for evangelism and missions.

Sadly, the seventy would be like lambs in the midst of wolves, being met with hostility for their message. On this journey they were to take nothing but depend solely on the Lord. They were to declare peace on the homes they entered, but peace would remain only if a son of peace (or a son of faith) was there. Otherwise, the home would receive no blessing. The disciples were to remain in one home, receiving provision from that family as workers worthy of support (see 1 Tim. 5:18).

If a town did not receive them, they were to proclaim judgment against them by wiping off the town's dust from their feet. The kingdom of God had come near in Christ Jesus. Those who rejected the King and His messengers would be worse off than Sodom, a city known for immorality, inhospitality, and rejection of God's people (see Genesis 19).[20] Sodom became the proverbial city of sinfulness in Scripture, but it did

18. Bock, *Luke*, 1:983.
19. Some translations read "seventy" and others read "seventy-two" due to variances in manuscripts.
20. Pao and Schnabel, "Luke," 317.

115

not receive the revelation that the towns Jesus and His disciples traveled through had, so it would not be held as highly accountable.

Most of us have been surrounded by Bible-believing churches all of our lives. We have experienced religious freedom and have access to numerous biblical resources, yet many of us are growing increasingly illiterate with regard to Scripture. Don't think we won't be held more accountable. Today is the day to repent and believe in the name of Jesus alone for salvation.

Jesus mentions three unrepentant cities by name: "Woe to you, Chorazin! Woe to you, Bethsaida!... And you, Capernaum" (Luke 10:13, 15). This is "an exclamation of pain and pity for the misfortune that awaits someone in a certain condition."[21] Remember, Bethsaida was the village in which Jesus fed the five thousand with the five loaves and the two fish (9:10–17). Sadly, this mighty work was not enough for the people to believe. Jesus compared Chorazin and Bethsaida with Tyre and Sidon, cities notorious for their sins (see Ezek. 26:1–28:24; especially their pride in 28:2). But they did not see the kingdom of God in their midst like Chorazin and Bethsaida did. Severer judgment comes on those who had greater revelation and rejected it.

Capernaum was the place Jesus had spent most of His time. He judged them for their pride and pronounced ultimate doom on those in that city who refused to see and hear the King of the kingdom. Significantly, this same doom had been pronounced on God's enemy Babylon (Isa. 14:13–15).

Jesus closed with a profound statement: "He who hears you hears Me, he who rejects you rejects Me, and he who rejects Me rejects Him who sent Me" (Luke 10:16). Jesus is claiming that His disciples speak the very words of God. They are proclaiming the message of the gospel, which is Jesus's message. Also, Jesus is saying that the one who rejects His disciples really rejects Him because they are ministering in His name for His name's sake. Most importantly, Jesus is claiming to be God. When someone rejects Him, they reject God the Father.

Joyfully, the seventy returned and reported to Jesus that even the demons were subject to them in His name. In saying that He saw Satan fall from heaven, Jesus alluded to Isaiah 14, which portrays the downfall of Babylon in language that many have understood as ultimately referring to Satan's fall from heaven (Isa. 14:12–15). From the wilderness to the cross, Jesus's ministry spells defeat for the devil (see Gen. 3:15). Additionally, His disciples' power to tread on serpents and scorpions (see Deut. 8:15; Ps. 91:13) and over all the power of the enemy was another way that Jesus saw Satan's doom coming to pass. But Satan's doom is not the greatest source of joy for the believer. Jesus reminded His disciples that their rejoicing should not be in their power but in their position in heaven.

Salvation should always be the disciple's greatest joy. Jesus did not just teach this; He practiced it. Jesus rejoiced in the Holy Spirit, thanking the Father for the sovereign decree of election for God's children (Luke 10:21–22). Jesus's prayer of thanksgiving

---

21. Bock, *Luke*, 1:583.

is the climax of all Israel's prayers and psalms of thanksgiving in the Old Testament.[22] The greatest and final Prophet, Priest, and King has come. The disciples were privileged to see and hear what many prophets and kings desired to experience but didn't. The kingdom of God was in their midst. How much more are we blessed: "The love of God has been poured out in our hearts by the Holy Spirit who was given to us" (Rom. 5:5). Rejoice and give thanks to the triune God, dear believer, for your salvation.

VIII. Jesus Shows Mercy (10:25–37)

On His journey to Jerusalem, Jesus encountered a lawyer who put Him to the test. Jesus had just been rejoicing that the Father has hidden salvation from the wise and understanding and revealed it to little children (Luke 10:21). Now He gives an example of someone who is wise and understanding according to the world's standards (a lawyer), but far from having childlike faith. The lawyer asked the question "Teacher, what shall I do to inherit eternal life?" (v. 25).

This lawyer didn't really want to hear Jesus's teaching. He was seeking only to justify his own behavior regarding the law and salvation. And people cannot do anything to inherit eternal life. Instead, they must believe in what Jesus has already done for them.

Jesus replied by appealing to the very authority that the scribes and Pharisees held in such high esteem, forcing the lawyer to consider what his own source of authority, the law, said about inheriting eternal life. The lawyer, knowing the law, responded correctly by quoting Deuteronomy 6:5 and the second part of Leviticus 19:18. Significantly, Deuteronomy 6:5 is a response to the first line of the Shema, the bedrock of Israel's faith: "The LORD our God, the LORD is one!" (Deut. 6:4). Also significant, Leviticus 19:18 falls within the context of God's commands for Israel to be holy since He is holy (Leviticus 17–26). And part of being holy is to love your neighbor as yourself.[23]

Jesus answers the lawyer on his own legal terms. The way to earn eternal life is to fulfill the law. But the New Testament is clear that nobody except Jesus could fulfill the law of God. Jesus's answer was true, but the lawyer could not accomplish it. He was pointing the lawyer to Himself, the sinless Son of God, who came to fulfill the law on our behalf.[24]

Sadly, the lawyer continued to focus on the law and self-justification, asking who his neighbor was. He wanted to reduce the requirements of the law by narrowing the definition of his neighbor. But God's word deals with the heart, and Jesus illustrated this with a story.

There was a man going down from Jerusalem to Jericho, a very dangerous and treacherous journey. The road was a steep descent (more than three thousand feet)

---

22. Pao and Schnabel, "Luke," 319.
23. Pao and Schnabel, "Luke," 320.
24. Ryken, *Luke*, 1:539.

through desolate country that was about seventeen miles long.[25] Robbers would often hide along this road because the terrain made it easy to attack people. Tragically, the robbers didn't just steal from the man; they left him half dead by stripping and beating him. Sadly, a priest, then a Levite, and finally a Samaritan passed by the injured man, but only the Samaritan stopped.

You can imagine the lawyer's shock when Jesus said it was the Samaritan who had compassion on the half-dead Jew. You may remember that Jews and Samaritans did not have a good relationship. There had been a long history of fighting between them, but the Samaritan recognized that this half-dead man was his neighbor. He bound his wounds, walked while the man rode on his animal, and took him to an inn. Then he paid the innkeeper to care for him, promising to come back, check on the man, and pay any outstanding balance. The shocked lawyer could not even say "the Samaritan" when Jesus asked which of the three was a neighbor to the victim of the thieves. Instead he replied, "He who showed mercy on him" (Luke 10:37). Jesus affirmed that his answer was correct by telling him to go and do likewise.

You and I know this is impossible. We need Jesus to do this on our behalf, and indeed He has. Jesus is far greater than the good Samaritan. When Jesus came to save us, we were not half dead but completely dead in our sins, hopeless and helpless to save ourselves. Jesus was not traveling down a road on His own business, but purposely left heaven to come and save sinners. Jesus did not just have compassion on us; He had abundant mercy on us by dying in our place. Jesus did not just bind up our physical wounds; He binds up our spiritual wounds, giving us eternal life through His life, death, resurrection, and ascension. Jesus did not bring us to an innkeeper; He spent His first night on earth in a stable, where there was no innkeeper. Jesus did not spend a couple of denarii but gave His very life for our salvation. As Philip Ryken writes, "Jesus traveled a much greater distance, to help people in much greater need, at much greater cost."[26]

If you are trying to earn your own salvation, stop. Turn to Jesus, the only Savior. If you are not displaying mercy to your neighbor, start. Jesus has first displayed compassion to us. Now, by His grace, we are to show mercy to others.

IX. Jesus's School (10:38–42)

Still on His way to Jerusalem, Jesus came to the village of Bethany (John 11:1). Martha welcomed Jesus into her house and got busy serving Him. Her sister, Mary, also welcomed Jesus, but she sat at the Lord's feet and listened to His teaching. Martha was distracted with much serving and frustrated that Mary was not helping her. She boldly approached the Lord about it: "Lord, do You not care that my sister has left me to serve alone? Therefore tell her to help me" (Luke 10:40). The Lord first answered her in tenderness, "Martha, Martha" (v. 41). According to R. C. Sproul, "It is one thing to

---

25. Morris, *Luke*, 207.
26. Ryken, *Luke*, 1:550.

address a person by their first name, but to repeat it is to use a Jewish form of affection and intimacy."[27] He then pointed out that her attitude was wrong: "You are worried and troubled about many things" (v. 41). Next, He reminded her that there is one thing necessary in life, a relationship with Him that leads to eternal life, and commended Mary's choice of the good portion, which is the Lord (see Pss. 16:5; 119:57; 142:5). Finally, He gives the reason for His approval of Mary's choice: "[It] will not be taken away from her" (Luke 10:42). A believer's relationship with the Lord is eternally secure.

Both Martha and Mary loved Jesus (see John 11), were faithful disciples, believed that Jesus was the Christ, and honored His presence.[28] Where Martha went wrong was in allowing service to take priority over seeking a deeper relationship with the Lord and in grumbling and complaining. There is a time to serve, and while we serve we can pray, meditate on Scripture, and sing hymns. There is also a time not to serve so that we can spend time in concentrated prayer and the study of the Bible. We must not make service the foundation of our faith; Christ alone is our foundation. Our eternal security depends not on our service but on our relationship with Him.

Do you see dependence on someone or something as mostly a weakness or a strength? Have you believed that you can save yourself from hardship by hard work? Do you try to satisfy your desires through your own means? In your work, do you depend on your knowledge and education? Are you trying to obtain financial security from wise investments? Do you have a tendency to isolate yourself instead of depending on others?

Dear reader, the gospel reveals that we are weak and utterly dependent on someone outside of ourselves to save us. Only in Christ do we find salvation, satisfaction, and strength. And only among Christ's people do we find true fellowship. As we learn to depend on Christ, we will also, by God's grace, experience the beauty of depending on one another. Together we can proclaim Christ, engage in mercy ministries, and seek to know Him more as we engage in corporate worship, attend women's Bible studies, and join together for prayer and fellowship.

---

27. Sproul, *Walk with God*, 207.
28. Ryle, *Luke*, 147.

Processing It Together . . .

1. What do we learn about God in Luke 9–10?

2. How does this reshape how we should view our present circumstances?

3. What do we learn about God's Son, Jesus Christ?

4. How should this impact our relationship with God and with others?

5. What do we learn about God's covenant with His people?

6. How are we to live in light of this?

7. How can we apply Luke 9–10 to our lives today and in the future?

8. How should we apply this passage in our churches?

9. Look back at "Put It in Perspective" in your personal study questions. What did you find challenging or encouraging about this lesson?

10. Look back at "Principles and Points of Application." How has this lesson impacted your life?

Something Greater Is Here

Luke 11–12

Purpose...

Head. What do I need to know from this passage in Scripture?

- Jesus teaches His disciples how to pray, reveals His greatness, and exhorts them to guard against sins such as hypocrisy, covetousness, and worry.

Heart. How does what I learn from this passage affect my internal relationship with the Lord?

- I am a kingdom disciple who has been given the privilege to pray to God the Father through Christ the Son by the Holy Spirit.

Hands. How does what I learn from this passage translate into action for God's kingdom?

- I will establish a habit of praying regularly.
- I will do justice in my family, church, and community.
- I will repent of hypocrisy, covetousness, and worry.
- I will boldly proclaim Christ, relying on the Holy Spirit to help me.
- I will store up treasure in heaven, not on earth.
- I will pray for the Lord to save my unbelieving family and friends.
- I will seek peace in strained relationships.

Personal Study...

Pray. Ask that God will open up your heart and mind as you study His Word. This is His story of redemption that He has revealed to us, and the Holy Spirit is our teacher.

Ponder the Passage. Read Luke 11–12.

- *Point:* What is the point of this passage? How does this relate to the point of the entire book?

- *Persons:* Who are the main people involved in this passage? What characterizes them?

- *Persons of the Trinity:* Where do you see God the Father, God the Son, and God the Holy Spirit in this passage?

- *Puzzling Parts:* Are there any parts of the passage that you don't quite understand or that seem interesting or confusing?

Put It in Perspective.

- *Place in Scripture:* What is the original context of this text? What is the redemptive-historical context—what has or hasn't happened in redemptive history at this point in Scripture? How does this text connect to Christ?

The following questions will help you if you got stuck on any of the previous questions, and they will help you dig a little deeper into the text, putting it all into perspective.

1. **11:1–4.** (a) How is the relationship between the Lord and His people sometimes portrayed in the Old Testament (see Ex. 4:22; Deut. 32:6; Isa. 63:16; Jer. 3:4; 31:9)?

   (b) Why is "hallowed be Your name" a prayer for God to fulfill His promises in Ezekiel 36:22–23, and through whom does God display His holiness?

   (c) What does it mean to pray "Your kingdom come" since Christ has already come and is coming again?

(d) How is the theme of God's daily provision displayed in Exodus 16:4–8 and Psalms 145:15–16; 146:5–7?

(e) Why should we be willing to forgive others?

(f) Who tempts us (see Gen. 3:1–7; Luke 4:1–2; James 1:13–14), and who tests us (see Ex. 16:4; 20:20; Deut. 8:2, 16; 13:3; 33:8; Judg. 2:22)?

2. **11:5–13.** (a) According to verse 8, what is the main point of this parable about prayer?

(b) What application does Jesus draw in verses 9–10?

(c) What parables does Jesus use to prove His promise in verses 9–10 (see vv. 11–12), and what is the main point of the parables according to verse 13?

(d) Why is the Holy Spirit the greatest of all gifts (see Rom. 8:13–14, 26)?

3. **11:14–23.** (a) What were the different responses to Jesus casting out a demon?

(b) How does Jesus respond to the people?

(c) How do Isaiah 49:25 and 53:12 provide background for verses 21–22?

(d) What application does Jesus make in verse 23, and how does this allude to Ezekiel 5:12 and 34:11–13?

4. **11:24–26.** (a) How does this illustration provide a conclusion to the previous passage in verses 14–23?

(b) What is the main point of this illustration (see 2 Peter 2:17–22)?

5. **11:27–28.** (a) How does Jesus correct the woman's view of blessedness?

(b) How were the woman's words true (see Luke 1:48)?

(c) What was Jesus's point?

6. **11:29–32.** (a) What comparison did Jesus make between the crowds and the wilderness generation (see Deut. 32:5, 20)?

(b) Of what is Jonah a sign (see Matt. 12:40)?

(c) Why will the queen of the South condemn this generation (see 1 Kings 10:1–13; 2 Chron. 9:1–12)?

(d) Why will the men of Nineveh condemn this generation (see Jonah 3:5)?

(e) Who is greater than Solomon and Jonah, and why?

7. **11:33–36.** What does this illustration reveal as the evil generation's problem?

8. **11:37–44.** (a) How did Jesus offend the Pharisee, and how did He use this to bring an indictment against him?

(b) What is Jesus's point in verse 41 (see 1 Sam. 16:7)?

(c) What does Jesus's first woe mean (see Lev. 27:30–32; Num. 18:21–32; Deut. 14:22–27)?

(d) Is Jesus condemning tithing—or something else? What is He actually condemning (see Mic. 6:8 and James 1:27)?

(e) What does the second woe mean (see Luke 14:7–11)?

(f) What is the meaning of the third woe (see Lev. 21:11; Num. 6:5–8; 9:6–7; 19:11–16)?

9. **11:45–54.** (a) What is the meaning of the first woe Jesus spoke to the lawyers (see Acts 15:10–11)? In contrast, what does Jesus offer (see Matt. 11:28–30)?

(b) What does the second woe mean (see Acts 7:51–52; Heb. 11:4; 1 John 3:12; Rev. 18:21, 24)?

(c) To what or whom does "the wisdom of God" refer in verse 49 (see 1 Cor. 1:30)?

(d) Why does Jesus refer to Abel and Zechariah (see Gen. 4:1–16; 2 Chron. 24:20–25)?

(e) What is the meaning of the third woe (see Rom. 2:17–24)?

(f) How did the scribes and Pharisees respond to Jesus, and why (see also Luke 20:20)?

10. **12:1–3.** (a) What was Jesus warning His disciples about?

(b) How did Jesus define the leaven of the Pharisees, and why were the disciples to watch out for it?

11. **12:4–7.** (a) Whom does Jesus tell his friends to fear, and why?

(b) How do the following passages help you better understand verse 5: Deuteronomy 32:22, 39; 1 Samuel 2:6; 2 Kings 5:7; 16:3; 21:6; 23:10; and Jeremiah 32:34–35?

(c) What illustrations does Jesus use to show the Father's love and care for His people?

(d) What does it mean to fear God (see Deut. 10:12–21)?

(e) How do the following passages help you better understand verses 6–7: 1 Samuel 14:45; 2 Samuel 14:11; 1 Kings 1:52; Job 38:37; Psalm 84:3; and Luke 21:18?

12. **12:8–12.** (a) How do Deuteronomy 30:15–20 and Daniel 7:13–14 provide background for verses 8–9?

(b) Skim Isaiah 63:7–64:11, then reread 63:10. What does it mean to blaspheme against the Holy Spirit?

(c) What is one of the ways the Holy Spirit helps believers (see also Ex. 4:12; Ps. 119:41–46; Jer. 1:9)?

13. **12:13–21.** (a) In light of the man's request, what does Jesus teach His disciples (see Ex. 20:17; Deut. 5:21; Job 31:24–25; Ps. 49; Eccl. 2:1–11; Rom. 7:7; 13:9; James 4:2)?

(b) What characterizes the rich fool (see also Job 27:16–22; Ps. 39:6; Eccl. 2:18–23)?

(c) What principle does Jesus draw from the parable?

14. 12:22–34. (a) Why are Jesus's disciples not to be anxious?

(b) In what ways does Jesus illustrate His command?

(c) How do 1 Kings 10:4–23 and Psalm 147:7–11 relate to Jesus's words?

(d) How are God's people to differ from the nations of the world?

(e) What is the Old Testament background for "little flock" (see Ps. 23:1; Isa. 40:11)?

(f) Since it is the Father's good pleasure to give His people the kingdom, what are they to do and why?

15. 12:35–48. (a) According to verse 35, what is the point of the parable in verses 36–38?

(b) According to verse 40, what is the point of the parable in verse 39 (see also Isa. 13:6; Ezek. 30:3; Joel 1:15; 2:1; Amos 5:18; Obad. 15; Zeph. 1:14–18; Mal. 4:5–6)?

(c) How is Peter's question in verse 41 answered indirectly in verse 48b?

(d) In light of the parable in verses 42–48, what is the main point? How do verses 42–46 allude to Genesis 39:4–5? How do verses 47–48 allude to Numbers 15:27–30?

16. **12:49–53.** (a) What does "fire on the earth" refer to (see Jer. 43:12; Ezek. 15:7; Hos. 8:14; Amos 1:4–14; 2:2, 5; Nah. 3:13; Zech. 13:9; Mal. 3:2–3)?

(b) To what does "baptism to be baptized with" refer (see Pss. 18:4, 16; 42:7; 69:1–2; Isa. 8:7–8; 30:27–28; Jonah 2:3–6; Mark 10:38)?

(c) What is Jesus's attitude toward this baptism, and how does it cause division between believers and nonbelievers (see also Mic. 7:1–7)?

17. **12:54–59.** (a) What does Jesus call the crowds He is addressing, and why?

(b) What two questions does Jesus ask the crowds?

(c) What is the point of the parable in verses 58–59 for the immediate audience?

(d) What is the point in the broader context of salvation history (see 2 Thess. 1:5–10)?

Principles and Points of Application

18. **11:1–13.** Seek to memorize the Lord's Prayer and incorporate it in your prayer life.

19. **11:14–26.** In what areas are you struggling with unbelief? Confess these to God.

20. **11:27–54.** How are you guilty of any or all of the following: neglecting the justice and love of God; displaying greed or wickedness; putting on a facade at church; loading others with expectations, rules, and burdens that you don't keep yourself; or hindering God's work in the life of a friend or family member? What will you do to make this right?

21. **12:1–12.** Whom or what do you fear, and why? Ask the Lord to replace these fears with the fear of the Lord.

22. **12:13–34.** (a) Before whom is it hard for you to acknowledge Christ? Before whom are you anxious to defend yourself? Ask the Lord to give you the opportunity to speak boldly for Him and thank Him that the Holy Spirit will help you know what to say.

(b) How are you seeking the treasures of this world instead of the kingdom of God?

23. **12:35–59.** (a) What divisions are in your family because of the gospel? How do Jesus's words help you expect and endure these? Spend time praying for your loved ones who are in need of salvation, asking the Lord to save them.

(b) Are you in right standing with God? If not, spend time in repentance. Are you in right standing with others? If not, seek peace.

Putting It All Together...

As Jesus walked among men, women, boys, and girls, proclaiming the kingdom of God and performing miracles, He taught many important truths that are imperative for the Christian growth of His disciples today. He is the Master Teacher, who continues to instruct us by His Spirit through the Holy Scriptures. Importantly, Jesus modeled prayer and taught His disciples how to pray. He also revealed His greatness and His victory over the kingdom of this world and His enemy the devil. But prayer and confidence in Christ's victory are not enough for the believer. Each day is a battle as we strive, by God's power, to subdue the sin that remains within us. Jesus acknowledges this battle by warning us against sins such as hypocrisy, covetousness, and worry— all of which seem to be at least somewhat excusable in our churches today. But Jesus will not excuse these sins. Instead, He warns us of their danger while comforting us with His care. It is a great encouragement to know that Jesus, the One who perfectly prays, is praying for us (Heb. 7:25) as we strive to put hypocrisy, covetousness, and worry to death.

I. Jesus Supplicates (11:1–13)

Prayer was a significant activity in Jesus's life (see Luke 3:21; 6:12; 9:18, 29). Certainly His disciples had made the connection between His time spent in prayer and His power in ministry. They too wanted to learn how to pray effectively, so they asked the Lord to teach them.

Jesus's beginning address, "Our Father in heaven," must have shocked the disciples. Although the concept of a father-son relationship was not new for God's people (see Ex. 4:22; Deut. 32:6; Isa. 63:16; Jer. 3:4; 31:9), there is no place in the Old Testament where God is addressed as Father in prayer. But with Jesus a new day had dawned— the age of the new covenant, the last days, the time between Jesus's first and second comings.[1] To call God "Father" respects His authority and suggests intimacy.[2] Our heavenly Father is far superior to all earthly fathers, yet He is approachable through His Son (Heb. 4:14–16).

Next, Jesus requests that God's name would be holy among His people. Sadly, God's name has been profaned both outside and inside the church. We must cry out that God's name would be seen as holy in the words and actions of God's people (see Ezek. 36:22–23).

Jesus also taught us to pray, "Your kingdom come." Although the kingdom has already been inaugurated with Jesus's first coming, it will not be consummated until He comes again. Until then, we pray that His rule would become greater in our hearts and in the hearts of our loved ones and that He would reign more and more in our churches, communities, countries, and continents. We ask that we would not seek the kingdoms of this world but would submit to the kingdom of God in our thoughts and actions.

The petition, "Give us day by day our daily bread" recalls Israel's grumbling in the wilderness and God's faithfulness to rain bread from heaven (see Ex. 16:4). The Lord always provides for His people, but He teaches us to depend on Him for our daily needs. Instead of giving us everything at once, He asks us to trust Him day by day to provide our necessities.

---

1. Pao and Schnabel, "Luke," 322.

2. Darrell L. Bock, *Luke*, vol. 2, *9:51–24:53*, Baker Exegetical Commentary on the New Testament (Grand Rapids: Baker, 1996), 1053.

In teaching us to pray, "And forgive us our sins, for we also forgive everyone who is indebted to us," Jesus argues from the lesser to the greater. If as sinful human beings we are able to forgive others, how much more is our heavenly Father, who is perfect, able to forgive our sins?[3] God is just and holy; He could not ignore sin. Payment was due and had to be paid, but Christ paid it in full, and now all those who are in Christ Jesus are forgiven.

In closing Jesus prays, "And do not lead us into temptation, but deliver us from the evil one." The Lord never tempts us (James 1:13–14), but He does test us. It was Satan who tempted Jesus in the wilderness (Luke 4:2), but it was the Spirit of God who led Him there (v. 1; see also Ex. 16:4; Rev. 2:10). We are asking that the Lord will not lead us into temptation by the world, our own flesh, or the evil one. When temptation comes, the Lord will provide a way of escape (1 Cor. 10:13). He also uses times of temptation to build our faith (James 1:2–3). But here we are taught to pray that we won't find ourselves in tempting situations that are very dangerous for sinners.[4] In the depths of suffering, the shame of sin, and the weariness of service, there is no greater place to turn than to our Father, who meets us with grace, mercy, and love.

To illustrate His teaching and demonstrate the importance of persistence in prayer, Jesus told a parable. Since it was common for people to travel during the night because it was cooler, and since hospitality was very important in that culture, it was not unusual that a friend would arrive at midnight. Families were expected to feed their guests, but since bread was made or bought on a daily basis, it was not uncommon to be out of bread by midnight, which is the case in this parable.

A friend is caught off guard by the arrival of a guest at midnight, and he has no bread to offer him. So he goes to another friend's home and asks to borrow three loaves of bread. At first the friend does not want to get up. In those days families slept in the same room, and if the friend got up to provide the three loaves, it would disturb his family. But the asker would not take any excuse for an answer. He was shamelessly presumptuous and persistent.

If a neighbor who does not want to get out of bed can be persuaded to do so by persistent asking, how much more will our heavenly Father, who desires to give good gifts to His children, do so? We never have to worry that we won't be able to rouse our heavenly Father in the middle of the night (Ps. 121:4) or that He will deny our request for daily needs (34:15) or for forgiveness (1 John 1:9).

Disciples are to continually ask, and it will be given; continually seek, and it will be found; continually knock, and it will be opened. Notably, there is a progression from asking, to seeking, to knocking down the door of heaven to request something from our Father. Strikingly, "everyone who asks receives, and he who seeks finds, and to him who knocks it will be opened" (Luke 11:10). Importantly, Scripture qualifies this

---

3. Morris, *Luke*, 213.
4. Ryken, *Luke*, 1:578.

promise: "If we ask anything *according to His will*, He hears us" (1 John 5:14, emphasis added; see also Matt. 6:10; James 4:15).

To illustrate the Father's graciousness in responding to persistent prayer, Jesus gives two more mini parables. First, would a father give a son a serpent if he asked for a fish? Second, would a father give his son a scorpion if he asked for an egg? In both cases, the answer is clearly no. If even earthly fathers, who are sinful, give good gifts to their children, how much more will the heavenly Father, who is perfect, give the greatest gift of all, the Holy Spirit, to His children?

Dear believer, we have already been given the greatest gift of all. The Holy Spirit indwells our hearts and seals us, guaranteeing our inheritance until we acquire possession of it (Eph. 1:14). Indeed, it is by the Spirit that we cry out, "Abba! Father!" The Holy Spirit "bears witness with our spirit that we are children of God," and fellow heirs with Christ (Rom. 8:15–17). We can boldly approach the throne of grace and find help in our time of need (Heb. 4:16).

II. Jesus Subdues (11:14–26)

As we've seen, Jesus's ministry in Galilee is behind Him, and He is now making His way to Jerusalem, where His ministry will climax in His death and resurrection. Just as He had cast out demons in Galilee, so too, on His way to Jerusalem, He cast out a demon from a mute man, and when he spoke, the people marveled. Sadly, not all the people marveled at Jesus's miraculous work. Some attributed Christ's power to Satan, "Beelzebub, the ruler of the demons."[5] Others were testing Him, seeking a sign from heaven to know who He was when they should have already recognized Him as the Christ, the Son of the living God. Not ignorant of their thoughts, Jesus addressed them.

First, He stated a principle: "Every kingdom divided against itself is brought to desolation, and a house divided against a house falls" (Luke 11:17). As in the case of a marriage that crumbles because a husband and wife have conflict or when owners of a company part ways because of disagreement, Satan's kingdom will not stand. The people's own words judge them. They cannot claim that their sons cast out demons in the name of God while denying that Jesus, the Son of God, casts out demons in God's name.

Jesus continued: "But if I cast out demons with the finger of God, surely the kingdom of God has come upon you" (Luke 11:20).[6] In other words, Jesus claimed that it was by the Spirit of God that He cast out demons, which proves that the kingdom of God had come upon them. Jesus illustrated this point by speaking of two men—one strong, and the other stronger. The strong man represents Satan. Notably, Jesus calls him strong, fully armed, a guard of his own palace, and one who keeps his goods

---

5. It is likely that the Jews understood Beelzebub, the name of a heathen deity, in terms of the similarly sounding Hebrew word that means "lord of the dung" and applied it to Satan. Morris, *Luke*, 215–16.

6. Both the "finger of God" and "the Spirit of God" (also translated "breath of His mouth" and "Spirit of the Lord") are used to refer to the same reality in the Old and New Testaments (see, e.g., Ex. 31:18; Pss. 8:3; 33:6; Ezek. 37:1; Matt. 12:28). Pao and Schnabel, "Luke," 323.

safe. Similarly, Peter says that our adversary is like a roaring lion seeking someone to devour (1 Peter 5:8; see also Eph. 6:11–18). But there is someone stronger than Satan. Through His life, death, and resurrection, Jesus took away Satan's armor and divided his spoil, claiming victory over sin (Isa. 53:12).

Dear friend, there is no neutral ground in this battle. We are either on the Lord's side or on Satan's side. On whose side are you? This is the most important question you will ever answer. Your future depends on it. Either you will live with Him forever in the Holy City, or you will be eternally separated from Him in hell.

In order to display that there is no neutral ground, Jesus gave a chilling illustration. Casting out demons is not the end of the story. When an unclean spirit goes out of a person, he seeks another place to rest, but on finding none, he goes back to the person he previously inhabited. But he does not go alone. He takes a whole entourage of evil spirits with him. Sadly, they find a moral person, clean and orderly, but not a Spirit-filled person. Morality does not guard a person from evil spirits, and when they reenter, it is much worse than the first time. Only the Spirit of God protects a person from being inhabited by evil spirits.

Complacency is deadly for the spiritual life. The state of those who have tasted of the heavenly gifts but never embraced them is far worse than those who never tasted them in the first place (Heb. 6:1–8). Many people have been surrounded by the truth of the gospel all their lives yet have failed to trust in Christ alone for salvation. Many people believe that morality saves. Do not be deceived, friend. Cry out today that your hearts and homes would not be just moral but would be filled with the Spirit of God and the love of Christ.

III. Jesus Signals (11:27–36)

As Jesus boldly claimed that He subdues Satan, a woman boldly blessed Jesus's mother, Mary, for her great Son. Without disagreeing (see Luke 1:39–45), Jesus made a contrast. He moved the focus from Mary to God. Those who hear the word of God and keep it are blessed (see also 8:8, 15, 21; 10:24; James 1:22).

Apart from God's grace, we are deaf to the word of God. We must pray and ask the Holy Spirit to open our ears and the ears of our family and friends to hear truth. Apart from grace, we are also unable to keep God's commandments. We must pray and ask Him to give us and our loved ones grace to obey Him each day.

As the crowds increased, Jesus spoke of them as an evil generation, recalling Israel's rebellion during the wilderness wanderings. They were evil because they were still seeking a sign when the greatest sign had appeared in their midst. Jesus had come preaching the kingdom of God, casting out demons, and healing the sick and the blind. But Jesus said that the sign of Jonah will be given to this evil generation.

Notably, Jesus uses the future tense, "will be." Also, this sign is spoken of in the context of judgment on an evil generation. The sign of Jonah, according to the Gospel of Matthew, is the death and resurrection of Jesus Christ (12:40). When Jonah preached to the Ninevites, they repented (Jonah 3:5). One greater than Jonah was preaching to this evil generation, but they were not repenting. For this reason, the Ninevites will rise up and condemn them, for they were pagan Gentiles who responded to the gospel, but the Jews refused to respond in repentance.

The queen of the South will also rise up at the final judgment and condemn the generation of Jesus's day. When the queen of Sheba heard of Solomon's fame, she came to Jerusalem to ask him hard questions. Once she saw his wisdom and wealth, she recognized that the Lord God had blessed Solomon (1 Kings 10:1–10; 2 Chron. 9:1–12). The Lord would bless this Gentile queen for blessing one of His people (Gen. 12:3). One greater than Jonah and Solomon stood in the midst of the Jews, yet they refused to recognize Him as the greater Prophet and King, the very Son of God.

If you are constantly seeking for more proof or another sign before you place your faith in Christ, stop. We have been given Scripture so that we might have certainty of the faith. All Scripture testifies that Jesus is the Christ, the promised Messiah who has accomplished the work of redemption.

Jesus continued to condemn the evil generation by illustrating how they had treated Him. Jesus is the light that has come into the world. Sadly, some want to extinguish His light. Others believe religious tradition is the true light when it is actually darkness. Those in spiritual darkness cannot see the light of Christ. Since their eye is spiritually bad, their body is full of darkness. But those who have had their eyes opened to the light by God's grace shine as lights for Him in this dark world.

IV. Jesus Scolds (11:37–54)

While Jesus was speaking, a Pharisee approached and asked Him to dine with him. Jesus, knowing the hypocrisy of his heart, graciously agreed. He didn't even have time to speak before the Pharisee started judging Him for not washing before dinner. The Pharisee wasn't interested in hygiene but rather in removing the defilement from contact with a sinful world.[7] Since Jesus knew Judaism's religious leaders were scrupulous about keeping external laws while ignoring the state of their hearts, He confronted the hypocrisy of the Pharisees: "Foolish ones! Did not He who made the outside make the inside also?" (Luke 11:40). In other words, God demands holiness of heart and hands. If the Pharisees would give their hearts, minds, and souls to the Lord, then their outward actions would be clean. Sadly, because their motives were impure, even the best external acts would be unclean.

The word that Jesus had for the Pharisees serves as a warning for us. God sees through our external acts into the motives of our hearts. When we put on a facade before walking into worship on Sunday morning, allow others to think that we are more righteous than we are, or put on an air of self-righteousness in an argument with our spouse, we are acting like the foolish Pharisees.

---

7. Morris, *Luke*, 221.

Jesus pronounced three woes, revealing His regret and grief over the Pharisees' attitudes and actions.[8] First, they had neglected the justice and love of God. Notably, Jesus commended them for keeping the tithe, but He was quick to point out that they should also have displayed the justice and love of God. The law commanded the Jews to tithe (see Lev. 27:30–32; Num. 18:21–32; Deut. 14:22–27), but they had gone beyond the law and developed a twelve-tithe system.[9] To go beyond the law in tithing and forsake the law in matters of justice and love is not walking with God (Mic. 6:8).

Second, they lusted after position. They loved to have the best seat in the synagogues, where others would recognize them as great religious leaders. They loved to be greeted in the marketplaces as noble men of the town. But sadly, they neglected their position before God as sinners in desperate need of grace.

Third, they deceived themselves and others in matters of spirituality. According to the Old Testament purity laws, the priests were not to go near dead bodies, not even their parents' (Lev. 21:11). The Nazirite vow forbade a person from going near a dead body, including a family member (Num. 6:6–8). Israelites could not keep the Passover if they had touched a dead body (9:6). There were laws for purification after touching a dead body so that the tabernacle of the Lord did not become defiled (19:11–14). So serious were the Jews about maintaining these laws that they would go around marking unmarked graves in order not to accidentally step on one. Ironically, Jesus said the Pharisees were like unmarked graves; people didn't realize they were following corrupt and spiritually dead religious leaders.

These three woes serve as a warning for us. Too often we neglect the love and justice of God while scrupulously keeping other spiritual disciplines. Or we lust after position, wanting others to know what we have accomplished so they will honor us. It's also a danger for all of us to think we are more spiritual than we really are.

Not surprisingly, other people were at the meal with Jesus and the Pharisee. Many house parties were open to those walking by, and one of the lawyers, a religious leader and scribe who had studied the law and explained what it meant, had joined them. He accused Jesus of insulting not only the Pharisees but lawyers as well. Jesus responded with three woes.

First, lawyers held others to a higher standard than they held themselves to. Second, they honored God's prophets with outward rituals while neglecting their teaching. Building tombs for the prophets was considered pious, but it was also an attempt to atone for their fathers' sins. Ironically, instead of honoring the prophets with tombs, they were really dishonoring them by refusing to heed their words from the Lord.[10] According to His wise and sovereign purposes, the Lord sent Israel prophets, from Abel (see Gen. 4:1–8) to Zechariah (see 2 Chron. 24:20–22), in order to point the way to the greatest Prophet of all, Jesus Christ. Sadly, Israel rejected these prophets by not

---

8. Morris, *Luke*, 222.

9. Pao and Schnabel, "Luke," 324.

10. Ryken, *Luke*, 1:636.

heeding their message and therefore rejected the God who had sent them. Even worse, the lawyers were ignoring the greatest and final Prophet, who stood before them. Jesus is not a prophet speaking on behalf of the Lord; He is the Lord who speaks.

Third, the lawyers engaged in false teaching. Although they spent their time studying Scripture and were supposed to teach others truth, they were blind to their sin and their need for the Savior. Instead of repenting, they sought to accuse Jesus.

Like the woes for the Pharisees, these woes for the lawyers serve as a warning for us. Too often we hold others to a higher standard than we hold ourselves to. Too often we honor God's preachers with our lips while rejecting the Scriptures they preach. And too often we remain blind to our sins while eagerly pointing out the sins of others.

V. Jesus Summons (12:1–12)

As Jesus traveled on toward Jerusalem, thousands of people gathered around Him, so many that they were trampling each another. He used this opportunity to warn His disciples about the leaven (hypocrisy) of the Pharisees. Leaven was a common household item used to make bread. A little leaven worked its way through the entire lump of dough, giving the bread what it needed to rise. In the same way, the Pharisees subtly worked their ways through the people, infesting the law with hypocrisy. But Jesus said that their secret ways would be revealed. Christ's second coming, the final judgment, will expose the hypocrisy of this world for all to see and hear.

Since believers are robed in the righteousness of Christ, their secret thoughts and sins are covered in the blood of the Lamb. This means that we can ask the Lord to reveal any areas of hypocrisy that are hindering our love for God and neighbor, knowing that He will extend grace and mercy to us. One of the ways that we can guard against hypocrisy is by having a proper fear of God. This is what Jesus addressed next with His disciples, His friends.

Jesus contrasted unbelievers who could persecute a believer even to death with God, who can judge persecutors and cast them into hell. He exhorted the disciples, in light of persecution and coming persecution, to fear God, who is the final Judge of where people spend eternity.

Jesus illustrated this by speaking of five sparrows, the most common and inexpensive of birds, which were sold for two pennies in the marketplace. If God takes care of such cheap and common birds, how much more will He take care of His people, who are of much more value than many sparrows (see Ps. 84:3)? God even numbers the hairs on our heads. If God knows such minute details of our lives, how much more will He care for the larger ones, like persecution and death?

Another way to guard against hypocrisy is to confess Christ before others. Jesus promised His disciples that if they acknowledged Him, the Son of Man (see Dan. 7:13–14), before others, He would acknowledge them before the angels of God, who will be involved on the final day of judgment. But whoever denies Jesus before others will be denied before the angels of God on the final day of judgment. Dear friend, have you confessed before others that Jesus is the Christ, the Son of the living God?

Anyone who speaks a word against the Son of Man will be forgiven, but the one who blasphemes against the Holy Spirit will not be forgiven (Luke 12:10). It is one thing to reject Jesus during His time on earth; some did this and came to believe in Him after His death, resurrection, and ascension. It is another thing to reject the Holy Spirit, which people do when they reject the working and saving power of God in their heart to bring them to salvation. This rejection is not momentary but is rather a lifestyle of rejecting the gospel (see Rom. 1:18–32; Heb. 6:4–6). Israel rejected God's presence with His people and

> rebelled and grieved His Holy Spirit;
> So He turned Himself against them as an enemy,
> And He fought against them. (Isa. 63:10)

In the same way, those who blaspheme against the Holy Spirit reject the very presence that has the power to save.[11]

For those who do not blaspheme the Holy Spirit, Jesus gives another promise. During times of persecution when they are brought before the synagogues, rulers, and authorities, they are not to be anxious about how to defend themselves because the Holy Spirit will teach them what to say. The Lord has always been with His people, teaching them what they are to say at critical times (see Ex. 4:12; Jer. 1:9). How much more will we believers who live after the day of Pentecost, when Jesus sent His Spirit, be assisted to speak boldly before our persecutors and accusers (see Acts 4:8; 7:51–56; 21:37–26:32)?

VI. Jesus Secures (12:13–34)

Someone in the crowd recognized Jesus as a teacher and asked Him to settle an inheritance dispute with his brother, but the motivation of the man's heart was revealed in Jesus's response. Jesus used the dispute to teach that a person must guard against covetousness by being rich toward God. By telling a parable, Jesus illustrated the principle that people's lives do not consist in their material possessions.

A rich man's land produced plentifully. Sadly, the rich man did not attribute his riches to the Lord. He planned to hoard everything for himself by building larger barns to store his goods in place of smaller ones. Then he was going to lead a relaxed life, relying on his stored wealth rather than continuing to be productive and give to those in need. But God said that he lacked wisdom: "Fool! This night your soul will be required of you; then whose will those things be which you have provided?" (Luke 12:20; see also Pss. 14:1; 53:1; Eccl. 2:1–11).

Wealth doesn't save us or stay with us. The most important thing in life is not possessions but a personal relationship with Jesus Christ. This love for God leads us to love

---

11. Pao and Schnabel, "Luke," 328.

our neighbor and share with people in need. The way to guard against covetousness (desiring anyone or anything above God) is to lay up treasure in God's kingdom by loving and serving Him with our time, talents, and treasures.

Covetousness is not the only sin Jesus addressed. He also confronted the sin of worry (Luke 12:22–34). Too many of us are worried about how life will turn out for our friend, what we are going to prepare for the next meal, how our bodies look, how our child is going to fit in at school, and how we are going to care for our aging parents. But Jesus said that life is more than these things.

To illustrate, He talked about the ravens. Ravens were considered one of the unclean and detestable animals (Lev. 11:13, 15; Deut. 14:12, 14), but the Lord provides food for them (Ps. 147:9; Job 38:41). If the Lord cares for ravens, how much more will He provide for His people?

Besides, anxiety cannot add a single hour to our lives. We must remember that our times are in the Lord's hand (Ps. 31:15). If we can't add a moment to our lives by what we do or don't do, we shouldn't worry about what we will eat and wear.

Or, Jesus said, think about the lilies. They neither toil nor spin, but they are arrayed more beautifully than Solomon was on his best days. This is quite something (see 1 Kings 10:4–23; 2 Chron. 9:13–21)! Additionally, if God clothes even grass, how much more will He clothe His people?

Significantly, unbelief is the root of anxiety. Jesus exclaims, "O you of little faith" (Luke 12:28). Most of us would not equate worry with unbelief. Many people wouldn't even consider worry sin. But Jesus says that worry is nothing less than a lack of faith in God's provision and bountiful care for His children. Anxiety and seeking after food and drink are what characterize unbelievers. Dear believer, since our heavenly Father knows what we need and is faithful to provide it, we should not worry but seek the kingdom of God and trust Him to provide.

Jesus closed with a tender exhortation: "Do not fear, little flock, for it is your Father's good pleasure to give you the kingdom" (Luke 12:32). As our Shepherd, the Lord gives us rest, leads us, restores us, comforts us, prepares good things for us, and chases us with goodness and mercy (Psalm 23). The next time you are tempted to worry, stop and worship God. Operate out of faith, not fear. Rest in God's promises and provision and recognize His sovereign plan.

To combat covetousness and worry, Jesus exhorted His disciples to sell their possessions and give to the needy. Then He told them to build their treasures in heaven. Where our treasure is, our heart is. Jesus wants our hearts to be fixed on the kingdom of God, not on the kingdoms of this world. Dear believer, build your treasure in heaven by using your time, talents, and treasures for God's glory by His grace.

VII. Jesus Separates (12:35–59)
Jesus next taught His disciples to guard against faithlessness by being ready for His second coming. "Let your waist be girded and your lamps burning" (Luke 12:35) is

an allusion to how Israel was to eat the Passover on their way out of Egypt (Ex. 12:11). Jesus, the inaugurator of the second exodus who redeems God's children by His death, resurrection, and ascension, spoke here of being ready for His second return. In that day men often wore long robes that hindered their ability to run, so they had to tie them up when running. In other words, they were to keep their waists girded. Also, people would let their lamps burn out when it was time to rest, but Christ reminded His disciples that they must always be ready for action.

Jesus illustrated his exhortation with a parable (Luke 12:36–38). Christ's disciples were to be like men who were waiting for their master to come home from a wedding feast. In Jesus's day a wedding feast could last up to a week, and the master often came home very late at night. So servants were to be ready to open the door to him at once when he knocked, despite the late hour. Surprisingly, the servants who are found awake will not serve their master. Instead, their master will serve them! The servants who are ready to meet their master are the ones who are blessed, and this is how it will be for those who are found ready on the day of Christ's return.

Continuing to teach about how to prepare for His coming, Jesus told a second parable (Luke 12:39), followed by an application (v. 40). No one would ever leave their home if they knew that it was going to be broken into while they were gone. Instead, they would stay and protect their home. Likewise, since Jesus's coming will be at an hour when no one expects, we must always be ready (see also Isa. 13:6; Ezek. 30:3; Joel 1:15; Amos 5:18; Obad. 15; Zeph. 1:14–18; Mal. 4:5–6). Peter asked the Lord whether He was telling the parable for the apostles or for everyone (Luke 12:41). Although Jesus didn't directly answer Peter, based on Jesus's words in verse 48, we must assume that He spoke in parables for everyone: "For everyone to whom much is given."

To continue emphasizing the importance of being ready for His return, Jesus told another parable (Luke 12:42–48). In each of the four examples, there is a master and a manager, or steward. In the first, the manager is faithful and wise and is blessed because of it (vv. 42–44; see, for example, Gen. 39:4–5). In the second, the manager is unfaithful and unprepared when his master comes and is therefore punished with the unfaithful (vv. 45–46). In the third, the manager knows his master's will but does not act accordingly or prepare for his coming, so he is beaten severely (v. 47). In the fourth, the manager does not know his master's will, does what deserves a beating, and is beaten, but lightly (v. 48a). The point is, the more a person has been given, the more he or she is held responsible.

Except for the second example, these scenarios speak of believers. Sadly, many of us have been given a good deal of resources and the freedom to serve in various ministries and capacities but are not the wise and faithful stewards we should be. Dear believer, ask God to help you be a faithful and wise steward of all He has entrusted to you.

Jesus now shifts His focus to the purpose of His first coming (Luke 12:49–50). Jesus came to baptize people with the Holy Spirit and with fire (3:16). In the Old Testament, the imagery of fire most often conveys judgment (see Jer. 15:14; Ezek. 15:7; Hos. 8:14;

Mal. 3:2–3), but it can also refer to refinement in order to purify an object or a people. When Jesus came He brought both. He came to seek and to save the lost, but those who refused to believe remained under God's judgment. Those who believed experienced His refinement. Jesus's baptism by John anticipated another baptism He would experience, His death. His distress until He accomplished redemption reflected His devotion to His Father's will.

Although in a sense Jesus brought peace to earth (Luke 1:79; 2:14), He also brought division (12:51). Those who believe in Jesus will be divided against those in their family who do not believe. Dear believer, if there is division in your home because you confess Christ but another family member does not, do not lose heart. Stand strong as a witness and worshiper of Christ with a heart of humility, words of grace, hands of service, and prayers for your loved one's salvation.

Jesus turned His attention from His disciples to the crowds in order to rebuke their hypocrisy (Luke 12:54–56). He accused them of knowing how to interpret the appearance of earth and sky but not the time. Although they could recognize when rain and scorching heat would come, they had failed to recognize the King in their midst.

Jesus closed with a parable that is both practical and profound (Luke 12:57–59). Before judgment falls, it is important that we get right with God and with our neighbor. Since every person has sinned and fallen short of God's glory (Rom. 3:23), each of us must settle with God. The only way to do this is through Jesus Christ. Believers can be confident that Jesus has paid the very last penny of our debt and has set us free. We will spend eternity with Him. But unbelievers will be put in the prison of hell forever.

We also need to settle with our neighbor. Since Christ has extended forgiveness and peace to us and reconciled us to God the Father, we should be eager to extend forgiveness and peace to others and seek reconciliation. We can do this only by God's grace. Ask Him to give you the strength to reach out to the one you have offended or who has offended you with a posture of peace and humility.

Dear believer, you will often be tempted to not pray, to doubt God's greatness and power, to live as a hypocrite, to covet what someone else has been given, or to worry about the things of this world. To fight this temptation, you must believe that Jesus is who He says He is. You must remember that He is praying for you that your faith will not fail. And you must obey God's commands and rest in His promises. Because Jesus is the Prophet who still speaks by His Spirit through Scripture, the Priest who "always lives to make intercession for" God's people (Heb. 7:25), and the King who reigns over all, we are faced with a decision to choose whom we will follow. For all those who repent of their sin and trust in Christ alone for their salvation, He has secured an eternal dwelling place with Him in which the godly will be separated from the ungodly and "the throne of God and of the Lamb shall be in it, and His servants shall serve Him." Most wonderfully of all, "they shall see His face" (Rev. 22:3–4).

Processing It Together...

1. What do we learn about God in Luke 11–12?

2. How does this reshape how we should view our present circumstances?

3. What do we learn about God's Son, Jesus Christ?

4. How should this impact our relationship with God and with others?

5. What do we learn about God's covenant with His people?

6. How are we to live in light of this?

7. How can we apply Luke 11–12 to our lives today and in the future?

8. How should we apply this passage in our churches?

9. Look back at "Put It in Perspective" in your personal study questions. What did you find challenging or encouraging about this lesson?

10. Look back at "Principles and Points of Application." How has this lesson impacted your life?

Glorious Things Done by Him

Luke 13–14

Purpose...

Head. What do I need to know from this passage in Scripture?

- Jesus calls people to repentance, teaching about the kingdom of God, salvation, and discipleship.

Heart. How does what I learn from this passage affect my internal relationship with the Lord?

- I am a kingdom disciple who has been exalted in Christ Jesus and welcomed by the Father as a guest at His table.

Hands. How does what I learn from this passage translate into action for God's kingdom?

- I will use my time, talents, and resources for the Lord this week.
- I will encourage others that God is growing His kingdom in His way.
- I will pray for the Lord to save my non-Christian family and friends.
- I will keep the Lord's Day holy, making time for corporate worship and acts of mercy.
- I will display humility in my interactions with others this week.
- I will help others count the cost of discipleship and follow Christ wholeheartedly.

Personal Study...

Pray. Ask that God will open up your heart and mind as you study His Word. This is His story of redemption that He has revealed to us, and the Holy Spirit is our teacher.

Ponder the Passage. Read Luke 13–14.

- *Point:* What is the point of this passage? How does this relate to the point of the entire book?

- *Persons:* Who are the main people involved in this passage? What characterizes them?

- *Persons of the Trinity:* Where do you see God the Father, God the Son, and God the Holy Spirit in this passage?

- *Puzzling Parts:* Are there any parts of the passage that you don't quite understand or that seem interesting or confusing?

Put It in Perspective.

- *Place in Scripture:* What is the original context of this text? What is the redemptive-historical context—what has or hasn't happened in redemptive history at this point in Scripture? How does this text connect to Christ?

The following questions will help you if you got stuck on any of the previous questions, and they will help you dig a little deeper into the text, putting it all into perspective.

1. 13:1–5. (a) What kind of suffering did the Galileans experience?

(b) What belief held by many Jews in that day does Jesus's question expose (see Ex. 20:5; Job 4:7–8; 8:4, 20; 22:5; Prov. 10:24–25)?

(c) What did Jesus use this incident as an opportunity to do (see also Ps. 7:11–16; Jer. 12:17)?

(d) How does the incident of the tower in Siloam differ from the incident in Luke 13:1, and how is it similar?

2. **13:6–9.** (a) In light of Exodus 15:16–17; Psalm 80:8–11; and Isaiah 5:1–7, who does the fig tree represent? Who does the owner represent?

(b) How does the plea of the vineyard keeper represent God's mercy (see also 2 Peter 3:9)?

(c) According to verse 9, what is the main point of the parable?

3. **13:10–17.** (a) How did Jesus respond to the disabled woman?

(b) Contrast the woman's response to Jesus's healing with the ruler of the synagogue's response. Why would he have responded this way (see Ex. 20:9–10; Deut. 5:13–14)?

(c) How does the Lord respond to both the synagogue ruler and the Jews?

(d) In calling the woman a "daughter of Abraham," what did Jesus imply (see also Luke 19:9)?

(e) Who does Jesus say had bound this woman for eighteen years, and how was Jesus's purpose for coming to earth displayed through this miracle (see Luke 4:18–19)?

4. 13:18–19. (a) Using a Bible resource, learn about mustard seeds.

(b) In what way does Jesus allude to both Ezekiel 17:22–24 and Daniel 4:10–15 in this parable?

(c) What is Jesus teaching about the kingdom of God in this parable?

5. 13:20–21. (a) How does this parable relate to the one in verses 18–19?

(b) What do you learn about leaven from a Bible resource?

(c) What is Jesus teaching about the kingdom of God in this parable?

6. 13:22–30. (a) Since Scripture is clear that salvation is by grace alone through faith alone, what does it mean to "strive to enter"?

(b) Who is the narrow door through whom people are saved (see John 10:7, 9; 14:6)?

(c) How are the following Old Testament passages that Jesus alludes to being fulfilled in verses 27–29?
- compare Jeremiah 1:5; Hosea 5:3; and Amos 3:2 with verse 27a
- compare Psalm 6:8 with verse 27b
- compare Psalm 112:10 with verse 28a
- compare Psalm 107:2–3; Isaiah 43:5–6; 45:6; and 59:19 with verses 28b–29

(d) What does verse 30 imply about Jews and Gentiles (see Acts 10:34–11:1)?

7. 13:31–35. (a) Why would the Pharisees tell Jesus about Herod's desire to kill Him, and do you think they were right (see Matt. 14:1–12)?

(b) Why would Jesus say that a prophet cannot perish away from Jerusalem (see 2 Kings 21:16; 2 Chron. 24:20–22; Jer. 26:20–23; 38:4–6)?

(c) How does Jesus identify with God's care of His covenant people (see Deut. 32:11; Ruth 2:12; Pss. 17:8; 57:1; 91:4)?

(d) How does Jesus's statement in verse 35a go further than Jeremiah's warning (see Jer. 12:7; 22:5)?

(e) What Old Testament passage does Jesus cite in verse 35b?

8. 14:1–6. (a) Using a Bible resource, find out what dropsy is.

(b) What question did Jesus pose to the lawyers and Pharisees before He healed the man, and how did they respond?

(c) What was the point of Jesus's second question to the lawyers and Pharisees, and what does their silence betray?

9. 14:7–11. (a) What prompted Jesus to tell this parable?

(b) What does the parable tell the guests not to do, and what does it tell them to do?

(c) How does verse 10 reflect Proverbs 25:6–7 and verse 11 reflect Ezekiel 21:25–27?

(d) What does this parable teach about the kingdom of God?

10. 14:12–14. (a) Who does Jesus tell the host not to invite to his dinners or banquets, and why?

(b) Who does Jesus tell the host to invite, and why?

(c) When is the resurrection of the just (see 1 Cor. 15:23–24)?

11. 14:15–24. (a) In the parable, who does the man giving the banquet represent, and who does the servant that the man sent represent?

(b) What three excuses did the servant receive, and what was the response of the master when the servant reported the excuses?

(c) How does verse 21 allude to Isaiah 29:18–19; 35:5–6; and 61:1–2?

(d) How does this parable relate to God's invitation to the Jews and to the Gentiles (see Rom. 9–11; 15:7–16)?

(e) What is the one requirement to attend God's great supper (see John 14:6)?

12. 14:25–33. (a) In light of Exodus 20:12 and Deuteronomy 5:16, what does it mean to hate one's family and life?

(b) What does it mean to bear one's own cross (see Luke 9:23–24; Acts 14:19–23; Heb. 13:12–14)?

(c) How are the two illustrations Jesus gives similar, and how are they different?

(d) What does it mean for disciples to forsake all that they have (see Phil. 3:7)?

13. 14:34–35. (a) Using a Bible resource, look up *salt* and describe what salt was like in Jesus's day.

(b) How is Jesus's question a warning to those who claim to follow Jesus?

(c) What does Jesus's call to hear emphasize?

(d) What makes it possible for a believer to be salt and light in this world (see, for example, Matt. 5:13–16; John 15:4–5)?

Principles and Points of Application

14. **13:1–9.** (a) What instruction does James 5:16 give about your continual need for repentance?

(b) How are you using your time, talents, and resources for the Lord's kingdom?

15. **13:10–17; 14:1–6.** How do you show that you honor the Lord on the Lord's Day?

16. **13:18–30.** Have you, dear friend, entered through the narrow door (see John 10:7, 9; 14:6)? If so, write out a brief testimony.

17. **13:31–35.** In what area(s) of your life are you facing grief and persecution that are challenging your perseverance?

18. **14:7–14.** How has our Christian culture promoted places of honor, and how do we need to grow instead in humility?

19. **14:15–25.** How are you giving your resources away to those who can never repay you? Ask the Lord to open your eyes to needs in your own church family and then to those in your community. Then take steps to meet those needs as you are able.

20. **14:26–35.** Read John 15:1–17. How does your life display that you are a disciple of Christ? In what area(s) do you need to grow?

Putting It All Together...

In his book *The Cost of Discipleship*, Dietrich Bonhoeffer (1906–1945) describes the difference between cheap grace and costly grace:

> Cheap grace is grace without discipleship, grace without the cross, grace without Jesus Christ.... Costly grace is the gospel which must be *sought* again and again, the gift which must be *asked* for, the door at which a man must *knock*.
>
> Such grace is *costly* because it calls us to follow, and it is grace because it calls us to follow *Jesus Christ*. It is costly because it costs a man his life, and it is grace because it gives a man the only true life. It is costly because it condemns sin, and grace because it justifies the sinner. Above all, it is *costly* because it cost God the life of his Son: "ye were bought at a price," and what has cost God much cannot be cheap for us. Above all, it is *grace* because God did not reckon his Son too dear a price to pay for our life, but delivered him up for us. Costly grace is the Incarnation of God.[1]

In Luke 13–14 Jesus teaches us the difference between cheap grace and costly grace. He teaches us to be kingdom disciples who display mercy on the Sabbath, approach God in humility, display generosity to others, and pledge our allegiance to Him above all other people and all other things.

I. Contrition (13:1–9)

While Jesus spoke on the importance of being ready for His second coming, some people told Him about the Galileans who had died under Pilate's command. By mingling their blood with the sacrifices that they were making to the Lord, Pilate took this crime even further. Although we know nothing else about the event from other passages in Scripture or Jewish literature, Pilate's actions are not surprising from what we know of him and of other historical incidents involving killing Jews.[2] Pilate was a cruel man, and he was the Roman administrator who had the capability of using force to accomplish his own selfish purposes.

Jesus exposed the motivation behind those who had told Him about this incident by asking whether this suffering had come to these Galileans because they were worse sinners. He put to rest the popular idea that people's suffering was a direct result of their sin and used this opportunity to warn them not to be concerned with the Galileans but to consider their own need to repent. He called them to repentance so that they wouldn't perish in the same way.

Jesus brought up another event, a tower in Siloam that had fallen and killed eighteen people, to call His listeners to evaluate their own lives. Instead of assuming that the death of others was because of their sin, they needed to repent of their own sin. Otherwise, they would perish.

---

1. Dietrich Bonhoeffer, *The Cost of Discipleship* (New York: Touchstone, 1995), 45.
2. Bock, *Luke*, 2:1204–5.

We must not draw conclusions about people's sin and their suffering (see John 9:2–3). God uses suffering in the lives of the righteous to sanctify them as much as He uses suffering in the lives of the disobedient to call them to repentance or to judge them. During times of suffering, believers should evaluate their relationship with the Lord, repenting as appropriate and rejoicing in the truth that God displays His power through our weakness.

The parable of the fruitless fig tree is closely connected with the previous exhortations to repent. Fig trees were abundant in the regions where Jesus lived and ministered. Jesus used the fig tree as a symbol for Israel. God had planted Israel to be a fruitful vine in the midst of the world in order to bear great fruit for His kingdom and glory (see Ps. 80:8–16). Sadly, Israel rebelled against the Lord, and even when Jesus came, most of the Israelites did not believe that He was the Messiah.

The owner of the fig tree had waited three long years, enough time for a fig tree to take root and produce figs, but none had grown. Since the tree was taking up valuable space and soil that could be used for a fruitful tree, the owner ordered it to be cut down. The vinedresser asked for one more year and committed to giving it extra nutrients. If it bore fruit, great; otherwise, it could be cut down.

Like the vinedresser, God is merciful and long-suffering. Although Israel was ripe for judgment, God is slow to judge. He is gracious in giving people more time to repent. But there is an end to His patience. For the generation of Jesus's day, there would be one more opportunity. They would witness Jesus's death and resurrection, and the gospel would be preached. Sadly, many still did not repent. In AD 70 the temple was destroyed and Israel was scattered again; many of the generation that saw and heard Jesus never believed in Him as Lord and Savior.[3] Dear friend, there is coming another day, the day of Christ's return, when the day of mercy will be over. When Christ comes again it will be for judgment. We must come before God with a contrite heart, recognizing we have sinned against a holy God and trusting in Christ alone for salvation. Otherwise, we will perish.

II. Cured (13:10–17)

Once again Jesus was teaching in a synagogue on the Sabbath. A woman was there who had a disabling spirit for eighteen years. She was bent over and could not straighten herself. Jesus, breaking all social norms in a society that did not value women, saw her, called her to Him, and spoke to her. Jesus freed her from her disability, laying His hands on her so that she became straight.

Jesus's act of healing on the Sabbath received three different responses. First, the healed woman glorified God. She represents the response of all true daughters of Abraham. Before we came to Christ, all of us had a disabling spirit. We were bent over in sin and could not straighten ourselves to walk in paths of obedience. We can be

---

3. Ryken, *Luke*, 2:11.

grateful that Jesus saw us, called us, and spoke to us, freeing us from our sin so that we can glorify God.

Second, the ruler of the synagogue was angry. Instead of addressing Jesus directly, he addressed those who had witnessed the healing. As a Jewish leader, he adhered strictly to the fourth commandment (Ex. 20:8–11; Deut. 5:12–15). Sadly, this man believed that Jesus's act of love and compassion should not be done on the Sabbath. What a tragedy that he was focused more on the rules of people than on the mercy of the Savior!

Jesus rebuked the ruler of the synagogue and his followers, calling them hypocrites. He exposed their inconsistency. If they found an ox or a donkey worthy of care on the Sabbath, how much more should they see this woman worthy of care? Jesus was fulfilling His purpose to free the oppressed (see Luke 4:18–19) and displaying His power over Satan, giving people a foretaste of the complete healing that will come in glory.

Third, the people rejoiced at the glorious things Jesus did. When we witness Jesus's mercy in someone's life, we should rejoice. When a loved one's cancer is in remission, someone gains relief from chronic pain, a friend's family is growing in peace, or a marriage has been restored, we should celebrate God's glorious grace. The Lord's Day is certainly a day for corporate worship, but it is also appropriate to engage in acts of mercy toward others and to celebrate God's mercy in their life.

III. Kingdom (13:18–30)

In the parables of the mustard seed and the leaven (Luke 13:18–19, 20–21), Jesus revealed that despite opposition from people like the synagogue ruler, the kingdom will continue to grow, and healings on the Sabbath anticipate a world that will one day be entirely restored and renewed.[4] In the first parable, Jesus revealed that God's kingdom is extending throughout the world, while in the second He taught that the kingdom of God is powerfully transforming the world.[5]

First, the kingdom of God is like a grain of mustard seed that a man sowed in his garden. The mustard seed was one of the smallest seeds, but it grew into a tree that was large enough for the birds to make nests in its branches. Although the kingdom of God starts off as small as a seed, it will grow to be large, and it will be a place of rest (a nesting place).

Jesus alluded to Ezekiel 17:22–24 (see also Dan. 4:10–15), a passage in which God promises to take a sprig from the lofty top of the cedar, break off from the topmost of its young twigs a tender one, and plant it so that it becomes a noble cedar. Under it will dwell every kind of bird that will nest in its shade. This speaks of the Lord raising up the Davidic King, Jesus Christ, who will be the one to break down the dividing wall and make one new man from both Jews and Gentiles who will find rest in Him.

---

4. Ryken, *Luke*, 2:28–29.
5. Morris, *Luke*, 242.

The image of the mustard seed contradicted the size of the kingdom that the Jews were anticipating. They were looking for a political Messiah to take over the kingdom of Israel. But Jesus did not come to set up a political kingdom on earth. His kingdom begins as a spiritual kingdom. He rules from heaven until His second coming, when all of His enemies will be destroyed and the kingdoms of this world become the kingdom of Christ. Until then, we are His ambassadors, taking the gospel into every sphere where the Lord calls us, being faithful to proclaim Christ in all that we do and say until He comes again.

The second parable compares the kingdom of God to leaven that a woman hid in three measures, or fifty pounds,[6] of flour, until gradually it was all leavened. Although there may be times when it doesn't look like the kingdom is growing, it is slowly working its way through all the earth, pervading every part of the world.

These parables teach us several things about God's kingdom. First, God's way seems foolish to people. God has always used seemingly insignificant things and people to shame the wisdom of this world. Second, we can be sure that the kingdom of God will grow. God is calling a people to Himself from every tribe, tongue, and nation. Third, the kingdom of God will grow in ways that are often hidden to us. Fourth, the kingdom of God spreads into all the nations. Fifth, the kingdom of God will permeate the world. This doesn't mean that the world will be Christianized; Christ must return before the kingdoms of this world become the kingdom of our Christ. But Christians are a fragrant aroma of Christ to all those around them and are impacting culture with the truths of the gospel as they pledge allegiance to Christ as their King.

Dear friend, if you are discouraged because your sin seems too great and your love for the Lord too small, you wish your husband was more spiritually mature, one of your children has wandered from the truth, or your ministry seems small and insignificant, remember the parables of the mustard seed and the leaven. Where God has begun a good work, He will complete it (Phil. 1:6). Keep proclaiming the gospel to those around you, believing that God is growing His kingdom.

As Jesus journeyed toward Jerusalem, an opportunity arose for Him to speak of the way of salvation in the kingdom of God (Luke 13:22–30). Someone asked if the saved would be few in number. Remember, the Jews in Jesus's day believed that they were the chosen people and that the Gentiles had no place in salvation. Instead of answering the question directly, Jesus exhorted the questioner to strive to enter through the narrow gate.

People who strive to enter the kingdom of God put all their effort toward it (see Prov. 2:1–5). This does not contradict the truth that salvation is by grace alone through faith alone. It means that until God saves us and the Holy Spirit assures us of our salvation, we are to put all of our effort toward seeking the way of salvation, reading the way of salvation in the Scriptures, hearing the way of salvation from teachers and

---

6. Bock, *Luke*, 2:1228.

preachers, and praying that God will illumine our hearts and minds.[7] How a person strives is important because many have gone about salvation the wrong way. The Jews were trusting in their status as God's chosen nation and were ignoring the truth that Jesus is the only way, the truth, and the life (see John 14:6).

In addition to the narrow gate, Jesus spoke of the master inside the house who is in charge of opening and shutting the door. There are people who stand outside the house knocking at the door, mistakenly believing that the way of salvation was through being God's chosen nation, eating and drinking in His presence, and hearing His teaching in the streets. The master will quickly tell them to depart because they never received Jesus Christ as Lord and Savior. Sadly, they are workers of iniquity (see also Ps. 6:8).

There are only two kinds of people in this world, the saved and the unsaved. No matter their morals, the unsaved are workers of iniquity and are destined for hell. Hell is a real place. The imagery of weeping and gnashing of teeth connotes both emotional and physical distress and agony. Unbelievers will not be annihilated in hell; it is a place of everlasting torment. And evidently those who are sent there will have some capability of seeing what they have lost and believers have gained.

Our culture doesn't like to talk about exclusions. Many people believe that there are different ways to enter through the door of heaven, and they think of it as a wide door that will include people from every religion. Many proclaim a god who displays his love by not sending anyone to hell. But that is not what Scripture teaches. Jesus is the only way of salvation, and hell is a real place. Christianity is exclusive in the sense that it excludes all those who reject Jesus Christ as the way of salvation, but it is inclusive in the sense that God saves a people from every tribe, tongue, and nation.

Gentiles, who have been last in God's plan of redemptive history, will be first, and Jews, who were first in God's plan of redemptive history, will be last. Even in the Old Testament, God was bringing Gentiles like Rahab and Ruth into His family, but He dealt mostly with Israel as His chosen nation. God opened up the floodgates to the Gentiles beginning on the day of Pentecost, however, and now through the church is proclaiming the gospel to every tribe, tongue, and nation.

There is a song I have sung with my children about one door with two sides. The question in the song is, "On which side are you?" I have used the song as an opportunity to talk with my children about the seriousness of knowing whether we are inside or outside of God's kingdom. Dear friend, I ask you the same question, "On which side are you?" Have you trusted in Christ alone for salvation? What about your loved ones? On which side are they? If they are on the outside, continue to pray that the Lord will save them. If they are on the inside, thank God for saving them.

---

7. Ryken, *Luke*, 2:43.

IV. Cries (13:31–35)

The same day that Jesus spoke parables of the kingdom, some Pharisees told Him to depart because Herod desired to kill him. Most commentators think that the Pharisees probably were not trying to help Jesus but rather to help Herod get Jesus out of the regions over which he ruled. Regardless, their attempt was not successful. Jesus sent the Pharisees to Herod with a message, prefacing it with an unflattering title ("fox"), which most likely referred to his destructive nature (see Luke 9:9; Acts 4:27).[8] Jesus made it clear that He had come to earth for a specific purpose and would not be deterred. Casting out demons and performing cures on His way to Jerusalem fulfilled one of His purposes in coming to earth (see Luke 4:18–19). Through these miracles, He displayed His power and authority over the evil and suffering in this world. Additionally, Jesus reminded Herod that He was a prophet, and like many other prophets, He would die in Jerusalem (see 2 Chron. 24:20–22; Jer. 26:20–23).

Jesus's cries over the city in which He would die were filled with emotion (Luke 13:34–35). Significantly, He used covenant language that the Lord used with His people in the Old Testament (see Deut. 32:11; Ruth 2:12; Pss. 17:8; 36:7; 57:1; 91:4), identifying Himself with Yahweh. Because Israel rebelled against the covenant Lord and refused to take shelter under His wings, their house was forsaken (see also Jer. 12:7). By rejecting their King, they rejected the only way of salvation.

Citing Psalm 118:26, Jesus told the Jews that they would not see Him again until they cried, "Blessed is he who comes in the name of the LORD." This psalm of thanksgiving, which celebrates God's steadfast love, was sung at the Feast of Tabernacles and Passover. It was sung when Jesus entered Jerusalem on Palm Sunday. And it was the last psalm that Jesus sang with His disciples at the Last Supper.[9] Perhaps Jesus was referring to His second coming, when Jerusalem would finally recognize Jesus as the Messiah, although it would be too late for the people to repent and believe. Or maybe He was referring to Palm Sunday, when many people sang Psalm 118 as He rode into the city. Sadly, many who sang His praises on Palm Sunday rejected Him on Good Friday.[10] Regardless, what is most important is whether we have cried out to the Lord, "You are my God, and I will praise You; You are my God, I will exalt You" (Ps. 118:28).

V. Confrontation (14:1–6)

Most likely Jesus, the lawyers, and the Pharisees attended the synagogue service in the morning, and Jesus was invited to join them for their noon meal. As you recall, the Pharisees were keeping a close eye on Jesus (Luke 11:53–54; 14:1). In fact, it's likely that the Pharisees arranged for the man with dropsy[11] to be at the house in order to

---

8. Bock, *Luke*, 2:1247.

9. C. John Collins, note to Psalm 118, in *ESV Study Bible* (Wheaton, Ill.: Crossway, 2008), 1091.

10. Ryken, *Luke*, 2:61.

11. *Dropsy* is not a disease but an indication that there is another underlying medical condition present. The symptoms of dropsy are "swollen limbs and tissue resulting from excess body fluids." It was often viewed by the Jews to be God's judgment for sin or uncleanness. Bock, *Luke*, 2:1256.

trap Him. But Jesus, knowing their motives, set a trap of His own, asking, "Is it lawful to heal on the Sabbath?" (14:3). If they said no, they would appear to be extremely compassionless, but if they said yes, they would betray their man-made religion. So they remained silent. Jesus answered yes to His question by His actions. He took the man, healed him, and sent him away.

Then Jesus asked the lawyers and Pharisees if they would pull out a donkey or an ox that had fallen into a pit on the Sabbath. They could not reply to this either. Again, if they replied yes they would betray their inconsistency of following their own man-made rules, but if they replied no they would expose their hard-heartedness. Their silence condemned them and called them to repentance.

How we observe the Lord's Day is important. We should all attend corporate worship. But how we engage in acts of mercy will look different for each of us. You may display mercy to your children by spending quality time with them on Sunday afternoon. You might invite a widow or a single person to share a meal. You might feed the homeless. The Lord's Day is a time for us to look around and ask the Lord to show us who in our lives needs compassion, and then be obedient to extend it.[12]

VI. Commitment (14:7–35)

Shifting His focus from the lawyers and Pharisees to those who were invited to the meal, Jesus addressed the guests who were rushing for places of honor. Typically, the closer a person sat to the host of the meal, the more honor he was given and the higher rank he was thought to have. But this is not how things work in God's kingdom, so Jesus told them a parable (Luke 14:7–11).

First, when guests were invited to a wedding feast, they should not seek out the places of honor. If someone more distinguished arrived later, they would have to shamefully give up their seat and move to one of lesser honor. Instead, they were to humbly sit in the lowest place of honor so that the host would invite them to move up to a higher place in front of the guests. The self-exalting will be humbled, but the humble will be exalted (Luke 14:14; see also Prov. 25:6–7).

The way to the kingdom of God is through Christ, the exalted One. We don't deserve any place at God's table, but because of God's grace, He sent His Son, who humbled Himself (see Phil. 2:1–11) so that we might be exalted with Him on the last day. As we humble ourselves in the presence of the Lord, we will be exalted in Him, not for anything that we have done but because of what He has done for us.

Once again Jesus switches His focus, this time to the host of the meal, a ruler of the Pharisees (Luke 14:1, 12–14). Jesus instructed him not to invite those who would be able to repay him, such as friends, siblings, relatives, or rich neighbors, but to invite the poor, the crippled, the lame, and the blind. Upon Jesus's return, such generosity will reap a blessing from God.

---

12. Ryken, *Luke*, 2:67.

Jesus's point is comparative. There is nothing wrong with inviting our family and friends to dinner; in fact, Scripture speaks of honoring our families often. But in light of how often we invite friends and family over, we should far more often extend an invitation to those who can never repay us. Believers should be characterized by generosity and selflessness in light of how God has dealt with us. We are the poor, the crippled, the lame, and the blind. We have lost the richness of communion with God. We are broken by our sin. We cannot see the truth of the gospel. We can never repay Jesus for what He has done. But through Christ we have received abundant riches, healing from brokenness, sight to see gospel truths, and freedom from our debt of sin.

Once again Jesus changes His focus, this time to one of the guests sitting at the table with Him who exclaimed, "Blessed is he who shall eat bread in the kingdom of God!" (Luke 14:15). Jesus was slow to endorse such an exclamation, not because it was untrue (see Isa. 25:6–10) but because it presumed on His grace. This Jewish man assumed that he would be at the banquet, but Jesus revealed through another parable that many who presume on God's grace will not be in the kingdom of heaven (Luke 14:16–24).

The man who gave a great banquet and invited many people represents God the Father, and the banquet represents God's kingdom. Throughout the Old Testament the Lord invited His chosen nation, as well as people from other nations, like Rahab, Ruth, and Naaman, to salvation in Him. The man sending his servant to tell those who had been invited to come represents God the Father sending His Son into this world to inaugurate the kingdom of God.

Sadly, the invitees make poor excuses. In Jesus's day it was improper for a person to make excuses when he had already committed to going to a banquet. Two invitations were sent. The first invitation was to secure the number of how many would be attending; the second invitation was to remind people on the day of the event to come because the host was prepared.

When the servant (Jesus) comes and tells his master (God the Father), the master becomes angry and tells his servant to go out to the streets of the city and bring in the poor, crippled, blind, and lame (those in Israel whom the Pharisees and other religious leaders were too proud to invite for dinner). Even after the servant does this, there is still more room. So the master tells the servant to go out to the highways and hedges and compel people to come in so that God's house will be filled.

God longs for people to repent and come into the kingdom of heaven. Sadly, because of hard-heartedness, many never repent of their sin and trust in Christ alone for their salvation. God's plan of salvation was not just for the Jews but also for the Gentiles (see Matt. 28:16–20; Acts 10:34–11:18). He has chosen a people for Himself from every tribe, tongue, and nation.

Jesus states, "For *I* say to you that none of those men who were invited shall taste *my* supper" (Luke 14:24; emphasis added). It is not just the banquet of God the Father but of the Son as well. Remember, Jesus was at a meal with Pharisees and other religious leaders who were trying to trap Him (v.1). He told them that they would never taste His banquet, the one of which their Scriptures prophesied and in which they believed. Sadly, they could not see that Jesus was the servant who had been sent by God, the One in whom they must believe in order to have a seat at the Lord's eternal feast.

Dear friend, we must not presume on God's grace. We must not assume that we are going to heaven because we were raised in a Christian home, attend church regularly, or put money in the offering plate. We must repent of our sin and run to Christ, trusting in Him alone for salvation.

No longer at the meal with the Pharisees, Jesus was once again en route to Jerusalem. With great crowds accompanying Him along the way, He seized the opportunity to teach about discipleship (Luke 14:25–35). He said that disciples must come to Him in total allegiance and love. We must love Jesus more than we love our life and family. We must be willing to say yes to Jesus even if that means saying no to our own dreams, goals, agendas, and family if their demands get in the way of Christ's call on our life.

Also, disciples must bear their own cross. We will suffer because of our faith. When we are treated unfairly because we are a believer, or when someone ridicules our Christian beliefs, or when our family rejects us or ridicules our beliefs, or when our career stops advancing because we took a stand for the truth in the workplace, or when our neighbor chides us for being too conservative as a Christian, we are bearing our cross.

Disciples must renounce all that they have. Jesus precedes this requirement with two parables. First, if a person desires to build a tower, he must first sit down and count the cost to determine whether there is enough money. Otherwise, the builder will be mocked for not finishing what he began. Second, when a king sees an army approaching that is greater in number than his, he has to decide whether his army should fight. If he does not think he can defeat the greater army, he must send a delegation and ask for terms of peace.

In the first parable, the question is, "Can we afford to follow Jesus?" In the second parable, the question is, "Can we afford not to?"[13] On the one hand, we must ask ourselves whether we are willing to give up everything that we have to follow Jesus, including our lives. On the other hand, we must ask whether, with the great army of God against us, we can afford not to follow Him. In the end His army will be acknowledged as victorious over all. Our only recourse is to ask for terms of peace, and the only way to have this peace is through Jesus Christ, the One through whom God reconciles us to Himself (2 Cor. 5:18).

Jesus closed with a warning. He used salt to illustrate that a disciple must align with God's definition of discipleship to be useful. In Jesus's day, salt was not the pure sodium chloride that you and I have in our kitchens today. It was a mixture of sodium chloride and other crystals that was produced by the evaporation of saltwater from the Dead Sea. The salt could leach out of the compound, leaving it useless for anything,

---

13. Ryken, *Luke*, 2:96.

including fertilizer.[14] Jesus's words to the church in Laodicea are similar and help explain this mini parable (see Rev. 3:15–17). In order to be a useful disciple, we must come to Jesus acknowledging our wretched state as sinners, our blindness to the truth, our shameful nakedness, and our poverty in spirit, pledging our allegiance to Him, putting Him above all else, and running hard after Him.

Bonhoeffer continues to explain the cost of discipleship by focusing on the cross:

> For God is a God who *bears*. The Son of God bore our flesh, he bore the cross, he bore our sins, thus making atonement for us. In the same way his followers are also called upon to bear, and that is precisely what it means to be a Christian. Just as Christ maintained his communion with the Father by his endurance, so his followers are to maintain their communion with Christ by their endurance. We can of course shake off the burden which is laid upon us, but only find that we have a still heavier burden to carry—a yoke of our own choosing, the yoke of our self. But Jesus invites all who travail and are heavy laden to throw off their own yoke and take his yoke upon them—and his yoke is easy, and his burden is light. The yoke and the burden of Christ are his cross. To go one's way under the sign of the cross is not misery and desperation, but peace and refreshment for the soul, it is the highest joy. Then we do not walk under our self-made laws and burdens, but under the yoke of him who knows us and who walks under the yoke with us. Under his yoke we are certain of his nearness and communion. It is he whom the disciple finds as he lifts up his cross.[15]

---

14. Ryken, *Luke*, 2:98.
15. Bonhoeffer, *Cost of Discipleship*, 92–93.

Processing It Together...

1. What do we learn about God in Luke 13–14?

2. How does this reshape how we should view our present circumstances?

3. What do we learn about God's Son, Jesus Christ?

4. How should this impact our relationship with God and with others?

5. What do we learn about God's covenant with His people?

6. How are we to live in light of this?

7. How can we apply Luke 13–14 to our lives today and in the future?

8. How should we apply this passage in our churches?

9. Look back at "Put It in Perspective" in your personal study questions. What did you find challenging or encouraging about this lesson?

10. Look back at "Principles and Points of Application." How has this lesson impacted your life?

Joy over Repentant Sinners

Luke 15–16

Purpose...

Head. What do I need to know from this passage in Scripture?

- God seeks those who are His own, calling them to repentance and rejoicing over their salvation. In response, we must love God more than the things of this world.

Heart. How does what I learn from this passage affect my internal relationship with the Lord?

- I am a kingdom disciple whose salvation has been celebrated by the triune God and is secured by the blood of Jesus.

Hands. How does what I learn from this passage translate into action for God's kingdom?

- I will ask the Lord to give me opportunities to share the gospel.
- I will pray for the Lord to save my lost family and friends.
- I will shepherd those under my care with love and grace.
- I will repent of any self-righteousness and squandering of time, money, and resources.
- I will be faithful in the small and large things my Father calls me to do.
- I will help others understand how God's law applies to the believer.
- I will care for the physically and spiritually poor in my midst.

Personal Study...

Pray. Ask that God will open up your heart and mind as you study His Word. This is His story of redemption that He has revealed to us, and the Holy Spirit is our teacher.

Ponder the Passage. Read Luke 15–16.

- *Point*: What is the point of this passage? How does this relate to the point of the entire book?

- *Persons*: Who are the main people involved in this passage? What characterizes them?

- *Persons of the Trinity*: Where do you see God the Father, God the Son, and God the Holy Spirit in this passage?

- *Puzzling Parts*: Are there any parts of the passage that you don't quite understand or that seem interesting or confusing?

Put It in Perspective.

- *Place in Scripture*: What is the original context of this text? What is the redemptive-historical context—what has or hasn't happened in redemptive history at this point in Scripture? How does this text connect to Christ?

The following questions will help you if you got stuck on any of the previous questions, and they will help you dig a little deeper into the text, putting it all into perspective.

1. **15:1–7.** (a) Contrast how the tax collectors and sinners responded to Jesus with how the Pharisees and the scribes responded.

(b) According to verse 3, how many parables does Jesus tell in verses 4–32?

(c) How do Jesus's words in verses 4–7 reflect the following passages: Genesis 49:24; Numbers 27:16–17; 2 Samuel 5:2; 7:7; Psalm 23; Isaiah 40:11; Jeremiah 23:2–5; Ezekiel 34:6, 11–12; Zechariah 10:2; 11:17; Matthew 2:6; John 10:1–18; Hebrews 13:20; 1 Peter 2:25; 5:4; and Revelation 7:17. How has Jesus fulfilled the attributes of a Good Shepherd?

(d) Since all humankind needs to repent (Rom. 3:23), who does Jesus mean by "just persons who need no repentance"?

2. **15:8–10.** (a) Compare the number of sheep in verse 4 with the number of coins in verse 8. What do you notice?

(b) What attributes of God are revealed in verses 8–10?

3. **15:11–16.** (a) Compare the number of sheep (v. 4) and the number of coins (v. 8) with the number of sons (v. 11). What do you notice?

(b) What does the younger son ask for in verse 12, and how does this reflect Deuteronomy 21:17?

(c) To whom did the younger son hire himself out, a Jew or a Gentile, and was this work appropriate for a Jewish person (see Lev. 11:7; Deut. 14:8)?

4. **15:17–24.** (a) How does the son's realization and plan display the beginning of repentance?

(b) Who initiates complete reconciliation?

(c) What verbs are used to depict the father's actions in verse 20?

(d) How does the father respond to his son's expression of unworthiness?

(e) Compare verse 23 with verses 7 and 10. What is the main point of all three stories in this parable?

5. **15:25–32.** (a) Where had the older son been the whole time his younger brother had been away?

(b) How did the older son respond to his father's grace, and who else's attitude does this display (see v. 2)?

(c) What was the older son overlooking about himself and about his brother?

6. **16:1–8.** (a) What charges were brought to the rich man against his steward (or manager), and did he believe them?

(b) What was the steward's dilemma when he learned that he had lost his job?

(c) What does the steward decide to do, and why?

(d) For what exactly does the rich man commend the steward?

(e) Contrast the sons of this world with the sons of light.

7. 16:9. (a) How does Jesus tell His disciples to make friends?

(b) In what events in the book of Luke do we see this lesson applied in a godly way (see 19:1–10) and in an ungodly way (see 16:19–31; 18:18–24)?

8. 16:10–12. (a) What specific example does Jesus give in verse 11 to illustrate His principle stated in verse 10?

(b) To what does "the true riches" refer (see Luke 12:32–34)?

(c) What is the second specific example that He gives in verse 12 to illustrate His principle stated in verse 10?

9. 16:13. (a) What is the general principle?

(b) Why can't a person serve two masters?

(c) What is the specific principle?

10. 16:14–18. (a) Describe the Pharisees. Where were they when Jesus was teaching the parable of the unjust steward to His disciples, and how did they respond?

(b) How does Jesus describe the Pharisees' view of themselves and God's view of them, and how does He explain these differences?

(c) How does Luke describe the age of promise and then the age of fulfillment?

(d) How does verse 17 clarify Jesus's words in verse 16?

(e) What specific example does Jesus give to prove that the law is still in effect? For more on this topic, see Matthew 5:31–32; 19:3–9; Mark 10:10–12; and 1 Corinthians 7:10–11, 15.

11. **16:19–31.** (a) According to verse 15, who is Jesus addressing in verses 19–31?

(b) What is the difference between the rich man and Lazarus?

(c) What are the rich man's prayers when he is in Hades, and how does Abraham respond to each one?

(d) How does the rich man argue with Abraham's response, and what is Abraham's final remark?

(e) Give a few examples from the Gospels of God raising someone from the dead. How do some of the people's responses to these miracles prove Abraham's answer is true?

Principles and Points of Application

12. **15:1–7.** (a) What actions can you take toward unbelievers in order to share the gospel with them? Ask the Lord to give you the opportunity and willingness to do so soon.

(b) How are you reflecting the attributes of the Great Shepherd to those under your care?

13. **15:8–10.** What can you learn from the woman who lost a coin about how you should pray for unbelievers?

14. **15:11–32.** (a) In what ways are you like the younger son before he came to repentance?

(b) In what ways are you like the younger son after he came to repentance?

(c) In what ways are you like the father?

(d) In what ways are you like the older brother?

15. **16:1–13.** (a) Spend time this week examining your use of money, time, and resources. Then record what you learned.

(b) How are you displaying your faithfulness to the Lord and to your neighbor in both small and large things?

(c) What master do you serve? (Think about the people or things that receive most of your time, money, resources, and attention.)

16. 16:14–18. (a) What in your life is an "abomination in the sight of God"? Spend time in repentance and confession.

(b) What is the purpose of God's law in your life? Since salvation is by grace alone through faith alone, how are believers to use the law?

(c) Have you entered the kingdom of God by faith alone in Christ alone? In what way does your life bear testimony of this?

17. 16:19–31. (a) How are you caring for the physically poor and the spiritually poor?

(b) Of the people you know, who needs to hear and believe in the gospel before they die? Pray for them, asking the Lord to save them. Ask Him for opportunities to share the gospel with them.

Putting It All Together...

One of the joys of being a believer is seeing the Lord provide for His people through the time, money, and resources of the covenant community. Years ago a friend shared with me her family's need for a vehicle. Money was tight, and they could not afford a new or used car, but they needed one for transportation. We prayed and prayed, asking the Lord to provide for their needs. As the weeks went by, our prayers were answered by church members loaning their vehicles out for a week or two at a time.

During this time the husband and wife learned that they were expecting their sixth child and would be in need of a vehicle that could carry eight people. They continued to pray as a family and asked their friends to pray. Not long afterward I was at a church event and my friend shared the wonderful news that a gentleman at our church had approached the deacons and told them he wanted to donate a van that had significant value. He could have sold the van and gotten a considerable amount of money for himself, but instead he wanted to use it to serve God's people. The deacons, who knew of my friend's need, called immediately and offered her family the van. That van was a testimony to her children and to our church family that the Lord hears our prayers and provides for our needs. It is also a reminder of how believers should use their time, money, and resources to glorify God and bless His people.

Jesus has much to say about being kingdom disciples who choose to love and be devoted to God rather than to money. We are to recognize that God alone secures our salvation, our true wealth, and that our resources are to be used for the building of His kingdom. Before we turn our attention to these truths, though, Jesus tells three different parables in order to reveal the grace and love of God.

I. Lost Sheep, Coin, and Son (15:1–32)

Not surprisingly, the Pharisees and the scribes were still among the crowds listening to Jesus, trying to catch Him in something He might say (see Luke 11:54; 15:2). Ironically, the tax collectors and sinners were drawing near to Jesus while the Pharisees and scribes were grumbling against Him. Like the discontented wilderness generation who grumbled against Moses (see Ex. 15:24), the Pharisees grumble against the greater Moses. In response, Jesus told them a parable made up of three different stories with the same main point (see Luke 15:7, 10, 24, 32), God's covenant love.

In the first story (Luke 15:1–7), a shepherd leaves ninety-nine sheep in the open country to find one that is lost. Like this shepherd, God the Father pursues His lost people in His great love and mercy, and His Son, Jesus Christ, keeps them safe (see John 10:14; 17:12). When the shepherd finds the lost sheep, he lays it on his shoulders, rejoicing. In his kindness, love, and compassion, he takes the burden on himself to bring the sheep back to the rest of the flock, where he belongs. Likewise, Jesus is the Good Shepherd who laid down His life on the cross of Calvary, bearing the burden of our sin, to deliver us from the bondage of sin and reconcile us to the Father (John 10:11).

When the shepherd comes home, he calls together his friends and neighbors to rejoice with him for finding the one lost sheep. The joy in heaven over one repentant sinner exceeds that of "ninety-nine just persons who need no repentance" (Luke 15:7). Since there is no person who doesn't need to repent (Rom. 3:23), Jesus is addressing the self-righteous Pharisees, who misunderstood both His purpose and the meaning of repentance. Jesus came to seek and to save the lost, so eating with sinners was part of His mission. And no one can get to heaven by good works; they must repent and believe in Jesus in order to be saved.

In bringing judgment against the bad shepherds of Israel through the prophecies of Ezekiel, the Lord had promised to be His people's shepherd (see Ezek. 34:11, 25, 30–31). As the Good Shepherd who gave His life for God's people, Jesus is the fulfillment of God's promise (John 10:11). He is the chief and Great Shepherd who oversees our souls, guides us to living water, and wipes away our tears (see Heb. 13:20; 1 Peter 2:25; 5:4; Rev. 7:17).

Dear friend, do you know this Shepherd? If you have wandered from the flock of God's people, Jesus wants to bring you home. If you have loved ones who have wandered away from the flock, you should know that Jesus has not forgotten about them. He hears the prayers you cry on their behalf. He seeks, claims, bears the burdens of, and rejoices over His own.

The second story in this parable is about the lost coin (Luke 15:8–10). Notably, the parable develops from focusing on one lost sheep out of a hundred to one lost coin out of ten. It also shifts from a male to a female, both of whom reveal something of God's character (see also Isa. 49:15; 66:13). Significantly, Jesus used illustrations that related to a woman's world as much as those that related to a man's world.[1] He had grave respect for women, delighting in teaching them His word and encouraging their gifts and their desire to learn.

This woman did three things to find her lost coin. First, she lit a lamp. Because her home probably had no windows, she needed a lamp to see. Second, she swept the house. The floors, which were made of dirt or straw, could easily hide a coin, so the broom would help uncover it. Third, the woman searched diligently until she found the coin. The coin, which was a drachma, would have been about one day's wage.[2] If the woman had only ten coins, she was not wealthy, so finding the lost coin would have been very important. Like the shepherd, she gathered her friends and neighbors to rejoice with her after she found her lost coin. The sinner's repentance brings both present (v.10) and future (v. 7) joy in God's kingdom.[3]

Like the coin, we are lost apart from the grace of Jesus Christ. We need God to turn on the light of the gospel in our souls, bringing us to saving faith. We need Him to sweep out the sin of our lives and make us clean through the blood of His righteousness. We need to be diligently sought and rescued from our bondage to sin. Gratefully, Jesus does this, and when He finds us, He seals us with His Spirit, who guarantees our inheritance (Eph. 1:13–14). Once saved, we are to shine the light of Christ into the lives of others by sharing the gospel with them. We are to help others sweep out their sin, asking God to deliver them from it. And we are to diligently pray for our unsaved family and friends, asking God to save them.

The third story in this parable is about a faithful father and two lost sons, one unrighteous and one self-righteous (Luke 15:11–32). Remember, Jesus is primarily addressing the grumbling Pharisees and scribes (v. 2). In this story the younger son symbolizes the sinners, the father symbolizes God, and the elder son symbolizes the self-righteous Pharisees.[4]

The younger son demanded his share of the property that would be his when his father died. Jewish law required the younger son to receive half of what the elder brother received, or one-third of the entire estate (Deut. 21:17). Sadly, the motive behind the younger son's request was not good. The father graciously granted his

---

1. Ryken, *Luke*, 2:117.
2. Ryken, *Luke*, 2:118.
3. Bock, *Luke*, 2:1304.
4. Ryken, *Luke*, 2:154.

younger son's request. Even though he probably suspected his son was not going to use his inheritance wisely, he did not try to coerce him to stay but gave him the freedom to go his own way.

Sadly, the son lost everything through reckless spending. Additionally, a severe famine arose in the land, leaving little food for anyone, much less for beggars like the destitute son. In desperation he did what no Jew did. He hired himself out to a Gentile owner of pigs; pigs were unclean animals and were not to be used for food (Lev. 11:7; Deut. 14:8).[5] Hungry and desperate, he longed to be fed with the pods that the pigs ate, but no one gave him anything.

Coming to the realization that even his father's hired servants were in a better situation than he was, he planned to go back to his father and confess his sin. He would plead unworthy to be called his son and would ask to be treated as a servant. Surprisingly, from a far distance, his father saw him, felt compassion for him, ran toward him, embraced him, and kissed him.

The father had been actively looking for his son, waiting for his return. The young man must have been nearly unrecognizable, but his father still knew his son. This elderly man, wearing long robes, picked them up and ran toward his son. The father was elated that his son had come home, expressing his emotion by repeatedly kissing him.

How great is the Father's love for us! We can't help but weep when we see the full import of these words for our lives! We too have taken a far journey into a country of sin and squandered our inheritance in sinful living. Yet the Father knows us, pursues us, accepts us, embraces us, and lavishes His love on us (see Zeph. 3:17).

The younger son must have been overwhelmed. Upon his confession of unworthiness, his father told his servants to bring four things—the best robe, a ring for his hand, shoes for his feet, and a fattened calf for him to eat. Likewise, our heavenly Father takes great delight in sinners coming to repentance.

It is important that the story doesn't end here. Jesus tells His listeners about the elder brother. He too received his share of the property (Luke 15:12). But in contrast to the younger son, he was a hard worker (v. 25) and had probably been working in the fields even before the younger brother left. As the sound of music reached his ears, he sought clarification. When the servant revealed that his younger brother had come home, he should have rejoiced at his safe return. Sadly, he was angry and refused to take part in the celebration.

It is significant that the father initiates contact with his older son just as he did with his younger son. He loved both sons greatly. But the elder son was bitter toward his father and brother (Luke 15:28–29). He was jealous of how his father had treated his younger brother, seemingly rewarding his scandalous behavior while ignoring his righteous behavior. But the father responded in love and faithfulness. He reminded his son of all that he had. He defended his celebratory actions. His son was once lost, but now he was found.

---

5. Pao and Schnabel, "Luke," 343.

Would the older son go inside and share in the celebration, or would he remain outside, lost in his own self-righteousness? Instead of telling His listeners, Jesus wanted them to walk away asking those questions about themselves. Those who remain in self-righteousness fail to recognize the grace of God. Dear reader, will you remain in your self-righteousness, or will you place your trust in Christ alone?

Before leaving the story, we need to reflect on who the true older brother is in our lives.[6] Jesus is our elder brother who is not ashamed to call us brothers and sisters (Heb. 2:10–18). He tells us of the faithful Father and sings His praise in the midst of His people. He became the God-man so that through His death He would deliver us from sin, Satan, and death. He robes us in His righteousness and celebrates our repentance with gladness and joy.

II. Lying Steward (16:1–13)

With the Pharisees and scribes still listening (Luke 16:14), Jesus now turns His attention to His disciples. Using a parable (vv. 1–8), He taught them how to be true sons of God. The parable begins by telling us about a rich man who received charges against his steward that he was wasting his goods. Without giving the steward an opportunity to defend himself, the rich man fired him.

Not surprisingly, the steward thought about what he should do to meet his needs. He first thought about digging, but he quickly decided he was not strong enough for such manual labor. Then he thought about begging, but he quickly determined that he would be too ashamed to do that. Finally, he settled on a plan. He would contact his master's debtors and significantly decrease their debts so that they would feel indebted to him and desire to repay his kindness when he was in need. The master's debtors had no idea that the manager was doing anything dishonest; they probably assumed that he had the authority to lower their debts and were thankful to him for doing so.

The first debtor owed one hundred measures of oil, about three years' worth of salary. The manager cut that debt in half, saving the debtor a year and a half of wages. The second debtor owed one hundred measures of wheat, between eight to ten years' worth of salary. The manager reduced his debt by 20 percent.[7] It is shocking that instead of being livid with the lying steward, the master commended him for his shrewdness. Notably, the steward's sin is recognized but not affirmed, and he is not commended for dishonesty but for shrewdness. Likewise, Jesus wanted His disciples, the sons of light, to be shrewd in the way they used their money on earth as they looked toward eternity.

This parable serves as an introduction to three lessons about money and discipleship (Luke 16:9–13). First, like the steward who made friends by reducing their debts,

---

6. I am indebted to Dr. Edmund Clowney and his sermon "Sharing the Father's Welcome: The Parable of the Prodigal Son" for first teaching me that this parable points to our true elder brother, Jesus Christ.

7. Bock, *Luke*, 2:1330–31.

believers are to make friends by giving their money to other believers.[8] These friends made by generosity will "receive you into an everlasting home" (v. 9). Whether this refers to Christian friends who once received the disciples' aid and welcome them into heaven, or to God who will reward the generous disciple by welcoming him into heaven, or both, it reminds us of the importance of generosity. Although God alone prepares for us an eternal home, in heaven we will learn how our generosity on earth blessed our brothers and sisters in Christ.[9] Jesus was reminding His disciples to have an eternal perspective with regard to wealth. Since we cannot take our possessions to heaven with us, we can bless others now while storing up eternal treasure in heaven.

The second lesson Jesus taught His disciples was to be faithful with money (Luke 16:10–12). People who prove faithful in small things are often those who receive increasing responsibility as time goes by, but people who are dishonest in little things never are entrusted with bigger things. Recall that the lying and unfaithful steward lost his job. If he had been honest and faithful, he would have received more responsibility.

Jesus gave two examples of faithfulness (Luke 16:11–12). First, He compared the wealth of this world with the wealth of the world to come (v. 11). Being able to manage the money of this world indicates an ability to handle heavenly riches. Second, Jesus compared people's use of others' money with their use of their own money (v. 12). If people cannot manage others' money well, then they won't manage their own wealth well. Likewise, believers are stewards of someone else's money—ultimately God's. If we are not faithful to use the resources that God has given us on earth, we will not be rewarded with riches in heaven.

The third lesson Jesus taught is that our hearts have room for only one master, and it should be Jesus Christ, not money or anything else (v. 13). Notably, the text doesn't say we *shouldn't* serve two masters but that we *can't*. We simply cannot love God and wealth. We have to choose, and our choice will have eternal ramifications. If we choose to serve money, we will hate and despise God. If we choose to serve God, we will love and obey Him. But we cannot serve both.

So how are we to view money? Think of Israel. God gave the tribes the land of promise as a gift. He had certain regulations and requirements to teach the people that the land was not their land but His. In the New Testament, we learn that the love of money is the root of wickedness (1 Tim. 6:10) and that we are to be eager to serve, not greedy for money (1 Peter 5:2). So we should give the Lord the first of our time, money, and resources. We should give to others in need. And we should keep our money in proper perspective, recognizing that it is the Lord's money, not ours; we are simply stewards of His wealth.

---

8. "Unrighteous mammon" (v. 8) is not wealth acquired in an unrighteous manner but rather denotes the money of this world that is so often used in an idolatrous way. S. G. De Graaf, *The Failure of Israel's Theocracy*, vol. 2 of Promise and Deliverance (St. Catharines, Ont.: Paideia Press, 1978), 405.

9. Ryken, *Luke*, 2:174–75.

III. Lovers of Self (16:14–18)

Even though Jesus was specifically addressing His disciples (Luke 16:1), the Pharisees were still hanging around seeking to accuse Him of wrongdoing or at least give Him a hard time. Sadly, these self-righteous lovers of money didn't want to choose between loving God and loving money. Jesus condemned their self-justification and idolatry. Their love of money was an abomination in the sight of God, for money had replaced Him on the throne of their hearts. Our God is a jealous God. He wants His covenant people to exalt Him for His glory and to enjoy doing so.

The purpose of the Law and the Prophets was to show people what God considered to be an abomination and to reveal how far short they fall in glorifying God. Most importantly, they point forward to Jesus Christ, the Savior of the world. But they cannot save. That is why John the Baptist, the last great prophet of the Old Testament period and the first great prophet of the New Testament period, preached the message he did. The kingdom of God had finally come! After many long years of promise, the fulfillment had come in the person and work of Jesus Christ. Now everyone is persistently urged to come into the kingdom.[10]

Although Jesus has fulfilled the Law and the Prophets, He did not abolish them. The Law still serves a useful purpose. It informs us of God's will. It reveals our sinfulness and our need for a Savior. It deters believers from sin and encourages them toward righteousness. In no way do these purposes compete with the gospel; rather, they comply with it. Christ's Spirit subdues our sin and enables us to keep God's commands (Westminster Confession of Faith 19.6–7).

Jesus gave an example of how the Law was still in effect during the time of fulfillment: "Whoever divorces his wife and marries another commits adultery; and whoever marries her who is divorced from her husband commits adultery" (Luke 16:18). There were two schools of rabbis that had different views on marriage, one conservative and one liberal. The liberal school believed that a husband could divorce his wife for just about anything, including burning dinner or not being as pretty as the next woman who came along. This is the mentality that Jesus was speaking against here. In other biblical passages, adultery and desertion are given as acceptable though not necessary reasons to divorce a spouse (see Matt. 5:31–32; 19:3–9; 1 Cor. 7:15).

Dear reader, if we are worshiping someone or something else other than God or even alongside God, we will fail to keep His commandments, enter His kingdom, and glorify God in our marriage. Until our hearts are right with God, they won't be right with other people or other things.

IV. Lazarus and the Selfish Man (16:19–31)

After confronting the Pharisees about their love of money and their self-justification and then speaking about the good news of the kingdom and the holiness of God, Jesus illustrated with a parable about the importance of loving God. Like the parable

---

10. Bock, *Luke*, 2:1353.

of the dishonest and shrewd steward, this parable begins with a rich man and forced Jesus's listeners to examine their relationship with wealth and with God. As his clothes, sumptuous meals, and home revealed, this rich man was extravagantly wealthy. Sadly, he was neither generous with his wealth nor interested in making friends with those in need. It is significant that Lazarus, the poor man in the story, is the only character Jesus named in His parables, and his name comes from the Hebrew Eleazar, which means "God helps."[11]

Lazarus was covered with sores, tended only by dogs, and was so hungry that he was willing to take the scraps from the rich man's table. But this man loved the Lord and was relieved of his earthly misery when he was carried by the angels to Abraham's side. The rich man also died and was buried. But sadly, instead of going to be with the saints, he was separated from them in Hades, a place where he suffered torment. Since the rich man could see Abraham far off and Lazarus at his side, he cried out to Abraham to help him, asking him to send Lazarus to cool his tongue with water in order to relieve his anguish. Ironically, the rich man, who hadn't acknowledged Lazarus's need for water, food, and provision, now asked Lazarus to nourish him. But Abraham could not send Lazarus. The rich man had chosen to love money rather than God, and death had closed the door on the opportunity to change his allegiance (Luke 16:24–26).

Not to be deterred, the rich man thought that at least he could save his five brothers from such anguish by asking Abraham to send Lazarus to warn them. Abraham replied that they had warning enough in Moses and the Prophets. In disbelief, the rich man argued that they needed someone to appear to them from the dead. But Abraham remained firm in his answer. If they wouldn't hear Moses and the Prophets, neither would someone coming back from the dead convince them.

Scripture proves this is true. There was a different Lazarus whom God raised from the dead, and his resurrection didn't convince everyone to believe (John 11). More importantly, Jesus Christ, who arose from the grave after three days and appeared to many, still faced rejection and unbelief from most people. Dear friend, today is the day of salvation. One day it will be too late to decide whether you love the Lord or the things of this world. Do not delay. Repent and trust in Christ alone for your salvation.

---

11. Morris, *Luke*, 269–70.

As much as my friend and her family were blessed by their new van, Scripture says the one who gave received the richer blessing (Acts 20:35). You might not have a car to donate to your church family, but there are lots of other ways to provide for others' needs. An elderly person may need a hot meal this week. A pregnant young wife and mom who feels sick might need you to clean her home. Missionaries might need financial support. How will you use your resources for God's kingdom? When He brings needs and opportunities across your path, be willing to part with your resources. Dear believer, it is more blessed to give than to receive. When we do so, we reflect the grace and love of God.

Processing It Together...

1. What do we learn about God in Luke 15–16?

2. How does this reshape how we should view our present circumstances?

3. What do we learn about God's Son, Jesus Christ?

4. How should this impact our relationship with God and with others?

5. What do we learn about God's covenant with His people?

6. How are we to live in light of this?

7. How can we apply Luke 15–16 to our lives today and in the future?

8. How should we apply this passage in our churches?

9. Look back at "Put It in Perspective" in your personal study questions. What did you find challenging or encouraging about this lesson?

10. Look back at "Principles and Points of Application." How has this lesson impacted your life?

All the People Gave Praise to God

Luke 17–18

Purpose...

Head. What do I need to know from this passage in Scripture?

- Jesus teaches His disciples to pursue holiness, persist in humble prayer, seek riches in heaven, and respond to His mercy by glorifying and praising God.

Heart. How does what I learn from this passage affect my internal relationship with the Lord?

- I am a kingdom disciple who has received God's mercy, leading to a heart of gratitude.

Hands. How does what I learn from this passage translate into action for God's kingdom?

- I will humbly and lovingly confront others' sin when necessary.
- I will readily extend forgiveness to others.
- I will engage in humble, persistent prayer.
- I will help others grow in gratitude.
- I will pray for those under my care and teach them God's word.
- I will share the gospel with the lost, praying for the Lord to open their blind eyes to see the truth.

Personal Study...

Pray. Ask that God will open up your heart and mind as you study His Word. This is His story of redemption that He has revealed to us, and the Holy Spirit is our teacher.

Ponder the Passage. Read Luke 17–18.

- *Point:* What is the point of this passage? How does this relate to the point of the entire book?

- *Persons:* Who are the main people involved in this passage? What characterizes them?

- *Persons of the Trinity:* Where do you see God the Father, God the Son, and God the Holy Spirit in this passage?

- *Puzzling Parts:* Are there any parts of the passage that you don't quite understand or that seem interesting or confusing?

Put It in Perspective.

- *Place in Scripture:* What is the original context of this text? What is the redemptive-historical context—what has or hasn't happened in redemptive history at this point in Scripture? How does this text connect to Christ?

The following questions will help you if you got stuck on any of the previous questions, and they will help you dig a little deeper into the text, putting it all into perspective.

1. **17:1–4.** (a) What does Jesus tell His disciples are certain to come (see also Rom. 11:9; 14:13; 1 John 2:10)?

(b) What illustration does Jesus use to compare the judgment people will receive if they cause a little one to stumble, and who are these little ones (see Matt. 8:10; Mark 10:24; Luke 10:21)?

(c) What is the background of verses 3–4 (see Lev. 19:17)?

(d) Why should we forgive others, and how are we able to forgive others (see Luke 23:34; John 20:23; Acts 2:38; 2 Cor. 2:5–11; Col. 3:13; Heb. 8:12; 9:22)?

2. 17:5–6. (a) For what do the apostles ask the Lord, and why?

(b) What is the point of Jesus's response? It may be helpful to look up *mustard seed* and *mulberry tree* in a reference tool.

3. 17:7–10. (a) According to verse 10, what is the point of this parable?

(b) How did Mary (see Luke 1:38) and the apostle Paul (see Eph. 3:7–13) exemplify this attitude?

(c) Contrast how Jesus tells us to view ourselves with what He says about us (Matt. 25:21, 34–40; 1 Cor. 4:5).

(d) How is Jesus the servant par excellence (see Phil. 2:5–11)?

4. 17:11–19. (a) Compare Jesus's location in verse 11 with Luke 9:51–56 and 10:38–42 (see also John 11:18). What do you notice?

(b) In light of Leviticus 13:49 and 14:2–4, why is Jesus's response to the ten lepers significant?

(c) Who was the one leper who returned to Jesus, and why is this significant?

(d) What do Jesus's words to the leper in verse 19 imply about the other nine?

(e) How does this story recall 2 Kings 5:1–19? What do both stories emphasize about God's plan of salvation?

5. **17:20–21.** (a) Whose question does Jesus answer?

(b) What does it mean that the kingdom of God is within you (or in the midst of you) (see Isa. 45:14; Luke 4:16–30; 7:22–28; 11:20; 16:16)?

6. **17:22–27.** (a) How were Jesus's followers to respond to false claims of seeing one of the days of the Son of Man, and why?

(b) What has to happen before Jesus can come to earth a second time (17:25)?

(c) What is the first example Jesus gave to describe the time of His second coming, and what was His point (see also Genesis 6–7)?

7. **17:28–37.** (a) What is the second example Jesus gave to describe the time of His second coming, and what was His point (see Gen. 13:12–13; 19:1–11, 16–17, 24, 26)?

(b) According to verse 37, from where will Christ return (see also Acts 1:10–11; 1 Thess. 4:16–17; Rev. 1:7)?

8. 18:1–8. (a) By telling the parable of the persistent widow, what was Jesus teaching His disciples?

(b) What do you learn from the Scriptures about God's justice and how His people are to perform justice (see Ex. 22:22–24; Lev. 19:9–10; Deut. 14:28–29; 2 Chron. 19:7; Ps. 68:5; James 1:27)?

(c) Contrast the unjust judge with God the Father.

(d) In light of the context of Luke 17:22–37, what is this parable teaching God's elect?

9. 18:9–14. (a) Who is the audience for this parable (see also Ezek. 33:13)?

(b) How did the Pharisees' fasting (see Lev. 16:29, 31; 23:27, 29, 32, where "afflict your souls" refers to fasting) and tithing (see Lev. 27:30–32; Num. 18:21–24; Deut. 14:22–27) exceed the law?

(c) Why can't the tax collector look up to heaven (see also Ezra 9:6)?

(d) How does the tax collector's cry echo Psalm 51:1, 3; Lamentations 3:42; and Daniel 9:19?

(e) According to verse 14b, what is the point of this parable (see also Luke 14:7–11)?

10. **18:15–17.** (a) What was Jesus teaching His disciples?

(b) How do you receive the kingdom of God like a child (see Ps. 131:2)?

11. **18:18–23.** (a) What does "no one is good but One, that is, God" have to do with Deuteronomy 6:4?

(b) From what commandments does Jesus quote (see Ex. 20:12–16; Deut. 5:16–20)?

(c) How is Jesus establishing the connection between God the Father, the law, and Himself?

12. **18:24–30.** (a) In light of the rich man's response, what principle does Jesus teach His disciples?

(b) How does Jesus's response to the question of who can be saved reflect the following: Genesis 18:14; Jeremiah 32:17, 27; Zechariah 8:6; and Luke 1:34–37?

(c) What is Peter's response to the Lord's teaching, and how does the Lord respond with both a present and a future promise?

13. 18:31–34. (a) What does Jesus teach His twelve apostles about His coming suffering (see also Luke 5:35; 9:22, 43–45; 12:50; 13:32–35; 17:25)?

(b) What did the prophets say about the Son of Man (see Isa. 53; Dan. 7:13–14)?

(c) How did the disciples respond to Jesus, and why?

14. 18:35–43. (a) What is the significance of the title "Jesus, Son of David" (v. 38; see 2 Sam. 7:12–16; Ps. 89:3–4)?

(b) Contrast the crowd's response to the blind man's cry with Jesus's response. How does the latter fulfill Isaiah 61:1–2, cited in Luke 4:18–19?

(c) How did the blind man and the people respond to this miracle?

Principles and Points of Application
15. 17:1–6. (a) Spend time in prayer today asking the Lord to guard and protect you and your loved ones from the evil one and asking for the grace to withstand temptations when they come.

(b) How may you be provoking others with your attitude? Repent of these sins, asking God to give you the grace to lead others in paths of righteousness for His name's sake.

(c) In what ways do you find a godly and loving rebuke difficult? What about forgiveness?

(d) In what area(s) do you need the Lord to increase your faith?

16. **17:7–10.** In what ways do you need to grow in humility and self-sacrifice?

17. **17:11–19.** Make an "I'm thankful for…" list this week, recording everything you can think of for which you are thankful to God.

18. **17:20–37.** How do you show that you are living each day in light of Christ's return, and how are you teaching those under your care to have an eternal perspective?

19. **18:1–8.** (a) Evaluate your personal, family, and corporate prayer life. In what area(s) of your prayer life have you lost heart? In what area(s) are you encouraged?

(b) Spend time praying for the persecuted church, children oppressed in human sex trafficking, orphans, and widows.

20. **18:9–14.** (a) In what ways are you self-righteous?

(b) In what ways are you, by God's grace, humble?

21. **18:15–17.** (a) Many of us encounter children on a regular basis, whether they are our own, those of a friend or neighbor, the students in our classroom, or the children we teach in Sunday school. In what ways are you leading the next generation to Christ?

(b) Thinking of the children you had in mind in the previous question, are there decisions you have made that might hinder them from knowing Christ? For example, perhaps it's uncomfortable for you to talk about Jesus with your neighbor and her child or invite them to church, but if you don't, who will?

(c) How does your walk with the Lord display wholehearted dependence, trust, and wonder?

22. 18:18–30. (a) How would you respond to someone who said that Jesus was only a good teacher?

(b) How do pursuing wealth, self-reliance, pride, addictions, and a sinful relationship hinder your relationship with the Lord and His people?

23. 18:31–34. How are you proclaiming the gospel to others, beginning with your own family?

24. 18:35–43. (a) In what area(s) of your life do you need God's mercy? Cry out for it.

(b) How are you responding to God when someone comes to saving faith?

(c) Spend time in prayer for those you know who need Jesus to open their blind eyes so that they see Him as Lord and Savior.

Putting It All Together...

Thankfully, when we become believers our growth in sanctification is not dependent on our own means. We would quickly become discouraged and disillusioned. It's likely that we would grow angry and bitter if we were trying to be godly in our own strength. But Jesus doesn't just save us by grace; He also sanctifies us by grace. To be sure, there is a difference between justification and sanctification. "Justification is an act of God's free grace," whereas "sanctification is the work of God's free grace" (Westminster Shorter Catechism 33, 35). The difference is important! In justification the righteousness of Christ is "imputed [or attributed] to us," whereas in sanctification we are "enabled more and more to die unto sin, and live unto righteousness." In Luke 17–18 we see both themes of justification and sanctification, but Luke 17 begins with an emphasis on sanctification. Jesus warns His disciples, "Temptations to sin are sure to come" (v. 1 ESV).

According to these chapters, believers, by God's grace, are to pursue purity. They are also to practice humility. Their lives are to be filled with praising God. It's important that they prepare for the parousia, Jesus's second coming. And they must persist in prayer. We cannot do this by our own power, but Scripture says, "His divine power has given to us all things that pertain to life and godliness" (2 Peter 1:3). So believers must "pursue peace with all people, and holiness, without which no one will see the Lord" (Heb. 12:14).

I. Pursuing Purity (17:1–6)

After addressing the Pharisees' love of money (Luke 16:14–31), Jesus now teaches His disciples what it means to follow Him. In a world full of stumbling blocks, disciples must have a heart for holiness and truth (17:1–3a). Following Jesus does not make us immune to temptations from the world, our own flesh, and the devil, but we are not to tempt others to sin. Jesus gives a grave warning. It would be better for a millstone to be hung around a person's neck and then be cast into the sea than to be a stumbling block to brand-new disciples who are not yet rooted and grounded in their faith. A *millstone* was a large, heavy stone used for grinding grain, and if it were hung around someone's neck, he or she would drown. But in comparison to experiencing God's judgment, drowning would be better.

Sadly, we can tempt someone else to sin by encouraging her in her pity party, provoking her to anger, pointing out someone else's faults to her, or leading her into a compromised situation. By God's grace, we must pursue purity, beginning with God's word, which arms us for the battle (see Luke 4:4, 8, 12; Eph. 6:10–20).

Jesus added an exhortation to His listeners to constantly pay attention to themselves and what they teach. I am so thankful that we have pastors at our church who are concerned enough to review the materials used in various ministries. We too should pay attention to what we are absorbing through books and media. It will affect how we disciple those under our care.

Disciples must also have a heart of forgiveness (Luke 17:3b–4). We must recognize our sin before humbly and lovingly pointing out another's sin (see Matt. 7:1–5). The Lord's people are not to have hatred toward one another but are to love each other (see Lev. 19:17). A humble and loving rebuke should always be given with the goal of repentance followed by reconciliation. Repentance requires turning away from sin to a different way of living. When this occurs, forgiveness should follow.

Jesus wants us to extend grace in a way that reflects His mercy. No matter how many times someone sins against us and then repents, we are to extend forgiveness. It is important to know that there are many situations in which forgiveness coexists with consequences. For example, the woman whose husband has abused her in the past and sought her forgiveness can forgive him without remaining in an unsafe home. Having a heart of forgiveness, overlooking minor offenses, working through major offenses, and not harboring anger or bitterness are not possible apart from Christ. We forgive because God has first forgiven us.

Disciples must also be people of faith (Luke 17:5–6). The disciples, sensing the impossibility of forgiving an offender as many times as he has offended, cried out to the Lord to increase their faith. Jesus uses two familiar things in their world to teach them that faith, no matter how small, is enough for God to do amazing things. The mustard seed was one of the smallest seeds, and the mulberry tree would remain planted for six hundred years. In other words, God will do mighty things with even the smallest faith. We may say, "Lord, I have only a small bit of faith, but I am going to step out and forgive this person who has hurt me once again." And He takes that small faith and does a mighty work of reconciliation.

II. Practicing Humility (17:7–10)
With a small parable, Jesus taught His disciples the importance of practicing humility. No one who has a servant plowing in the field or shepherding sheep would fix dinner for him and invite him to sit at the table. Instead, the master would want his servant to fix dinner for him so that he could sit at the table. Only then would the servant be able to eat. Also, the master would not thank his servant because it was the servant's duty to serve him. The point of the parable is that disciples are servants of the Lord Jesus Christ. It is our humble duty to serve Him. He owes us nothing. Yet because of His grace, He has given us everything by becoming a servant and humbling Himself to the point of death (see Phil. 2:7–11).

III. Praising God (17:11–19)
Jesus was still on His way to Jerusalem, traveling in and out of regions around the city and doing works of mercy. As He entered a village, ten lepers cried out to Him from a distance, asking for mercy. Because they were lepers, they were unclean and could not approach Him (Lev. 13:3). Leprous people were to wear torn clothes, keep their head bare, cover their mustache, cry out that they were unclean, and live alone outside the camp of Israel (vv. 45–46).

Think of women who have been involved in sex trafficking since an early age, women whose husbands have abused and then left them, women who battle a same-sex attraction, women whose husbands have been unemployed for years, or women who

191

have been raised by mothers who hated them and told them they would never amount to anything good. Like these ten lepers, they know shame.

More than anyone else, Jesus knew shame. He was spit on, ridiculed and rejected by His own people, and betrayed by one of His disciples. Another disciple denied he knew Him. Led like a lamb to the slaughter, He died a cursed death on the cross. Strikingly, the One who knows shame best reaches out to us, offering us His robes of righteousness in exchange for our shameful ones. This is our hope, and this is the hope that we give to our sisters who are filled with shame.

According to the law, the ten lepers had to go and show themselves to the priests in order to be pronounced clean (Lev. 14:1–32). But before they reached the priests, Jesus miraculously cleansed them from a distance. Sadly, although all ten were healed, only one turned back to praise God and give Him thanks, and he was a Samaritan. The Samaritans worshiped on their own mountain, Mount Gerizim (John 4:20), and were followers of the Old Testament Law of Moses only, not the Prophets. The Jews did not consider them to be part of the chosen people of God and did not associate with them (v. 9). So what made this Samaritan different from the other nine lepers?

He was different because he recognized that God had done a mighty work of healing in his body and took the time to turn back. Also, he praised God, falling on his face at Jesus's feet, giving Him thanks, and displaying his faith in Jesus as God's Son.

Jesus's questions to the Samaritan are revealing. Since there were ten cleansed, the other nine should have turned back to thank Him, but only the foreigner did. Sadly, the Jews, God's chosen people, should have been at the front of the line to express their gratitude, but they were nowhere to be found. Although these nine lepers were cleansed and healed of their leprosy, only the thankful Samaritan was healed from his leprosy *and his sins*.

You may recall another foreigner who was healed from leprosy in or near the region of Samaria (2 Kings 5:1–19).[1] Naaman too received great words of healing from a prophet and was healed from a distance. He too returned to the healer and praised God. Even in the Old Testament, God's plan was to save a people from every tribe, tongue, and nation. But the story of Elisha healing Namaan pales in comparison to the story of Jesus healing the Samaritan leper. Elisha did not have the power to forgive sins. Only the final and greatest Prophet, Jesus Christ, can save people from their sins. And in response, believers should praise God and give Him thanks.

IV. Preparing for the Parousia (17:20–37)

The Pharisees were still hanging around, asking questions and trying to stir up controversy. They continued to doubt that Jesus was the Son of God, the King of the kingdom. They continued to hope for a political kingdom that the Messiah would set up on earth to deliver them from the power of Rome. Many believed that the kingdom

---

1. Pao and Schnabel, "Luke," 346.

would come with signs of glory and would be recognized by all. But Jesus corrected their thinking.

He explained that the kingdom of God is not coming with signs to be observed. Also, He said, the kingdom of God is not something that one will be able to point to as here or there. Finally, the kingdom of God was in the midst of them. In other words, the King of the kingdom (Jesus) had come, and where the King is, so is the kingdom.

Jesus turned His attention to His disciples to explain. He told them that the days were coming when He would ascend into heaven and they would be left longing to see one of the days of the Son of Man (His parousia, or second coming), but they wouldn't see it. False teachers would urge people to look here or there, but the disciples were not to follow them. Christ's return will be universally visible to all humankind. Like they could not miss lightning in the sky, people would not be able to miss His return. And no one could predict the parousia.

Jesus also says that something very important must happen before the kingdom of God can come in all of its fullness: He must die on the cross and be rejected by the Jews ("this generation"; v. 25). The Jews did not understand that the kingdom of God in its inaugural stage was one of suffering. They were looking for the kingdom in its consummated glory.

Jesus gave two examples from the Old Testament to explain when the kingdom would be consummated. First, the second coming of Christ can be likened to the flood coming in the days of Noah (Genesis 6–7). Notably, Luke's focus is not on sinful activities but on the everyday activities that went on until the day Noah entered the ark. Then the flood came suddenly. Sadly, all those who had not prepared were drowned.

The second example is taken from the days of Lot (see Genesis 13 and 19). Again, Luke focuses on everyday, good activities such as eating and drinking, buying and selling, planting and building. There was no warning that destructive fire and sulfur would rain down from heaven. All the unrighteous were caught off guard and destroyed. This is how Jesus said it is going to be at the time of His second coming.

When Jesus comes again there will not be time to collect belongings or indulge in worldly ways. To illustrate, Jesus reminds us of what happened to Lot's wife (Gen. 19:26). She was almost free from destruction, but she longed for the world more than she longed for the Lord and was lost for all eternity because of it.

How do we prepare for such a coming? We must lose our lives now. We are not to focus on everyday activities, as important as those things are. Instead, we are to focus on Christ and do all things for His glory (see 1 Cor. 10:31).

All people are held responsible for the choices they make. People will be divided on the last day according to their faith in Christ. Each person will be accountable before the Judge of all the earth, Jesus Christ.

Jesus tells us where this judgment will take place: "Wherever the body is, there the eagles will be gathered together" (Luke 17:37). Philip Ryken thinks this is perhaps best understood as a proverb about spiritual life and death. The places where people are dead spiritually is the very place where judgment will occur, just as vultures feed off dead carcasses. This then is a warning to examine whether you are dead in sin or alive in Christ.[2] Dear friend, will you be found with saving faith on the day of judgment? We will be prepared for Christ's return only by being in right standing with God through the atoning blood of Jesus Christ. And until that day, we must recognize that suffering comes before glory.

V. Persistence in Prayer (18:1–8)

Jesus told His disciples a parable to encourage them to always pray and not lose heart as they awaited His second coming. Notably, Jesus explained the point of the parable before He told it. Although God's people will endure much suffering for the sake of the kingdom, God will act justly in His perfect time.

In a certain city there was a judge who did not fear God or respect humankind. In the same city was a widow who asked the judge to give her justice against her adversary. The unjust judge cared nothing at all about giving the widow justice. But after experiencing her continual requests and realizing that she would eventually wear him down, he decided it was in his best interest to grant her request for justice.

If even an unjust judge will dispense justice, how much more will the righteous Judge of all the earth, our heavenly Father, give justice? During the time between the first and second comings of Christ, God's people can be sure that God is just and will bring justice speedily. Since God's days are not like ours (2 Peter 3:8), we must not lose hope or think that God has forgotten us. His plan is fixed, and justice is certain. What is important is that believers are faithfully persisting in prayer, not losing heart at His promises, and eagerly awaiting His return.

Unlike the unjust judge, God is perfectly righteous in His judgments (see 2 Chron. 19:7). He cares for the widow, the orphan, and the alien (see Ex. 22:22–24; Lev. 19:9–10; 23:22; Deut. 5:6, 15; 14:28–29; Ps. 68:5; James 1:27). God will give justice to His elect. Like the martyred saints who cry out for God's justice (see Rev. 6:10), you and I often cry for the same, and we can be sure that God will answer on the last day.

When the Son of Man comes, He will come with the clouds of heaven; be presented before God the Father, the Ancient of Days; and will be given the glorious kingdom in which people from every nation will serve Him for all eternity (Dan. 7:13–14). Dear believer, are you eager for this day, awaiting it with great excitement in your heart? We must place our faith in the just Judge, our only hope on the day of judgment. There is nothing but the blood of Jesus that can save us from the wrath of God.

VI. Problems with Pride (18:9–14)

Addressing the self-righteous, Jesus told a parable of a Pharisee and a tax collector. Like the previous parable this one also addresses one's posture in prayer. It is important to remember that the Pharisees were known as the religious elite, while the tax

---

2. Ryken, *Luke*, 2:242.

collectors worked for the Romans and were known for keeping others' tax money for themselves.

The prayers of the Pharisee and the tax collector could not be more different. The self-righteous Pharisee began his prayer by thanking God that he was not like the ungodly, including the tax collector who was also praying at the temple. To prove his righteousness, the Pharisee gave God a list of his righteous acts regarding fasting and tithing. Ironically, his acts went beyond what the law required. Jews were required to fast only before the Day of Atonement, once a year (see Lev. 16:29, 31; 23:27, 29, 32). And Jews had to tithe from only certain crops (Lev. 27:30–32; Num. 18:21–24; Deut. 14:22–27). Sadly, this Pharisee had added man-made religion to God's law, and he was not only proud of it but also relied on it to prove his righteousness.

In contrast, the tax collector, standing far off in the temple, most likely by the court of the Gentiles and far away from the Holy Place, would not even lift his eyes to heaven because of his sins. Instead, he beat his breast, crying out to God to be merciful to him, a sinner. Significantly, the word translated *merciful* means "to propitiate or to expiate" (to atone for sin by means of a blood sacrifice). In the Old Testament sacrificial system, there were two things that blood accomplished. First, it covered the sin of the people (expiation). Second, it turned away the wrath of God (propitiation).[3] So when the tax collector beat his breast and asked God to be merciful to him, he was asking that his sin be covered and that God would turn away His wrath from him. We too are in desperate need of God's mercy. And He has given it to us in His Son, Jesus Christ. Christ covered our sin by His blood and turned away God's wrath at the cross.

Both men went to the temple. Both men prayed. But only one man humbly acknowledged he was a sinner, so only one man was saved. The self-exalting will be humbled before God, but the humble will be exalted. Believers must pray not only persistently but also in humility (see also Ezek. 18:2–5, 10–13; 21:26; 33:13).

VII. Permitting the Children (18:15–17)

As Jesus continued His journey to Jerusalem, the crowds were bringing their infants to Him, hoping He would touch them, bless them, and pray over them (see Matt. 19:13–15). Misunderstanding the priorities of God's kingdom, the disciples rebuked the crowds for doing this. But Jesus was greatly displeased with His disciples for rebuking the crowds (Mark 10:14). Instead, He welcomed the children to come. Do you do the same? When you receive a request to serve in Sunday school or a children's ministry, are you eager to show the covenant children in your church the love of Jesus? Mothers, when you witness your children being baptized, do you recognize that they are precious in God's eyes? Bringing our children to Jesus means teaching them God's word formally and informally whenever the opportunity arises. It means praying with them, singing hymns with them, and teaching them a biblical worldview.

---

3. Ryken, *Luke*, 2:261–64.

As He blessed the infants, Jesus taught His disciples that they must receive the kingdom of God like a little child. This does not mean we remain as infants in our faith, failing to mature in learning and applying sound doctrine (see Heb. 5:12–13), but that we are never to lose our childlike dependence and trust in Christ, our wonder of who He is, and our joy and freedom in delighting to come to His arms. Think about what it is like when children are infants. They are completely dependent on their mothers to feed, clothe, change, and protect them. They look up at their moms with a smile of love and trust. They have joy in their mother's presence and feel secure in their arms. Likewise, disciples should look to Jesus in wholehearted dependence, trust, and wonder.

VIII. Profitable Pursuit (18:18–30)

As Jesus continued toward Jerusalem, a ruler asked Him, "Good Teacher, what shall I do to inherit eternal life?" (Luke 18:18; see also 10:25). Jesus asked the ruler, "Why do you call Me good? No one is good but One, that is, God" (18:19). He began with the Old Testament assertion that God alone is good, revealing that He Himself is God (see Deut. 6:4). Then, listing the last five of the Ten Commandments out of order, He pointed the man to the law, displaying that no one is good except God alone, and no one but God can keep the law. Sadly, the ruler did not realize that he had broken the law. He proudly declared that he had kept it from his youth. Without arguing, Jesus told him of one thing he still lacked—the hardest for him to do. The rich ruler must sell all his possessions and distribute them to the poor. Then he must follow Jesus.

The rich ruler became very sorrowful. He cared more about riches on earth than riches in heaven. Jesus was not surprised. He knew how difficult it was for the wealthy to enter the kingdom of God. Jesus illustrated with the largest animal in that area, the camel, and the common household needle. Think of an enormous camel trying to fit through the eye of a sewing needle! But Jesus said that would be easier than a rich man entering the kingdom of God.

Those who heard it were astonished. The prominent belief among the Jews was that the more riches one had, the greater God had blessed them. Jesus turned this prosperity gospel upside down. Importantly, though, the salvation of the rich is possible with God. He can save the wealthiest person or the poorest, just as He can bring a baby into this world through a young virgin (Luke 1:34–38) or an old woman (Gen. 18:14). He can welcome little children (Luke 18:15–17) or a wealthy ruler into His kingdom. "Salvation is of the LORD" (Jonah 2:9).

Probably speaking for all the disciples, Peter was quick to point out that they had left their homes to follow Jesus. He wanted to know what they would have (Matt. 19:27). Remarkably, Jesus does not rebuke him, but assures him. Whoever leaves anything or anyone for the sake of God's kingdom will receive many times more both in the present and in the future in heaven. Saying no to comfort, convenience, and relationships in order to say yes to God is a blessed life indeed. To do so, we must recognize that Jesus is more than a good teacher and follow Him as Savior and Lord.

IX. Predicting the Plan (18:31–34)

Although Jesus had mentioned His death to His twelve apostles before this occasion (see Luke 5:35; 9:22, 44–45; 13:33; 17:25), He now reveals a more detailed description of His death and resurrection. They are going up to Jerusalem, and everything written about Him, the Son of Man, by the prophets would be accomplished (see Isa. 52:13–53:12; Dan. 7:13–14). This included being delivered over to the Gentiles, mocked, shamefully treated, spit on, flogged, killed, and, most importantly, rising again from the dead.

Since it was not yet God's time to reveal the meaning of these things to the apostles, they did not understand the things about which Jesus spoke. But it wouldn't be hidden from them forever. After His resurrection, Jesus appeared to His disciples before ascending into heaven and opened their minds to understand all that the Old Testament had spoken about His death and resurrection (see Luke 24:44–47).

Dear believer, give thanks to God that you can study and read the Old and New Testaments and that God has opened your eyes to understand truth. For many today are still blinded to the truth of the Bible and think that the cross is foolishness. If you and your loved ones understand and grasp the gospel message, this is a testimony of God's grace. As believers, we have been commissioned to make disciples of all nations, teaching them about Jesus's death and resurrection. Seize every opportunity to share the gospel with the lost, praying for the Lord to save them.

X. Pleading for Mercy (18:35–43)

On His journey, Jesus came near Jericho, which was eighteen miles away from Jerusalem. Located on the main highway to Jerusalem, it served as a tax collection center and was located about a mile and a half away from the site of ancient Jericho.[4] There was a blind man begging by the road.[5] We don't know how long he had been there begging, but he must have gotten his hopes up when he heard a crowd going by, and he inquired what it meant. When the crowd told him Jesus of Nazareth was passing by, he cried out, "Son of David, have mercy on me!" (Luke 18:39).

Significantly, the title "Son of David" recalls that Joseph, Jesus's earthly father, was of the house of David (Luke 1:27; 2:4; 3:31). Also, the angel had revealed that the Lord God would give Jesus the throne of His father David forever (1:32). Zacharias had prophesied that Jesus was a horn of salvation in the house of David (v. 69). Jesus was born in the city of David (2:11). Furthermore, Jesus is the greater David, the very Son

---

4. Bock, *Luke*, 2:1505.

5. If you read the parallel accounts in Matthew 20:29–34 and Mark 10:46–52, you will notice some significant differences in the story that have caused much discussion among commentators. Most likely, all three gospel writers record the same event, although with differences in details. For a more comprehensive discussion of the views, see Bock, *Luke*, 2:1502–4.

of Man, who is Lord of the Sabbath (6:3). All of these references in Luke recall God's covenant with David in which He promised him an eternal heir on his throne (2 Sam. 7:12–16). But the Son of David is also the Suffering Servant, who was sent to recover the sight of the blind (see Isa. 61; Luke 4:18–19). Importantly, both roles (king and servant) are now linked. The physically blind beggar could see what spiritually blind people could not see: Jesus is the promised Son of David. No wonder he cried out for this promised One to have mercy on him!

The blind man's cry for mercy recalls David's cry for mercy after the prophet Nathan confronted him for committing adultery with Bathsheba (see Ps. 51:1–2). Sadly, those who were in front of the blind man rebuked him, telling him to be silent. But the blind man recognized that Jesus, Son of David, was his only hope of ever seeing again, so he cried out all the more. His repetitive cries brought Jesus to a stop, and He commanded that the blind man be brought to Him. Then He asked the blind man what he wanted Him to do for him. Addressing Him as "Lord," the blind man told Him that he wanted to regain his sight, a miracle Jesus performed.

It is significant that this man's faith pointed to the deeper healing. Yes, he could now see, but most importantly he had believed in Jesus as the Son of David, Lord of all. In response to Jesus's mercy, the man and the people glorified God. This is how it should be for every believer. All of us were blind to the truth of the gospel, in need of Jesus's mercy. In response to the miracle of our new birth, we are to glorify God and enjoy a relationship with Him through the means of grace (the word of God, prayer, and the sacraments).

❦ ❦ ❦ ❦

Do you feel discouraged and disillusioned because you have believed the lie that your growth in sanctification is dependent on your own means? Have you grown angry and bitter because you are trying to be godly in your own strength? Dear believer, Jesus doesn't just save us by grace alone; He also sanctifies us by grace. This is good news! As you face the temptations that come daily from the world, the flesh, and the devil, you have God's "divine power" at work within you so that you can say yes to righteousness (2 Peter 1:3). Choose today to pursue peace, practice humility, praise God, prepare for His parousia, and persist in prayer.

Processing It Together...

1. What do we learn about God in Luke 17–18?

2. How does this reshape how we should view our present circumstances?

3. What do we learn about God's Son, Jesus Christ?

4. How should this impact our relationship with God and with others?

5. What do we learn about God's covenant with His people?

6. How are we to live in light of this?

7. How can we apply Luke 17–18 to our lives today and in the future?

8. How should we apply this passage in our churches?

9. Look back at "Put It in Perspective" in your personal study questions. What did you find challenging or encouraging about this lesson?

10. Look back at "Principles and Points of Application." How has this lesson impacted your life?

The King Who Comes

Luke 19:1–21:4

Purpose...

Head. What do I need to know from this passage in Scripture?

- Jesus is the King who comes in the name of the Lord, bringing both salvation and judgment.

Heart. How does what I learn from this passage affect my internal relationship with the Lord?

- I am a kingdom disciple who has received salvation with joy.

Hands. How does what I learn from this passage translate into action for God's kingdom?

- I will seek the lost, sharing the gospel with them and asking Jesus to save them.
- I will obey God's word, exalting Him as King and praising Him for His works.
- I will weep over the sin around me and pray for God's kingdom to come.
- I will submit to God's authority and offer Him my time, money, and resources.
- I will interact with others in humility, not hypocrisy.

Personal Study...

Pray. Ask that God will open up your heart and mind as you study His Word. This is His story of redemption that He has revealed to us, and the Holy Spirit is our teacher.

Ponder the Passage. Read Luke 19:1–21:4.

- *Point:* What is the point of this passage? How does this relate to the point of the entire book?

- *Persons:* Who are the main people involved in this passage? What characterizes them?

- *Persons of the Trinity:* Where do you see God the Father, God the Son, and God the Holy Spirit in this passage?

- *Puzzling Parts:* Are there any parts of the passage that you don't quite understand or that seem interesting or confusing?

Put It in Perspective.

- *Place in Scripture:* What is the original context of this text? What is the redemptive-historical context—what has or hasn't happened in redemptive history at this point in Scripture? How does this text connect to Christ?

The following questions will help you if you got stuck on any of the previous questions, and they will help you dig a little deeper into the text, putting it all into perspective.

1. 19:1–10. (a) What was Zacchaeus's profession and status?

(b) Who initiated the conversation between Jesus and Zacchaeus?

(c) Contrast Zacchaeus's response to Jesus with the Pharisees' response ("they" in v. 7).

(d) How did Zacchaeus prove his repentance, and how did this relate to the law (see Ex. 22:1; 2 Sam. 12:6)?

(e) How does this story show Jesus continuing to fulfill His mission (Luke 4:18–19, 43)?

2. **19:11–27.** (a) For what two reasons did Jesus tell His disciples this parable?

(b) Who do each of the following represent: the nobleman, the servants, and the ten minas?

(c) What were the ten servants to do while the nobleman was away?

(d) For what were the commended servants praised, and what does the return on their investment show about God's character?

(e) According to verses 26–27, what is the point of the parable?

3. **19:28–40.** (a) Use a Bible resource to learn more about the mountain called Olivet. What do you learn?

(b) What did the two disciples find when they reached the village, and how did the owners respond?

(c) What do the two disciples do when they return from the village, and how does this fulfill Zechariah 9:9?

(d) What do the other disciples do, and what role is Jesus fulfilling (see 2 Kings 9:13)?

(e) How do the disciples respond when they see Jesus coming down the Mount of Olives (see also Pss. 118:26; 148:1; Luke 2:14)?

(f) How does Jesus respond to the Pharisees' exhortation to rebuke His disciples (see also Ps. 96:11–13; Isa. 55:12; Rom. 8:19–22)?

4. **19:41–44.** (a) In the Bible, who else weeps over sin (see 2 Kings 8:7–11; Jer. 9:1)?

(b) Why does Jesus weep (see also Luke 13:34–35)?

(c) In verses 43–44 Jesus prophesies of "the attack of Rome that led to the collapse of Jerusalem in A.D. 70."[1] How will this judgment be like earlier ones recorded in the Old Testament (see, e.g., 2 Kings 25:1–21)? What ultimate event does this foreshadow?

5. **19:45–48.** (a) What is Jesus's first stop in Jerusalem, what does He do there, and why?

(b) Look up Isaiah 56:7 and Jeremiah 7:11. How does Jesus use these verses?

---

1. Bock, *Luke*, 2:1562.

(c) What was Jesus doing daily in the temple, and who was seeking to destroy him (see also Luke 11:53–54)?

(d) What kept Jesus's enemies from doing anything to Him?

6. **20:1–8.** (a) What was Jesus doing in Jerusalem that upset the Jewish leaders, and what have we learned about these men already (see Luke 5:17, 21, 30; 6:7; 9:22; 11:53; 15:2; 19:47)?

(b) Why would Jesus have responded to the Jewish leaders with a question regarding John the Baptist?

(c) What was the motivation behind the leaders' response?

(d) How did Jesus respond to them, and why?

7. **20:9–18.** (a) Who do the following represent in this parable?
   - the man who planted the vineyard (see Ex. 19:3–6; Deut. 7:6–11)
   - the vineyard (see Ps. 80:8–13; Isa. 5:1–7)
   - the tenants (see Luke 5:17, 21, 30; 6:7; 9:22; 11:53; 15:2; 19:47; 20:19)
   - the servants (see Luke 13:34a; Acts 7:52–53)
   - the beloved son (see Luke 3:22)

(b) For the primary Old Testament background of this parable, look up Isaiah 5:1–7. What do you learn?

(c) How is 20:15a fulfilled in Luke 23:33?

(d) How is 20:16a fulfilled in Acts 8:4–40; 10:44–48; 11:19–26; 13:42–52?

(e) What passage from the Old Testament does Jesus cite in answer to the people's exclamation?

(f) Look up Isaiah 8:14–15 and Daniel 2:34, 44–45. How does Jesus allude to these passages?

8. **20:19–26.** (a) What action did the scribes and the Pharisees take against Jesus, and why?

(b) How did the spies interact with Jesus, and why did Jesus respond the way He did?

(c) In light of Genesis 1:26–27; Psalm 24:1; Romans 11:36; 13:1–7; 1 Corinthians 10:31; and 1 Timothy 2:1–3, what does Jesus's statement in verses 24–25 mean?

(d) How did the spies respond to Jesus's answer (see also 2:47 and 14:4, 6)?

9. **20:27–40.** (a) What do you learn about the Sadducees' beliefs?

(b) What do you learn about the law of levirate marriage from Deuteronomy 25:5–10?

(c) To what Old Testament passage does Jesus refer to prove that there is a resurrection, and why is it important that He chose something Moses wrote?

(d) Compare the response of the scribes with verse 26 (see question 8d). What do you notice?

10. **20:41–44.** (a) What does Jesus ask the scribes, and what Old Testament passage does He cite?

(b) What are the answers to Jesus's question (Luke 22:69; Acts 2:22–36)?

11. **20:45–47.** (a) Of whom does Jesus warn His disciples, and why?

(b) What should the scribes have been doing (see Deut. 10:18–19; Isa. 1:17, 23; Luke 6:20–23; 13:22–30; 14:7–11; James 1:27)?

(c) What is the "greater condemnation" the scribes will receive, and why (see James 3:1)?

12. **21:1–4.** (a) Contrast the actions of the scribes (20:47) and the rich (21:1) with the poor widow.

(b) Using the example of the poor widow's offering, Jesus teaches what principle?

Principles and Points of Application

13. **19:1–10.** Since Jesus came to seek and to save the lost, His people are to do the same. How are you using hospitality to share the gospel with others?

14. **19:11–27.** (a) In what ways are you engaging in kingdom service?

    (b) How can you grow in your relationship with Christ through the disciplines of grace?

    (c) Spend time in prayer for those you know who have rejected Christ as King, asking God to save them.

15. **19:28–40.** Spend time rejoicing and praising God for His wonderful attributes, His mighty works, and His Son, Jesus Christ.

16. **19:41–44.** How do you react to the sin around you?

17. **19:45–48.** (a) How do you prepare your heart for corporate worship each Sunday?

    (b) To whom do you teach God's word? Pray that they will listen diligently and apply what they learn.

18. **20:1–8.** In what area(s) do you need to submit to Jesus's authority?

19. **20:9–18.** With whom do you need to share the gospel? Pray that the Lord would give you the opportunity and the boldness to do so.

20. **20:19–26.** How are you rendering to Caesar the things that are Caesar's (see Rom. 13:1–7; 1 Tim. 2:1–3) and to God the things that are God's (see 1 Cor. 10:31)?

21. **20:27–44.** How does the hope that the resurrected Christ will one day return and resurrect our bodies change your outlook on your present circumstances?

22. **20:45–21:4.** (a) In what areas of your life do you need to replace hypocrisy with humility? Ask God to give you the grace to do so.

(b) How can you become a more cheerful and generous giver with your time, money, and resources?

Putting It All Together…

If you were to consider your words and actions throughout the week, what would you learn about what or whom you worship, for what or whom you work, and for what or whom you witness? Some of us worship appearance and achievement, work to be successful and satisfied, and witness to others about people or products we want them to like. Others worship comfort and convenience, work for money, and witness to others about favorite musicians or sports teams. We all worship someone or something. We all work for someone or something. And we all witness about someone or something. We need God's grace to worship Him alone, work for His glory, and witness for His great name.

Luke 19–20 addresses all three of these. With regard to worship, Jesus teaches us to celebrate His kingship, stand on the good news of Christ, surrender to God, and subscribe to correct doctrine. Concerning work, He teaches us to serve Him, submit to His authority, and sacrifice everything to follow Him. In regard to witness, Jesus teaches us to seek the lost. As we share the gospel with family, friends, and neighbors and pray for the Lord to save them, it's likely that we will weep over their sin. Jesus was deeply grieved over Israel's rejection of the only way of salvation, as they failed to recognize Him as "the way, the truth, and the life" (John 14:6).

I. Seek the Lost (19:1–10)

Jesus healed a blind beggar near Jericho (Luke 18:35). Now He enters Jericho to seek and to save a sinner. Since Jericho was a tax collection center situated on the major highway to Jerusalem, about eighteen miles northeast of the city, it was a prime place for a tax collector to live in order to get rich.[2] In this city there was a tax collector trying to see Jesus. Not tall enough to see Jesus through the crowd, he ran ahead and climbed up a sycamore tree, knowing He would pass by.

Although Zacchaeus was too short to see Jesus, he was not too short for Jesus to see him. Jesus knew exactly where Zacchaeus would be because God had called this tax collector to be a son of Abraham. Jesus called Zacchaeus down from the tree and told him that He had to stay at his house that day. Zacchaeus hurriedly climbed down the tree and joyfully received Jesus. Unlike the sad, rich ruler who could not receive Jesus because he loved his riches (Luke 18:23), Zacchaeus received Jesus joyfully, recognizing Him as the true riches.

It is sad that the Pharisees grumbled about Jesus sitting at a sinner's table. They misunderstood His mission to seek and to save sinners (Luke 4:18–19, 43; 5:31–32). Zacchaeus repented of his sin, recognizing Jesus was Lord over his life, including his wealth. He was eager to make things right with the Lord and with others, especially the poor he had wronged. Zacchaeus went above and beyond what the law required in a remarkable way. God's people were required to give up to only one-fifth of their property to the poor, but Zacchaeus gave away half of his possessions.[3] In addition, even though double restitution was the standard, Zacchaeus offered those he had wronged fourfold restitution, the amount required in the case of stealing an animal (Ex. 22:1).[4]

By God's grace salvation came to Zacchaeus's house on that day. From before the foundation of the world, Zacchaeus had been chosen as a son of Abraham. God sent His Son into the world as the Good Shepherd to seek and to save His lost sheep (see Ezek. 34:15–16; John 10:11). Dear believer, give thanks that Jesus sought you and saved you. Then go and seek the lost, opening your door to sinners in order to share the gospel.

II. Serve the King (19:11–27)

Remember that Jesus was near Jerusalem, where His purpose for coming to earth would climax in His death and resurrection. Also recall that the disciples incorrectly thought the kingdom of God was going to appear immediately. The Jews were looking for a messiah who would come and be a political ruler, setting up his kingdom on

---

2. Bock, *Luke*, 2:1505.
3. Ryken, *Luke*, 2:311.
4. Ryken, *Luke*, 2:312.

earth and reigning in glory. Despite the prophecy in Isaiah 53 of a Suffering Servant, they did not realize that Jesus's kingship would be far different than they imagined. They didn't understand that His cross would precede His glory or that the kingdom was inaugurated but not yet consummated. For these reasons, Jesus taught them the parable of the ten minas.

A nobleman went into a far country to receive for himself a kingdom with the plan to later return home. He called ten of his servants, gave them ten minas, and commanded them to engage in business until he returned. But his citizens hated him and sent a delegation to say that they did not want him as king. At his return from receiving the kingdom, he called his servants to account for what business they had done. Two of the servants were commended for their faithfulness and given responsibility according to their return on his money. One of the servants was condemned for not being a good steward, and his one mina was taken away from him. The other seven are not mentioned, but we can be sure that they were either commended or condemned. The enemies of the nobleman who had sent the delegation were slaughtered.

Jesus is the nobleman who left heaven for the far country of earth to receive a kingdom through His death and resurrection. He then returned home by ascending into heaven, where He is now seated at the right hand of God the Father, ruling over His inaugurated kingdom, awaiting its consummation. All of God's people are His servants who have been given a mina, the gospel message.[5] Believers are to engage in the business of making disciples until He returns.

It is a sad reality that many people do not want Jesus to reign over them. When He returns, two groups of people will be revealed, those who accepted Him as King and those who rejected Him. His enemies will spend an eternity in hell, while His servants will spend an eternity in heaven. All of His servants will receive heaven by grace, but according to their faithfulness, they will receive differences in responsibility as they continue serving their King for a lifetime of spiritual employment.[6]

The people had misunderstood the timing of the kingdom, and they were in danger of being poor stewards while Jesus was gone. Jesus wants His disciples to learn the importance of kingdom-minded living during the time when His kingdom has already been inaugurated but not yet consummated. As those who have received the gospel, we are to share it with others and live according to God's word. By God's grace, we are to serve the King with our time, money, and resources for His glory and the good of His people.

III. Celebrate the King (19:28–40)

Jesus left Jericho and headed toward Jerusalem. When He drew near Bethphage and Bethany, at the mountain called Olivet, He sent two of His disciples to the village opposite them. Upon arrival they would find a colt that no one had ever sat on, tied up. The

---

5. Ryken, *Luke*, 2:319.
6. Ryle, *Luke*, 246.

disciples were to untie it and bring it to the Lord. If questioned, they were simply to say the Lord had need of it.

The two disciples found the colt just as Jesus said, and when they were questioned, they replied that the Lord had need of it. On their return, they put their cloaks on the back of the colt to provide a saddle for Jesus. Then the two disciples put Him on it, exalting Him as King. As Jesus rode along, the other disciples took their cloaks and put them down on the road, along with palm branches (see Matt. 21:8), to make a royal carpet for the King (see 2 Kings 9:11–13).

It is significant that the Mount of Olives Jesus descended toward Jerusalem is the same mountain from which He ascended into heaven after His death and resurrection. And it may be the mount on which He will return (Acts 1:11–12). As Jesus drew near Jerusalem, the whole multitude of His disciples recognized Him as King. In fulfillment of Psalm 118:26 and Zechariah 9:9, they rejoiced and praised God with a loud voice for all the mighty works they had seen Jesus perform (see also Ps. 148:1; Luke 2:14).

Christ was given a foretaste of what He will receive when He comes again and every knee bows and every tongue confesses that He is Lord (see Phil. 2:10–11). But first He had to suffer on the cross to atone for the sins of God's people. Not surprisingly, the Pharisees told Jesus to rebuke His disciples for praising Him. But He replied that if His disciples ceased to praise Him, the stones would cry out (see Ps. 96:11–13; Isa. 55:12; Rom. 8:19).

Dear Christian, let us never cease to celebrate Christ as King. Let us exalt Him continually for who He is and all that He has done. Let us give Him our obedience, respect, honor, and praise.

IV. Sob over Sin (19:41–44)

In contrast to His disciples, who were rejoicing, praising God, and exalting Him as King, Jesus, the greatest Prophet, wept over Jerusalem's sin (see also 2 Kings 8:12; Jer. 9:1; Luke 13:34–35). Jesus lamented that the Jews failed to recognize Him as the King of peace. Their rejection of Him had further hardened their hearts. Like the judgment Israel suffered by being exiled at the hands of Assyria and Babylon (see 2 Kings 6:14; Ps. 137:9; Isa. 29:3; Jer. 52:5; Ezek. 4:2; 21:22; Mic. 3:12), the time of judgment would come for them.

If the Jews had accepted Jesus's arrival, His visit would have been a blessing (see Gen. 50:24–25; Ex. 3:7, 16; Job 10:12; 29:4), but since they rejected Him, it was now a curse (see Isa. 10:3; Jer. 6:15; 10:15). In AD 70 Jerusalem was utterly destroyed by the Romans. As horrific as this event was, it was only a foretaste of the judgment to come at Christ's second coming. On that day much more than Jerusalem will be destroyed, "but the day of the Lord will come as a thief in the night, in which the heavens will pass away with a great noise, and the elements will melt with fervent heat; both the earth and the works that are in it will be burned up" (2 Peter 3:10).

Dear friend, are you ready for the day of Christ's visitation? Do you sob over your sin because it is against the holy God? Today is the day to receive Christ as King. Remember, He weeps over your sin. He longs for you to turn to Him in repentance and faith. He longs to gather you in His arms as the loving Shepherd who knows His sheep by name. Do not run from Him in your shame; run to Him for your salvation.

V. Sanctify the Temple (19:45–48)

Jesus, the greatest and final Prophet, is now in Jerusalem, the city where the prophets die (Luke 13:33). He entered the temple and drove out the buyers and sellers, fulfilling what the prophets Malachi and Zechariah had spoken: "And the Lord, whom you seek, will suddenly come to His temple" (Mal. 3:1). "In that day there shall no longer be a Canaanite ["trader," ESV] in the house of the LORD of hosts" (Zech. 14:21). As Jesus drove them out, He quoted from Isaiah 56:7, which anticipated Jews and Gentiles worshiping together in the temple, and Jeremiah 7:11, which indicted the Israelites for making the temple a place of idolatry.

Although the sellers and money changers were needed to sell animals for sacrifice during the time of the feast and to make change for half shekels to pay the temple tax,[7] they should not have been doing business for extortion or inside the temple, which was holy to the Lord. We should note that Jesus called the temple His house. He not only claimed to be God but also pointed to the truth that He is the true temple (see also John 2:18–22). The temple in which they stood would be destroyed, but He would last forever.

Jesus was not just driving out money changers and sellers in the temple; He was also teaching and preaching the gospel (see also Luke 2:41–52). Sadly, the chief priests, scribes, and leaders sought to destroy Him. But since the people wanted to hear Him, they were unable to do anything. As always, Jesus divided the crowds. They were either for Him or against Him. He does the same today. We must choose whether we are for Jesus, following Him as King, or against Him, rejecting His kingship.

Believers are called to sanctify the temple. No longer do we go to the temple. Our bodies have become a temple of God by the indwelling of the Holy Spirit (1 Cor. 6:19–20). As such, we are to conduct ourselves honorably so that we are holy as God is holy (1 Peter 1:14–16). Each Lord's Day we should gather together with God's people, listening to the preaching of God's word, praying with other believers, and engaging in the sacraments. And daily we should proclaim the gospel to those around us, beginning with our children and grandchildren.

VI. Submit to Authority (20:1–8)

On one of the days Jesus was teaching in the temple, the chief priests, scribes, and elders confronted Him, questioning His authority (see also Luke 5:17, 30; 6:7; 9:22; 11:53; 15:2; 19:47). Since Jesus knew their motives, He refused to give them an answer.

---

7. Ryken, *Luke*, 2:343.

Instead, He asked them a question regarding whether the baptism of John was from heaven or from man.

Why would Jesus ask them a question about John? The ministries of John and Jesus were united. John was to prepare the people for Jesus's arrival (Luke 1:16–17). He proclaimed Jesus's might and power, His salvation and judgment (3:16–17). And he baptized Jesus (v. 21). Jesus affirmed that their ministries were linked, exalting John as more than a prophet in his role of preparing for His arrival (7:24–35). In fact, their ministries were so closely related that Jesus could ask the leaders a question about John and its answer would also apply to Him.

The chief priests, scribes, and elders were trapped. If they answered that John was from heaven, they would also be acknowledging that Jesus was from heaven, something they did not want to do. But if they said that John was from man, they were in danger of being stoned to death because the people were convinced that John was a prophet sent by God. So they answered that they did not know. But sadly, they did know. They had heard Jesus teach and had seen His work, but they refused to believe.

Because of their unbelief, Jesus would not give them any more answers. Instead, He gave His answer to the people in the form of a parable (Luke 20:9–18), with the scribes and chief priests overhearing (v. 19). He would later give His answer by citing Psalm 110:1 on two occasions (Luke 20:41–44; 22:66–71).[8] Jesus was not on trial before men; men were on trial before Jesus. This is as true today as it was then. We cannot put Jesus on trial. He is God's Son, the Lord of heaven and earth. We can either submit to His authority and be saved or reject His authority and be judged.

VII. Stand on the Stone (20:9–18)

Although no longer directly addressing the chief priests, scribes, and elders, Jesus told a parable to answer their question, "Tell us, by what authority are You doing these things? Or who is he who gave You this authority?" (Luke 20:2).

First, a vineyard owner (representing God the Father) planted a vineyard (representing Israel) and let it out to vinedressers (representing the leadership of Israel). Then the owner went into another country for a long while (representing Israel's history). When the time came, the owner sent a servant (servants represent Old Testament prophets) to the vinedressers so that they would give him some of the fruit (representing good spiritual fruit) of the vineyard. But the vinedressers beat the servant and sent him away. So the owner sent another servant, but the vinedressers treated him shamefully also. Then the owner sent a third servant, but the vinedressers cast him out also. So finally the owner sent his beloved son, hoping that the vinedressers would respect him. This parable is showing that God the Father sent the Old Testament prophets and finally His beloved Son, Jesus. But Israel's leadership rejected Him, just as they had rejected the Old Testament prophets. So God the Father would come and destroy those vinedressers (the destruction of Jerusalem in AD 70 was a partial fulfillment of

---

8. Bock, *Luke*, 2:1589.

this, but the complete fulfillment awaits the final day of judgment) and give the vineyard to others (the Gentiles).

God the Father had planted Israel for a purpose. He delivered them from Egypt so that they would be a kingdom of priests and a holy nation (Ex. 19:4–6; Deut. 7:6–11). He had planted Israel as a vineyard and had done everything He could to care for them, yet they rebelled against Him, and there was nothing left for Him to do but bring judgment (Isa. 5:1–7; see also Ps. 80:8–13; Ezek. 15). God held the leadership of Israel most accountable for the people's rebellion (see, for example, Ezek. 13–14; Mic. 3; Zech. 10:1–5; 11:1–3; Mal. 2:1–9). The Lord God sent prophet after prophet to Israel and Judah, but Israel would not listen, and the prophets suffered severe persecution at their hands (see 1 Kings 19:1–5; 2 Chron. 24:20–22; Jer. 38:1–6; Luke 13:34a; Acts 7:52–53). From the beginning God the Father had planned to send His beloved Son as the final and perfect Prophet, Priest, and King (2 Cor. 1:20). God has always intended for His people to be made up of both Jews and Gentiles (see Gen. 12:1–3; Acts 2:39).

Not surprisingly, the people responded to the parable with shock. Remember, the Israelites were God's privileged people (Rom. 9:4–5). Was God really going to give the vineyard to others? To prove His point, Jesus quoted from Psalm 118:22 and alluded to Isaiah 8:14–15 and Daniel 2:34, 44–45.

Psalm 118 was a joyful song of thanksgiving used at the great Jewish festivals throughout the year, especially Passover, which celebrated God's deliverance of Israel from Egypt.[9] The Jewish people considered themselves to be the rejected stone among the Gentile nations, but they were certain that God would vindicate them and display that they were His chosen nation and treasured possession. Christ, the true Israel, applied this verse to Himself, claiming that God would fulfill His promises to exalt His Son as the cornerstone.

Isaiah 8:14–15 warns Israel to fear the Lord of hosts, or He will become a trap in which they will be taken. And Daniel 2:34, 44–45 reveals that the stone that struck the image in Nebuchadnezzar's dream became a great mountain that filled the entire earth, symbolizing the truth that God's kingdom would eventually become the only kingdom.

By quoting from the Old Testament, Jesus proved the truth behind the parable. He showed that Israel's rebellion, their horrific treatment of God's prophets, the wicked leadership of the nation, and Christ's suffering had not taken God by surprise. He ordains everything that comes to pass. Also, He pointed out that the day of rejection is followed by the day of resurrection. The rejected stone becomes the cornerstone. He proclaimed judgment on those who reject Him. Further, He warned the people that they were not to follow in the footsteps of Israel's leaders or they would be in danger of judgment as well. Jesus professed that despite the rejection around Him, He was the cornerstone for Israel. Finally, God would still be glorified through Israel's rejection by bringing the Gentiles, "who once were far off…near by the blood of Christ…so as

9. C. John Collins, note to Psalm 113, in *ESV Study Bible*, 1087.

to create in Himself one new man from the two" and "reconcile them both to God in one body through the cross" (Eph. 2:13–16).[10]

Dear believer, we must stand on the stone. No matter our suffering, battles with sin, or weariness in service, we can be certain that God's sovereign plan continues to unfold. Like Christ, we will experience days of suffering followed by glory. Do not forsake His warning. Those who stumble over the stone will face judgment. But those who stand on the stone will enjoy the blessing of God's favor forever.

VIII. Surrender to God (20:19–26)

The scribes and the chief priests, rightly perceiving that Jesus had told this parable against them, were angry and sought to lay hands on Him. Ironically, although they didn't fear God, they did fear man. So they used others to do their scandalous work for them. They sent spies in order to catch Jesus in something He said so that they could deliver Him over to the authority and jurisdiction of the governor, Pilate.

The spies, pretending to be righteous, asked Jesus a question prefaced with flattery: "Teacher, we know that You say and teach rightly, and You do not show personal favoritism, but teach the way of God in truth: Is it lawful for us to pay taxes to Caesar or not?" (Luke 20:21–22). Jesus, knowing the intention of people's hearts, perceived their craftiness (see vv. 1–8) and again asked a question of His opponents instead of giving an answer.

First, he told the spies to show Him a denarius. A *denarius* was a Roman silver coin with the imprint of Emperor Tiberius on it. The people were required to pay their taxes with Roman coins. Other coins circulated in Rome at that time, including Jewish ones, and many Jews probably tried to use Jewish coinage as much as possible. But when it came to paying taxes, they had to use Roman coins.[11] Then Jesus asked them whose likeness and inscription was on the coin. They answered, "Caesar's" (Tiberius Caesar).

Jesus replied, "Render therefore to Caesar the things that are Caesar's, and to God the things that are God's" (Luke 20:25). Scripture makes it clear that men and women are made in the image of God and are to glorify Him in all that they say and do (Gen. 1:26–27; Ps. 24:1; Rom. 11:36; 1 Cor. 10:31). But we also know that God has ordained governing authorities, using them to bring about His purposes and requiring us to submit to them as long as they do not ask us to do something that is against His commands (see Rom. 13:1–7). We also have a responsibility to pray for our political leaders (1 Tim. 2:1–3). So everything that is Caesar's is also God's. Jesus is teaching us what it means to be citizens of heaven and earth simultaneously, loyal to God and loyal to the state, as far as it complies with Scripture.[12]

---

10. Pao and Schnabel, "Luke," 364.

11. Morris, *Luke*, 306.

12. Morris, *Luke*, 306.

Ironically, instead of seizing on Jesus's words, the spies were silenced by them (see also Luke 2:47; 14:4, 6). We cannot silence God, but He can silence us. His Word is the authority that stands over our lives, and we must surrender to it. If we don't, there will come a day when we will be forced to bow to Him, acknowledging Him as Lord (Phil. 2:10–11), but on that day it will be too late for salvation. Today is the day to surrender to Jesus as Savior and Lord. Then embrace your responsibility to be loyal citizens of both heaven and earth. Pray for your governing authorities, as well as your pastors and elders. Be faithful to pay your taxes on time and correctly, and be cheerful givers when the offering plate is passed. Care for your brothers and sisters in Christ and be kind and do good to your unbelieving neighbor.

IX. Subscribe to the Resurrection (20:27–44)

For the first time in the book of Luke, the Sadducees are mentioned. But this is not the first time they have encountered John and Jesus. Many of the Sadducees and Pharisees came to the River Jordan, where John was baptizing people who were confessing their sins. He called them a "brood of vipers" because they presumed their salvation was secure based on their ancestry. It is likely many of them were still standing near John when Jesus came to be baptized (Matt. 3:7–17). The Sadducees, along with the Pharisees, were testing Jesus, asking Him to show them signs from heaven, but Jesus refused, saying that the sign of Jonah would be the only one given (16:1–4). Also, Jesus warned His disciples about the leaven of the Sadducees and Pharisees, referring to their teaching that was not in accord with His (vv. 5–12). In contrast to the Pharisees, the Sadducees did not believe in a resurrection (Acts 23:8). Not surprisingly then, the Sadducees approached Jesus to question Him about this important doctrine.

The Sadducees begin with the law of levirate marriage (see Deut. 25:5–10). This law preserved the family name of a man who died without a son to carry on his name. The dead man's brother would marry the dead man's widow in order to preserve his brother's name in Israel. Since the Sadducees believed in the writings of Moses, they used this law to try to prove what they perceived to be the absurdity of the doctrine of the resurrection. The story they told Jesus was of a family with seven brothers, all of whom followed through with the levirate marriage law, but none of whom left a son to preserve their brother's name. They wondered, therefore, whose wife the woman would be in the resurrection since she had seven husbands on earth.

Jesus did not directly answer their question. Instead, He taught them about the nature of the age to come. While people live on this earth, marriage is appropriate, especially for the purpose of procreation. But in heaven marriage will no longer be necessary because believers no longer die (so there is no need for procreation), believers are equal to angels (who don't die and don't marry), and resurrected believers are sons of God (so we are secure in His family).[13]

---

13. Ryken, *Luke*, 2:381–82.

In order to prove His point, Jesus turned to the writings of Moses that the Sadducees believed. Referring to the passage about the burning bush, He specifically cited Exodus 3:6, in which Moses called the Lord "the God of Abraham, the God of Isaac, and the God of Jacob" (Luke 20:37). In other words, the Lord is "not the God of the dead but of the living, for all live to Him" (v. 38). When the Lord spoke these words to Moses, the patriarchs had already died. It is significant that He used the present tense: "I *am* the God of your father…" (Ex. 3:6; emphasis added). Abraham, Isaac, and Jacob were sons of God whose souls were already in heaven and whose bodies awaited the resurrection.

Some of the scribes commended His answer, and after that they no longer dared ask Him a question. But Jesus was not done asking questions. He asked them how the Jews can say that the Christ is the Son of David. This was a traditional Jewish teaching deeply rooted in the Old Testament. The Jews of the first century had their hopes fixed on a political deliverer, a king who would reign on the throne of David and make the kingdom better than it was in Solomon's beginning days (see 2 Samuel 7).

Instead of waiting for a reply, Jesus answered His own question by citing Psalm 110:1. It is notable that this is a royal psalm sung by Jews who were looking for a Davidic king to come. Jesus's point is not that the Messiah is merely David's son, a point that has already been affirmed in Luke (see 1:27, 32, 69; 2:4, 11; 3:31; 18:38–39), but that He is also David's Lord.[14] In other words, Jesus Christ is the final and perfect Davidic King, but He is more; He is Yahweh come in the flesh, King of kings and Lord of lords.

In verse 44, Jesus left the audience to ponder a question: "Therefore David calls Him 'Lord'; how is He then his Son?" The answer to this question would be revealed at Jesus's resurrection and ascension. How the people answered would determine whether they would be loyal servants of the King or rebellious tenants who lost the vineyard forever.

We can have certainty through the Scriptures that Jesus died and rose again: "But now Christ is risen from the dead, and has become the firstfruits of those who have fallen asleep" (1 Cor. 15:20). When Christ returns we too will be raised from the dead. The question is whether we will be raised to eternal life or eternal death. What we do with Jesus determines the answer. Is He just a good teacher, a son of David? Or is He also David's Lord—and Lord of all?

X. Sacrifice Everything (20:45–21:4)

Turning His attention to His disciples but still in the hearing of all the people, Jesus warned them of the scribes. Regardless of how high a view the scribes had of the Old Testament, their lifestyles condemned them. They liked to walk around in long robes that were part of a large, expensive wardrobe. The scribes liked other people to notice their wealthy attire. Also, they loved greetings in the marketplaces. Rabbis in Jesus's

---

14. Pao and Schnabel, "Luke," 372.

day were supposed to be greeted in the marketplace with respect, but these scribes wallowed in such favoritism and attention. The scribes loved the best seats in the synagogues. They enjoyed being treated with honor for their special knowledge. They also loved the places of honor at feasts. They did not follow Jesus's teaching of humbly taking the lowest place at a banquet; instead, they presumptuously sat in the place of honor and felt that they deserved to do so. They devoured widows' houses. The scribes, as the leaders of Israel, should have been displaying God's covenantal kindness toward widows (see Ex. 22:22; Deut. 10:18–19), but instead they were taking advantage of them, using them for their own selfish gain. Finally, the scribes made long prayers to look good in front of others. Sadly, when they should have been humbly conversing with God, they were proudly promoting their spirituality before others. Since the scribes should have been leading the nation in integrity and godliness but instead were leading them in ungodliness, Jesus said that they would receive the greater condemnation (see also James 3:1).

Even though the scribes were devouring widows' houses, there was one widow who remained faithful to give the Lord what she had. Such graciousness and faithfulness caught Jesus's attention. Remember, it was Passover week. Jews had made the journey to Jerusalem from all over Israel so that they could pay their vows to God.[15] There were thirteen receptacles in the shape of a trumpet that were located in the Court of Women so that people could walk up at any time to give an offering.[16] Jesus, who was near the temple (Luke 20:1), looked up and saw the rich putting in their gifts. If Jesus had been one of the chief priests or scribes, He would have favored the rich. Instead, He favored a poor widow who put in two mites, or small copper coins. Each was worth one one-hundredth of the average daily wage.[17] Based on percentages, the poor widow put in far more than the rich.

As much as we don't want to think we are like the scribes, we must admit, if we are honest, that many similarities exist between the scribes of Jesus's day and the leaders of the church today. Think of the prosperity preachers who like to live in extraordinary homes and drive nice sports cars. In my personal experience, when I was a director of women's ministry in the local church, I received glamour shots in the mail promoting speakers for women's events. Their pictures, astronomical fees, and rigid requirements saddened me. Too often women flock around personalities and programs. We tend to expect the red-carpet treatment while ignoring the widow's carpet that needs to be cleaned. In the area of giving, we often think in terms of how little time, money, and resources we can give to the church instead of how much. Jesus reveals that true greatness and true riches come by sacrificing everything to Him, including our very

---

15. Ryken, *Luke*, 2:404.
16. Bock, *Luke*, 2:1645.
17. Bock, *Luke*, 2:1645.

lives. The poor widow understood this. Oh, that you and I would understand this too! In our poverty, His riches shine brightest.

As a mom of four children, I still love to sing Bible songs, and one of my favorites is still "Zacchaeus." I want my children to learn the same truth I did: Jesus seeks and saves the lost. And I want them to seek the lost, telling them about the one who saves, Jesus Christ. This is what we all should want for our children, grandchildren, and the covenant children in our churches—to know Christ as their Savior and to make disciples of all nations.

Processing It Together...

1. What do we learn about God in Luke 19:1–21:4?

2. How does this reshape how we should view our present circumstances?

3. What do we learn about God's Son, Jesus Christ?

4. How should this impact our relationship with God and with others?

5. What do we learn about God's covenant with His people?

6. How are we to live in light of this?

7. How can we apply Luke 19:1–21:4 to our lives today and in the future?

8. How should we apply this passage in our churches?

9. Look back at "Put It in Perspective" in your personal study questions. What did you find challenging or encouraging about this lesson?

10. Look back at "Principles and Points of Application." How has this lesson impacted your life?

The New Covenant in My Blood

Luke 21:5–22:62

Purpose...

Head. What do I need to know from this passage in Scripture?

- Jesus exhorts His disciples about how to live in times of persecution and eats His last Passover with them before His death.

Heart. How does what I learn from this passage affect my internal relationship with the Lord?

- I am a kingdom disciple who has received forgiveness and grace for my sins.

Hands. How does what I learn from this passage translate into action for God's kingdom?

- I will pray for my persecuted brothers and sisters regularly.
- I will view every trial as an opportunity to bear witness for Christ.
- I will participate in the Lord's Supper during corporate worship in a worthy manner.
- I will be a servant leader in areas of influence.
- I will strengthen my sisters against sin by praying for them and encouraging them.

Personal Study...

Pray. Ask that God will open up your heart and mind as you study His Word. This is His story of redemption that He has revealed to us, and the Holy Spirit is our teacher.

Ponder the Passage. Read Luke 21:5–22:62.

- *Point:* What is the point of this passage? How does this relate to the point of the entire book?

- *Persons:* Who are the main people involved in this passage? What characterizes them?

- *Persons of the Trinity:* Where do you see God the Father, God the Son, and God the Holy Spirit in this passage?

- *Puzzling Parts:* Are there any parts of the passage that you don't quite understand or that seem interesting or confusing?

Put It in Perspective.

- *Place in Scripture:* What is the original context of this text? What is the redemptive-historical context—what has or hasn't happened in redemptive history at this point in Scripture? How does this text connect to Christ?

The following questions will help you if you got stuck on any of the previous questions, and they will help you dig a little deeper into the text, putting it all into perspective.

1. **21:5–6.** (a) Where is Jesus going when this discussion takes place, and with whom is He speaking (see Matt. 24:1–3)?

   (b) What does Jesus predict will happen to the temple, and when had this happened before (see 2 Kings 25:1–21)?

2. **21:7–9.** (a) Where is Jesus when the conversation in verses 7–36 takes place, and to whom is He speaking (see Matt. 24:3)?

   (b) How does Jesus respond to the disciples' questions, and why?

(c) What else does the New Testament say about deceivers (see, for example, 2 Thess. 2:3–12)?

3. **21:10–19.** (a) What does Jesus foretell in verse 10, and how does this allude to Isaiah 19:2?

(b) What does Jesus foretell in verse 11, and what is the purpose of such judgment (see Ezek. 38:19–22)?

(c) What does Jesus say will occur before the events in verses 10–11, and why?

(d) What does Jesus exhort His disciples to do, and why?

(e) Who will betray Jesus's disciples, and why?

(f) What is the promise in verses 18–19 (see also Dan. 11:32, 35; 12:1, 12; Mic. 7:7)?

4. **21:20–24.** (a) How does verse 20 recall Daniel 12:11?

(b) What does Jesus tell His disciples to do (see also Gen. 19:17, 19; Jer. 51:45), and why (see also Lev. 26:31–33; Deut. 28:49–57, 64; Jer. 20:4–6; 51:6; Hos. 9:7; Zech. 12:3)?

(c) Why is judgment coming, and what will happen to Jerusalem (see also Deut. 28:58–68; Jer. 20:4; 27:7; Dan. 8:13–14; 12:5–13; Zech. 12:3)?

5. 21:25–28. (a) What will precede Jesus's second coming (see also Ps. 46:3; Isa. 13:6–11; 24:19; 34:4; Joel 2:30–31)?

(b) How does verse 27 allude to Daniel 7:13?

(c) How has the believers' redemption already drawn near, but not yet in its fullness (see Rom. 8:23; 1 Cor. 15:20–23)?

6. 21:29–33. (a) What does the parable teach about the kingdom of God?

(b) What does it mean that Jesus's words won't pass away (see Pss. 102:25–26; 119:89, 160; Isa. 40:8; 51:6; 55:10–11)?

7. 21:34–38. (a) What does Jesus exhort His disciples to do, and why (see also Isa. 24:20; Rev. 14:8)?

(b) How is one counted worthy to escape God's judgment (see Acts 4:10–12)?

(c) How was Jesus spending His time during the day? At night?

8. 22:1–6. (a) What do you learn about the Feast of Unleavened Bread and Passover from Exodus 12:1–28, 43–51; 13:3–10; 23:14–15; 34:18; Leviticus 23:4–8; Numbers 9:1–14; and Deuteronomy 16:1–8.

(b) Who was seeking to put Jesus to death, and why were they concerned about how to do it?

(c) Why is the timing of Jesus's death significant (see 1 Cor. 5:6–8; Heb. 9:11–10:18)?

(d) Into whom did Satan enter, and when was the last time Satan was mentioned in the book of Luke (see 4:1–13)?

(e) Contrast what Judas did with what he should have done (see James 4:7).

9. **22:7–13.** What do Jesus's instructions reveal about the sovereignty of God, especially with regard to Jesus's death and resurrection (see Luke 18:31–34)?

10. **22:14–23.** (a) To what does "the hour" refer (see John 13:1–4)?

(b) What does it mean that Jesus will no longer eat of the Passover until it is fulfilled in the kingdom of God (see Rev. 19:6–10)?

(c) How does Jesus fulfill Exodus 24:8; Isaiah 53; and Jeremiah 31:31–34?

(d) Read chapter 29 of the Westminster Confession of Faith or articles 33 and 35 of the Belgic Confession. What do you learn about the Lord's Supper?

(e) How does this event fulfill Psalm 41:9–12?

11. 22:24–30. (a) What dispute arose among the apostles (see also Matt. 20:20–24; Mark 9:34; Luke 9:46–48)?

(b) How were the apostles to be different from the world's leaders, and how did Jesus set the example for them (see John 13:1–20)?

(c) For what does Jesus commend His disciples? Give examples of this from the book of Luke.

(d) What does Jesus promise His apostles (see also Eph. 2:20; Rev. 21:14)?

12. 22:31–34. (a) What battle lies behind this event in Peter's life (see Eph. 6:11–12)?

(b) How do we know from Jesus's words that Peter's denial will end differently from Judas's betrayal?

(c) How does Peter respond to Jesus's words, and how was this the beginning of his downfall (see Prov. 16:18)?

(d) How is Jesus's prediction fulfilled (see 22:54–62)?

13. 22:35–38. (a) How does Jesus change His directions from His previous ones, and why (see Luke 9:1–6; 10:1–12)?

(b) What Scripture will Jesus accomplish?

14. 22:39–46. (a) To what place did Jesus and His apostles come (see Matt. 26:36)?

(b) What are they to pray for (see also Luke 11:1–4)?

(c) What is Jesus's prayer, and what does the cup signify (see Isa. 51:17, 22; Jer. 25:15; Ezek. 23:31–34; Zech. 12:2; Rev. 14:10)?

(d) Who appeared to Jesus, and for what reason (compare this with Heb. 1:7, 14)? How does this incident display Jesus's humanity?

(e) Why should Peter in particular have stayed awake and prayed (see v. 31)?

15. 22:47–53. (a) Who cut off the servant's ear, and how did Jesus respond (see John 18:10)?

(b) What does Jesus mean when He says, "This is your hour, and the power of darkness" (see Eph. 6:12; Col. 1:13)?

(c) How was it also Jesus's hour, and the power of light (see John 12:46; 13:1; 17:1)?

16. 22:54–62. (a) What choices led up to Peter's three denials (see 22:33, 45–46, 54, 55)?

(b) Briefly describe Peter's three denials. How does this incident fulfill Jesus's words (22:34)?

(c) What did the Lord do when the rooster crowed, and what did Peter remember and do?

Principles and Points of Application

17. **21:5–9.** In what way are you finding your security in some type of external beauty? Ask God to give you wisdom and discernment to recognize the true value of things.

18. **21:10–19.** Spend time in prayer for our persecuted brothers and sisters, asking the Lord to strengthen their witness, help them respond wisely to their persecutors, and grant them endurance and patience with joy.

19. **21:20–24.** How have you suffered for Christ's sake, and what lessons did you learn in the midst of it?

20. **21:25–28.** Are you ready to meet the Son of Man, Jesus Christ, at His second coming, and why?

21. **21:29–38.** (a) In what ways are the cares of this life weighing you down?

(b) How can the means of grace help you to guard against the things of this world?

22. **22:1–6.** In what area(s) are you tempted to betray your loyalty to Christ? Repent of these and turn to the Lord, meditating on 1 Peter 5:8–9.

23. 22:7–38. (a) In what area(s) has God called you to be a servant leader, and how are you doing?

(b) How does it encourage you to know that Jesus is praying for you in the midst of temptation?

(c) How are you strengthening your brothers and sisters in Christ with lessons you have learned from past times of temptation?

24. 22:39–46. Spend time in prayer that you and your loved ones will not enter into temptation. Also pray for the Lord's will to be done, especially with regard to any suffering in your life that you are asking Him to remove.

25. 22:47–53. Give an example of when you have defended Jesus or the Scriptures in the wrong way instead of in love and humility.

26. 22:54–62. (a) In what ways have you failed to acknowledge your love of Jesus before others? What contributed to your failure?

(b) How can you be bold in your witness for Jesus in an increasingly hostile world? How can you encourage others to do the same?

Putting It All Together...

Think of the last time you were tempted to do what the Bible says you should not do and you carried through with it. Instead of showing compassion, you were harsh in your tone. You spoke an unkind word instead of building up another person in love. You displayed pride instead of humility. You refused to forgive someone when they asked your forgiveness. You settled for strife instead of pursuing peace. You engaged

231

in impure thoughts or actions. Instead of complimenting a sister for her hard work, you envied her. Or you were embarrassed to confess you were a Christian in front of your peers.

Sadly, many believers are unprepared for temptation. We are often unaware of our potential to fall into deep and grievous sin. We often fail to pray that we will not enter into temptation. Many times we pursue the things of this world instead of Christ. We often hang around the wrong company and miss the edification and encouragement of godly friendships. And we often fail to confess Christ before the crowd, being more concerned about our reputation than His.

What do we do when we sin? We must flee to Christ. In His presence, we will find an advocate full of compassion and love. We will learn that there is nothing we can do to separate us from the grip of God's grace. Our Father loves us, our Savior prays for us, and the Holy Spirit convicts us to repent and return to a relationship with the triune God.

These chapters in Luke remind us how important it is to pray that we will not enter into temptation and of the Savior's love for us when we do. It's a balm for every woman who has wondered if Christ will take her back after she has fallen into sin. Yes, His mercies are new each morning, and His grace is greater than all our sin.

I. Prediction of the Temple's Destruction (21:5–9)

Jesus had been teaching in the temple in Jerusalem (Luke 19:45–21:4) and was now heading toward the Mount of Olives. Before He left, His disciples pointed out to Him the beautiful buildings of the temple (Matt. 24:1–3; Mark 13:1). The temple in Jerusalem was one of the wonders of the ancient world and the religious center of the nation. Herod the Great had renovated it beginning in 19 BC, building new foundation walls and enlarging it to two times its original size. The renovation was finally completed over eighty years later in AD 63–64, only to be destroyed in AD 70. Herod the Great used white marble stones that were as long as sixty-seven feet, as high as twelve feet, and as wide as eighteen feet. The temple was decorated with offerings and gifts, which included gold- and silver-plated gates and gold-plated doors.[1] It must have been shocking then for the disciples to hear Jesus predict the destruction of the temple, even if they remembered the Scriptures recounting the destruction of Jerusalem at the hands of Nebuchadnezzar in 586 BC (2 Kings 25:1–21; Ezek. 24:1–14; 33:21–33).

Sadly, Israel had worshiped the external beauty of the temple, putting their trust in its magnificence and symbolism instead of in the Lord. They should have recognized that the true temple had come in Jesus Christ, but instead they rejected Him and faced judgment. After Christ's ascension, God would not allow the Jews to continue going about life as though He had not sent His Son into the world as the final and perfect sacrifice. He would destroy the temple in Jerusalem because it was no longer serving the purpose that it once had in the days before Christ's death as a type of the person

---

1. Bock, *Luke*, 2:1660–61.

and sacrifice to come. Rather than dwelling in a temple built by human hands, God would dwell with His people through the Holy Spirit.

As Jesus sat on the Mount of Olives, the disciples came to Him privately and asked when the destruction of the temple would be and what would be the sign before it took place (Matt. 24:3). Jesus did not answer their question directly. Instead, He warned His disciples about false teachers and prophets. He also exhorted His disciples not to be terrified when they heard of wars and commotions because these would come well before the end. Sadly, Israel had not learned their lesson from previous generations. The Jews still did not recognize their true King, and the destruction of the temple and exile would occur again in AD 70, a microcosm of the final judgment when Christ returns.

It's so easy to be fooled by the beauty of buildings and the wonder of worship services. But we must be on guard against false teachers who have an air of external religiosity but lack inward transformation of the heart (see 1 John 2:18, 26; Jude 4). It's also easy to be terrified of wars and commotions as we read the news, but we should find great hope and peace if we are hidden in Christ. Christ's return will be the believer's day of joy, when we will see our Lord and Savior face-to-face and enter into glory with souls and bodies that are fully redeemed.

II. Persecution (21:10–19)

Jesus prophesies that "nation will rise against nation, and kingdom against kingdom" (Luke 21:10), an allusion to Isaiah 19:2.[2] He also predicts that there will be great earthquakes, famines, pestilences, terrors, and great signs from heaven, which recalls Ezekiel's prophecy against Gog, of the land of Magog, the purpose of which is to display God's greatness and holiness to the nations (Ezek. 38:23).[3] Likewise, the purpose of the final day of wrath is that all people will confess the lordship of Christ to the glory of God the Father (Phil. 2:10–11).

Before such wars, though, Jesus's disciples would undergo intense persecution. They would be delivered up to the synagogues and prisons and brought before kings and rulers for His name's sake. It would be their opportunity to bear witness for Christ. They could trust the Lord to give them a mouth and wisdom that none of their adversaries would be able to withstand or contradict.

Persecution would not just come from without; it would also come from within. Persecutors could be parents, brothers, relatives, or friends. They would betray believers or worse—put them to death for their faith. Disciples would be hated for His name's sake. But although some of Jesus's disciples would die physically, they would not die spiritually. After they endured to the end, they would enter into eternal fellowship with

2. Pao and Schnabel, "Luke," 374.
3. Pao and Schnabel, "Luke," 375.

Christ in heaven. Notably, we know from church history that ten of the eleven disciples suffered martyrdom, John died in exile of old age, and Paul was beheaded in Rome.[4]

Let us not cease to pray for our persecuted brothers and sisters around the world to bear witness for Christ's name's sake, respond to their persecution with God's words and wisdom, endure hatred, and be willing to lose their life in order to gain eternal life. In your own life, use your trials and sufferings as an opportunity to bear witness for Christ. It may be that infertility, a broken marriage, a debilitating disease, a horrific prognosis, the care of an aging parent, or a special-needs child provides your God-given opportunity to bear witness for Him. Trust Him to give you the words to speak as you witness about His great name in a broken world.

III. Prediction of Jerusalem's Destruction (21:20–24)

Jesus told His disciples that when they saw Jerusalem surrounded by armies, they would know that its desolation had come near. This "abomination of desolation" (Matt. 24:15), spoken of by the prophet Daniel (Dan. 12:11), refers to a horrific event that occurred in 167 BC. The Greek king Antiochus IV Epiphanes conquered Jerusalem, placed a statue of the pagan god Zeus in the temple courts, and sacrificed pigs in the Holy of Holies—an outrageous abomination in the eyes of the Jews.[5] Now Jesus says another horrible event is coming. The temple would again become desolate, but this time it would be at the hands of the Romans, not the Greeks.

About forty years after Jesus foretold the destruction of Jerusalem, Titus marched on Jerusalem and the enemy laid siege, surrounding it for almost six months. At the end, the famine was so severe that the citizens were eating the dust. Nursing mothers had no food to eat so that their bodies would produce milk for their babies, so some babies died of starvation while others were killed. By the time the Romans broke through the city walls, the people had no resistance left. The historian Josephus wrote that as many as one million Jews were killed with another one hundred thousand taken prisoner. The Jews who survived were led into captivity, leaving scarcely one Jew in the city.[6] God brought judgment against His covenant people because they had rejected His Son. The Old Testament recounts an entire history of rebellion, but it is in the pages of the New Testament that we see Israel's most horrific sin of rejecting God's perfect sacrifice, His beloved Son, nailing Him to a cross.

Ironically, the disciples were to flee from the city, the very place country folk usually fled to for protection. God's people did not forget these words. About three years before Titus's attack on Jerusalem, another Roman general marched against the city but did not succeed. The early church fled across the Jordan River to a city called Pella, where they were still living when Titus attacked and burned the city in AD 70. God, in His providence and grace, spared a remnant, the true believers, and carried forward

---

4. Sproul, *Walk with God*, 340.
5. Ryken, *Luke*, 2:424.
6. Ryken, *Luke*, 2:425.

His plan of redemption as they spread across the regions proclaiming the gospel, some of them returning to Jerusalem after it had been destroyed in order to evangelize.[7]

These days of vengeance were in fulfillment of the curses God had promised would come on His people if they were not faithful to Him (see Lev. 26:31–33; Deut. 28:49–57; Jer. 20:4–6; 51:6; Hos. 9:7; Zech. 12:3). Because Israel had failed to be a light to the nations, they would be led away captive into all nations. Jerusalem would be trampled by Gentiles until the times of the Gentiles were fulfilled, referring either to the Romans who occupied Jerusalem for centuries or to the time between Christ's first and second coming, during which the church is to make disciples of all nations.[8]

You and I do not have to flee to the countryside but rather to the cross of Calvary. Jesus Christ is now seated at the right hand of God the Father, interceding for us and watching over us. Those of us who are hidden in Christ do not need to fear the destruction of our bodies or of this world. With our eyes focused on glory, we can glorify God and enjoy Him now, just as we will do forever.

IV. Powerful Coming (21:25–28)

The destruction of Jerusalem in AD 70 was a day of judgment, but it was not the final day of judgment. Now Jesus tells His disciples about His second coming, when He will judge the living and the dead. There will be signs that precede His coming in the heavens and on earth. The sun, moon, and stars will be different and the heavens shaken. On earth, the people of the nations will be perplexed and distressed (see also Ps. 46:1–3; Isa. 13:6–11; 24:19; 34:4; Joel 2:30–31).

After these signs in the heavens and on earth, which will be greater than any before in history, the Son of Man will be seen coming in a cloud with power and great glory, an allusion to Daniel 7:13. When Christ comes again, He will consummate His kingdom. The kingdoms of this world will become the kingdom of Christ. It will be the believers' most glorious day, for their redemption will be consummated. Although we are already redeemed by the blood of the Lamb, the full benefits of our redemption, especially a new and glorious body, await Christ's second coming (see Rom. 8:23). This is why Jesus tells His disciples to straighten up and raise their heads. In Christ, they have nothing to fear and nothing of which to be ashamed, for they are covered in the blood of Jesus.

Dear friend, when Christ returns, will you be able to raise your head because the fullness of your redemption is drawing near? If not, cry out to the Lord to save you today. If so, thank Him for the gift of salvation.

V. Pious Living (21:29–38)

Jesus continued to teach about the second coming by telling His disciples a parable. When trees get leaves, those who pass by know that summer is near. In the same way,

---

7. Ryken, *Luke*, 2:428.
8. Ryken, *Luke*, 2:429.

when the disciples saw the signs He described, they should know the kingdom of God was near.

Jesus stated, "This generation will by no means pass away till all things take place" (Luke 21:32). To what does "this generation" refer? It can't mean Jesus's disciples because He knew they would die before He returned. So He was either speaking about a certain race of people, the Jews; about an evil generation, unbelievers; or about a godly generation, God's people. Regardless, everything that Jesus says is true, and we can believe that the end will come just as He has said it will (see also Pss. 102:25–26; 119:89, 160).

In the meantime, Jesus warned His disciples not to let their hearts be weighed down with dissipation and drunkenness and the cares of this life so that the day of His return would catch them off guard. Remember, Jesus was speaking to His closest friends, His disciples. He knows how easy it is for His followers to take their focus off eternity and be consumed with temporal cares and immorality (see Isa. 24:20; Rev. 14:8).

Not one person will escape the day of Christ's coming. For those in Christ, this will be a wonderful day of beholding their Savior, but for those not found in Him, it will be the day of judgment leading to eternal suffering. To avoid the pitfall of sin and worldliness, we must first trust in Christ as our Lord and Savior and then continue to pray for His return, watching and waiting with eager hearts (Rev. 22:20).

Leading up to His death, Jesus was teaching in the temple every day, but at night He was lodging on the mountain called Olivet. We can be sure that these nights were spent in prayer to His Father, preparing for the next day of ministry when the people came to the temple early in the morning to hear Him teach. We also need to be teaching others the word of God, spending time in prayer, and coming together as a covenant community to hear the preaching of God's word.

VI. Plot of Judas (22:1–6)

The Feast of Unleavened Bread, which is called Passover, was near (see Ex. 12:1–27, 43–49; 23:14–15; 34:18; Lev. 23:4–8; Num. 9:1–14; Deut. 16:1–8). To show the importance of this feast, God commanded Israel to make "the month of Abib" (Deut. 16:1), in which it was celebrated, "the first month of the year" on the Jewish calendar (Ex. 12:2). Each household was to take an unblemished, one-year-old male lamb and keep it until the fourteenth day of the month, when the whole assembly of the congregation of Israel would kill their lambs (vv. 1–6). On the very first Passover, the people had to smear some of the blood from the lamb on the two doorposts and the lintel of the house in which they ate (v. 7). Also, they were to eat the lamb in haste, with their belt fastened, sandals on their feet, and their staff in their hand, ready to flee Egypt (v. 11). The blood on the doorposts and lintel would be a sign for the Lord to pass over their home and not kill their firstborn, which was the final plague that the Lord was bringing on Egypt (Exodus 11). Significantly, our Lord and Savior's suffering and death occurred at Passover. He is the Lamb of God who takes away the sins of the world, our Passover Lamb that has been sacrificed for us (1 Cor. 5:7–8).

Sadly, the chief priests and the scribes sought to kill Jesus. But saddest of all, Satan entered into Judas Iscariot, one of the twelve apostles. Remember that after Satan had tempted Jesus in the wilderness, he left Him alone until an opportune time (Luke 4:13). Now is the opportune time.

God had sovereignly ordained the time of the Passover to be when Jesus was handed over to His enemies and crucified (Acts 2:23), but at the same time, Judas, the betrayer, and those who crucified Christ are fully responsible for their sin. Judas was not innocent. He gave the devil a foothold (Eph. 4:27) and did not resist him (James 4:7); he did not stand firm in his faith (1 Peter 5:9).

Judas conferred with the chief priest and scribes about how he might betray Jesus to them. Delighted, they agreed to give him money, the biggest motivator behind Judas's betrayal (see John 12:5–6). Sadly, Judas worshiped money more than God, and this moment of decision would prove to be his downfall.

These verses should give us pause. It was the religious elite and one of the twelve apostles who killed Jesus. Jesus repeatedly warns us that there will be those in the midst of the covenant community who will not be loyal to Him. We must make sure we are not among them. We cannot serve two masters. We must choose between Christ and the things of this world.

VII. Passover (22:7–38)

In anticipation of eating the last Passover with His apostles, Jesus sent Peter and John to prepare the meal. If all of the apostles had known where the Passover would take place, Judas could have betrayed Jesus earlier than God had planned (see Luke 18:31–34). So only Peter and John knew where the meal would take place beforehand.

Jesus had made the preparations for His triumphal entry (Luke 19:30–32), and likewise He was fully in control of the Passover meal. It seems that He had prearranged the entire meal with the master of the house. Since women usually carried jars of water, a man carrying a jar would have been easy for Peter and John to spot. They were to follow this man into his master's house and say, "The Teacher says to you, 'Where is the guest room where I may eat the Passover with My disciples?'" (22:11). The master would show Peter and John where to prepare it; it would be a large upper room that was furnished. Church tradition says that this was the home of Mary, mother of John Mark.[9] We don't know for sure, but it was surely the home of someone who acknowledged Jesus as the Messiah.

When the time came for the meal, Jesus reclined at the table with His apostles, a posture that reminded them that Israel had been delivered from Egypt and was no longer in slavery. This was different from the first Passover, when Israel ate in haste, dressed and ready to flee from Egypt (Ex. 12:11). It is significant that before Jesus

---

9. Bock, *Luke*, 2:1713.

died, He wanted to share one last meal with His closest friends in order to help them understand why He had to suffer. The Passover, which looked back to the great exodus event in the Old Testament, was now becoming the Lord's Supper, which celebrated the great exodus event in the New Testament, Christ's death and resurrection.

To inaugurate the new covenant, Jesus took the cup of thanksgiving and told His apostles that He would not drink of the fruit of the vine until the kingdom of God comes, at the marriage supper of the Lamb (Rev. 19:9). Then He took bread, gave thanks, broke it, and gave it to them, saying, "This is My body which is given for you; do this in remembrance of Me" (Luke 22:19). He took another cup after supper, saying, "This cup is the new covenant in My blood, which is shed for you" (v. 20; see Ex. 24:8; Isa. 53; Jer. 31:31–34).

The apostle John tells us that after supper was finished, Jesus laid aside His outer garments, took a towel, poured water into a basin, and began to wash the disciples' feet and dry them, setting an example of servant leadership (John 13:1–20). Luke simply tells us that Jesus revealed to His disciples that one of them would betray Him. How shocking this news must have been to everyone except Judas, who knew what he was about to do.

The disciples began to question one another as to which one of them was going to betray Jesus. The apostle John tells us that Simon Peter motioned to him to ask Jesus who He was talking about. John leaned back against Jesus and asked Him, but nobody else at the table heard the question or the answer. Jesus told John that the betrayer was the one to whom He would give a morsel of bread after dipping it. And after Jesus gave Judas the piece of bread, He told him to quickly do his evil deed. Judas immediately went out at night to betray Jesus (see John 13:21–30).

Sadly, while the apostles were still around the table, a dispute arose among them as to which one of them was to be regarded as the greatest (Luke 22:24–30). This wasn't the first time this dispute had occurred. You may remember that earlier an argument arose as to which one of them was the greatest, and Jesus used a child to teach them that small means great in God's kingdom (Luke 9:48). Here Jesus pointed to the way the Gentiles lead to tell His apostles to be different. They were not to be as the Gentile kings, who lord their authority over their people and require them to call them bene-factors. Instead, the apostles were to become servant leaders like Him.

He also encouraged His apostles by reminding them of their faithfulness in remain-ing with Him. They had given up everything for Jesus and followed Him. Yes, they were sinful, but they loved Jesus. He promised them a kingdom in which they will eat and drink at His table and judge the twelve tribes of Israel. The word translated *bestow* (NKJV) or *assign* (ESV) in verse 29 is the same verb for "making a covenant" in the Greek, and this promise was specifically given to the twelve apostles (see Eph. 2:19–20; Rev. 21:14).[10] But Jesus has also promised all believers a kingdom with all of the glori-ous benefits of His inheritance (Eph. 1:3–14).

---

10. Ryken, *Luke*, 2:483.

Knowing that suffering comes before glory, Jesus reminded His apostles that they have an adversary and accuser who desires to sift them like wheat. Jesus specifically addressed Simon Peter by name, but the "you" in the phrase "Satan has asked for you" (Luke 22:31) is plural in the Greek, so His address included all of the apostles.[11] Satan has desired to sift humankind like wheat since the garden of Eden (see Gen. 3:1–7; see also Job 1:6–12; Zech. 3:1). Our adversary the devil prowls around us like a roaring lion, seeking to devour us (1 Peter 5:8). Satan is the deceiver of the whole world, accusing believers day and night before God (Rev. 12:9–10). But his defeat is certain (vv. 7–17). Christ triumphed over Him on the cross (Col. 2:15).

Remarkably, Jesus is praying for His apostles so that their faith may not fail. He told Peter that after he had turned again, he was to strengthen his brothers. This is instructive. First, it shows us that Peter would fail, just like you and I will fail. Second, it shows that the Lord would preserve Peter's faith, just like He preserves yours and mine. Third, it shows that when we repent, we are to use our past failures to encourage and strengthen fellow believers who are tempted to falter in their faith.

In pride Peter defended his faith and made it sound much stronger than it was. Sadly, Jesus predicted his downfall: "I tell you, Peter, the rooster shall not crow this day before you will deny three times that you know Me" (Luke 22:34). Beware, believer, pride is destructive (Prov. 16:18). Apart from the grace of God, we are all capable of falling into sin. We must humble ourselves before God, seek His grace in moments of temptation, flee from and resist the devil, and run to our advocate Christ.

Before leaving the upper room, Jesus covered one more topic with His apostles. He recalled the time that He sent them out with no money bag, knapsack, or sandals (see Luke 9:1–6; 10:1–12). At that time the apostles were in places where many people followed Jesus. They lacked nothing. But now they would face much hostility.[12] The prophet Isaiah's words were being fulfilled. Jesus would be numbered with the transgressors (Isa. 53:12). The Suffering Servant would suffer at the hands of sinful men for the sins of God's people.

The apostles misunderstood the nature of Jesus's suffering. They did not realize that He would be as a lamb led to the slaughter with no sword in His hand. Though they offered Christ two swords, He did not accept them. He would go without sword, sinless, to suffer for the sins of the sinful.

VIII. Prayer on the Mount of Olives (22:39–46)

Jesus left the upper room and went to the Mount of Olives, the place where He was accustomed to spend time in prayer. This was the mountain from which He had come down to enter Jerusalem (Luke 19:28–29) and on which He spent each night after His days of teaching in the temple (21:37). The disciples also followed him. When He came

---

11. Ryken, *Luke*, 2:486.
12. Ryken, *Luke*, 2:493.

to Gethsemane (Matt. 26:36), He told His disciples to pray that they may not enter into temptation (see also Luke 11:4; 22:31–32).

Jesus went a short distance away from them to pray. Kneeling down, He asked the Father to remove the cup of His wrath from Him if He was willing. We should note that He submitted to the Father's plan the entire time. The cup He wanted removed was that of God's wrath and judgment against all the sins of His people. Since God is just, someone had to pay for His people's sins, and that person had to be perfect to stand in our place. Jesus alone qualified since He is the perfect God-man. As He looked toward the cross, His agony was so great that His tears were like drops of blood falling to the ground, and an angel from heaven appeared to strengthen Him.

Sadly, while the disciples were supposed to be praying, they fell asleep. Knowing what He was about to endure and having just poured out His soul in agony to His Father, Jesus questioned why they were sleeping. Then He repeated His exhortation, "Rise and pray, lest you enter into temptation" (Luke 22:46).

We need to pray often for the Lord to deliver us from temptation. It's so easy to sleep when we should be praying or get distracted with things we need to do. But prayer should be a top priority. It's vital for the Christian life, a means of grace God has given us so that we might be strengthened against temptation.

IX. Power of Darkness (22:47–53)

While Jesus was still speaking to His disciples in the garden of Gethsemane, a multitude came ("the chief priests and captains," Luke 22:4) with Judas, one of the twelve, leading them. He drew near to Jesus to betray Him, just as Jesus had predicted, with a kiss. This was the sign Judas had given so that they could identify Jesus in the dark and seize him (see Mark 14:44–45). The kiss, usually a greeting of love and friendship, was now used in a deep betrayal of Jesus.

Having misunderstood Jesus's earlier refusal to use swords (see Luke 22:35–38), the disciples asked if they should strike with a sword. But Jesus knew this would be the worst thing they could do. He could be accused of causing an uproar. Sadly, Peter didn't wait for Jesus to answer (John 18:10). He struck the servant of the high priest, cutting off his ear. Immediately, Jesus put a stop to such violence and healed the servant's ear. Then He addressed His enemies, questioning why they were treating Him as a robber and informing them that this was their hour, and the power of darkness. Significantly, it would also prove to be God's hour, and the power of light (Col. 1:13).

It's easy to relate to Peter, isn't it? Whether we use an unkind word, give an ungracious look, or commit an unloving action, we can seek to defend the Lord, the church, or sound doctrine in the wrong way. Instead, we must ask God to give us the grace to respond in kindness and graciousness to those who are hostile to the gospel.

X. Peter's Denials (22:54–62)

The chief priests and officers who had come with Judas seized Jesus and led Him to the high priest's house. Only two disciples followed, Peter and presumably John (John

18:15–16), and Peter followed at a distance. On arriving at the high priest's house, the chief priests and captains kindled a fire in the middle of the courtyard and sat down together. Peter took his place among them, commingling with the enemy.

Peter's first denial occurred when a servant girl saw him in the light and told the others that he had been with Jesus, but Peter denied that he knew Him. A little time went by before Peter's second denial. Someone else recognized him as a disciple of Jesus, but he denied it. Roughly another hour went by, and another insisted that Peter was with Jesus because he was a Galilean, but Peter said that he did not know what he was talking about. Notably, all of Jesus's disciples, except for Judas, were from Galilee, and the Judeans in Jerusalem looked down on Galileans.[13]

While Peter was still in the middle of denying that he knew the Lord, the rooster crowed. At this moment, Jesus looked at Peter. Jesus's look reminded Peter of the Lord's prediction of his denials, which led him to go out and weep bitterly. Ultimately this brought Peter to repentance, and he then helped spread the gospel. Based on what we have seen of Jesus in the book of Luke, we can assume that Jesus's look was probably one of love and compassion. This is what all believers receive when they flee to Christ after falling into temptation. Dear sinner, when you fail, you will be tempted to run away from Christ. Don't—run to Him in repentance and rest in His compassion and love. And then turn and strengthen your fellow believers who have fallen into temptation, urging them to flee to Christ.

We often experience great grief and weeping after the Holy Spirit convicts us of sin, and rightly so. But eventually our weeping should turn to joy as we rest in God's forgiveness and grace. We will fail to be faithful many times in our lives, but like Peter, we have a Lord and Savior who is interceding for us—praying that our faith will not fail and preserving it until the end. When He looks at you, remember that it's a look of compassion and love. He is eager to receive our repentance and ready to forgive. Dear sinner, flee to the compassionate Christ.

---

13. Wayne Grudem and Thomas R. Schreiner, note to Luke 22:59, in *ESV Study Bible*, 2008.

Processing It Together...

1. What do we learn about God in Luke 21:5–22:62?

2. How does this reshape how we should view our present circumstances?

3. What do we learn about God's Son, Jesus Christ?

4. How should this impact our relationship with God and with others?

5. What do we learn about God's covenant with His people?

6. How are we to live in light of this?

7. How can we apply Luke 21:5–22:62 to our lives today and in the future?

8. How should we apply this passage in our churches?

9. Look back at "Put It in Perspective" in your personal study questions. What did you find challenging or encouraging about this lesson?

10. Look back at "Principles and Points of Application." How has this lesson impacted your life?

The Lord Is Risen Indeed

Luke 22:63–24:53

Purpose . . .

Head. What do I need to know from this passage in Scripture?

- The Jews demand Jesus's crucifixion, after which He is revealed as the Redeemer through His resurrection, the Prophet through proclaiming Himself in all of Scripture, the Priest through blessing His disciples, and the King through His ascension.

Heart. How does what I learn from this passage affect my internal relationship with the Lord?

- I am a kingdom disciple who has been called to suffer and then enter into glory.

Hands. How does what I learn from this passage translate into action for God's kingdom?

- I will respond to unjust suffering in a godly way.
- I will pray for my persecuted brothers and sisters.
- I will pray for my political leaders and spiritual leaders to make godly and just decisions.
- I will worship the Lord and rest on the Sabbath.
- I will show others how to see Christ in all of Scripture.
- I will rely on the Holy Spirit as I share the gospel with unbelieving friends and neighbors.

Personal Study...

Pray. Ask that God will open up your heart and mind as you study His Word. This is His story of redemption that He has revealed to us, and the Holy Spirit is our teacher.

Ponder the Passage. Read Luke 22:63–24:53.

- *Point:* What is the point of this passage? How does this relate to the point of the entire book?

- *Persons:* Who are the main people involved in this passage? What characterizes them?

- *Persons of the Trinity:* Where do you see God the Father, God the Son, and God the Holy Spirit in this passage?

- *Puzzling Parts:* Are there any parts of the passage that you don't quite understand or that seem interesting or confusing?

Put It in Perspective.

- *Place in Scripture:* What is the original context of this text? What is the redemptive-historical context—what has or hasn't happened in redemptive history at this point in Scripture? How does this text connect to Christ?

The following questions will help you if you got stuck on any of the previous questions, and they will help you dig a little deeper into the text, putting it all into perspective.

1. 22:63–65. (a) Where is Jesus, and who is mocking and beating Him (22:52–54)?

(b) How did their request point to one of the three offices that Jesus came to fulfill (see also Luke 4:24; 6:22–23; 11:47–51; 13:33–35; 20:9–18)?

(c) What other two events most likely occurred during this night (see John 18:13; Mark 14:55–64, respectively)?

2. 22:66–71. (a) In Jesus's response to the leaders, how did He use Psalm 110:1 and Daniel 7:13?

(b) How does the council's question in verse 70 recall Psalm 2:7, and how did Jesus respond?

(c) What was the council's conclusion?

3. 23:1–5. (a) Of what three things did the chief priests and scribes accuse Jesus before Pilate?

(b) With which one of the three accusations was Pilate concerned, and how did Jesus respond?

(c) How did the chief priests and scribes respond to Pilate's verdict?

4. 23:6–12. (a) Why would Herod have been in Jerusalem (see 22:1)?

(b) Why was Herod glad to see Jesus, and was his desire fulfilled?

(c) How did Herod's treatment of Jesus affect his relationship with Pilate, and how does this fulfill Psalm 2:2?

5. 23:13–17. (a) How does verse 14 inform us of the answer to the first two charges brought against Jesus in verse 2?

(b) Was Pilate's second verdict the same as the first (compare v. 4 with vv. 14–16)?

6. 23:18–25. (a) How does the response of the chief priests, rulers, and people allude to Isaiah 53:8?

(b) Who was Barabbas (see also Acts 3:14)?

(c) What was Pilate's third verdict, and how did the crowd respond?

(d) What was Pilate's final decision, and how does this allude to Isaiah 53:6, 12?

(e) How does this exchange (freedom for a criminal and crucifixion for an innocent man) illustrate the truth of 2 Corinthians 5:21?

7. 23:26–31. (a) Who was forced to carry Jesus's cross?

(b) What does Jesus tell the daughters of Jerusalem to do, and why (see also Jer. 9:17–19)?

(c) To what event does Jesus refer in verses 29–30 (see also Lam. 4:4; Hos. 10:8)?

(d) In the proverb, who does the green wood represent, and who does the dry wood represent (see Jer. 11:16)?

8. **23:32–38.** (a) Where were Jesus and the two criminals crucified?

(b) What does Jesus pray, and how does this fulfill Isaiah 53:12?

(c) What did the rulers do with His garments, and how did this fulfill Psalm 22:18?

(d) How does verse 35 allude to Psalm 22:7–8 and verse 36 recall Psalm 69:21?

(e) What inscription hung over Jesus, and why was this ironic?

9. **23:39–43.** (a) Contrast the two criminals on each side of Jesus.

(b) How does Jesus fulfill His mission even in His dying hour (compare Luke 4:18–19 with 23:43)?

(c) How is Jesus the second and greater Adam (see Gen. 2:8; Rom. 5:12–21; Rev. 2:7)?

10. **23:44–49.** (a) What did the signs in the sky signify (see Joel 2:10; Amos 8:9; Zeph. 1:15)?

(b) What did the torn veil signify (see Heb. 6:19; 9:3, 8, 26; 10:19–22)?

(c) How does verse 46 fulfill Psalm 31:5?

(d) What were the different responses to Jesus's crucifixion, and how does verse 47 begin to fulfill Luke 2:32?

11. 23:50–56. (a) What do you learn about Joseph?

(b) What details do you learn about Jesus's burial?

(c) How do the women display obedience to God's commands (see Ex. 20:8–11)?

12. 24:1–12. (a) Who came to the tomb, and what did they find and not find?

(b) When did Jesus speak about His death (see Luke 9:22, 44)?

(c) How did the women respond to the angels' words, and to whom did they go?

(d) How did Peter's response differ from the others, and why is this significant (see 22:61–62)?

13. 24:13–24. (a) Who was going to Emmaus, and what were they discussing?

(b) Why didn't they recognize Jesus?

(c) How were Cleopas's words about who Jesus is true but incomplete?

(d) Who does Cleopas say is responsible for Jesus's death?

(e) What were Cleopas and others hoping Jesus would do?

14. **24:25–32.** (a) How does Jesus respond to the two disciples?

(b) How did Christ enter into His glory (Acts 2:29–36)?

(c) What does Jesus reveal as the key for interpreting the Old Testament?

(d) What did Jesus do while He was at the table with the two disciples (compare this with Luke 9:16 and 22:19)?

(e) Who opened the eyes of the disciples, and how does this continue to fulfill His mission (see Luke 4:18–19)?

15. **24:33–43.** (a) What were the eleven and those gathered with them saying when Cleopas and the other disciple arrived (see also 1 Cor. 15:5)?

(b) How do Jesus's words fulfill Luke 1:79; 2:14; and 19:38?

(c) How did Jesus respond to the disciples' terror and fright, and what does this reveal about Him?

16. 24:44–49. (a) In light of verses 44–46, read Luke 9:22; 18:31–33; and 22:22. What do you notice?

(b) How did the disciples come to understand the Scriptures?

(c) Give two examples of places in the Old Testament that proclaim Christ. You might want to refer to previous lessons to find some examples.

(d) How does "beginning at Jerusalem" reverse the Jewish expectation (see Isa. 2:2–5)?

(e) What does Jesus tell His disciples they are (see also Acts 1:8b)?

(f) What will Jesus send (see Isa. 32:15; Ezek. 39:29; Joel 2:28; Acts 1:4–5, 8; 2:4), and what are they to do until then?

17. 24:50–53. (a) Where is Bethany located (see Luke 19:29; John 11:18; Acts 1:12)?

(b) What role does Jesus display in lifting up His hands and blessing His apostles (see Lev. 9:22)?

(c) How did the disciples respond to Jesus's ascension, and how was this different from their response to His resurrection? What had made the difference?

(d) How did the disciples display their obedience to Jesus's command, and what were they doing (see also Acts 1:12–26)?

18. Luke does not record all the appearances that Jesus made during His forty days on earth after His resurrection. Write down what you learn from the following Scripture references: (1) Mark 16:9/John 20:14–18; (2) Matt. 28:9–10; (3) Luke 24:34; (4) Luke 24:15; (5) John 20:19; (6) John 20:26, 29; (7) John 21:1; (8) Matt. 28:16–20; (9) 1 Cor. 15:6; (10) 1 Cor. 15:7; and (11) Luke 24:51.

Principles and Points of Application
19. **22:63–23:17.** (a) In what areas of your life are you undergoing unjust suffering, and how are you responding?

(b) Pray for our persecuted brothers and sisters in Christ around the world, asking the Lord to give them strength to stand strong as witnesses and worshipers of Him.

20. **23:18–25.** (a) In what spheres of influence are the voices of the people prevailing to bring about ungodly and unjust decisions?

(b) Pray for our leaders to have wisdom, discernment, conviction, and strength to say no to the people when they are wrong.

21. **23:26–43.** (a) For what or for whom are you weeping? For what or for whom should you be weeping?

(b) Pray for unbelievers you know, asking God to save them.

22. **23:44–49.** (a) What are some different ways people have responded to Christ's crucifixion?

(b) How would you answer someone who asks you why Jesus's death matters?

23. **23:50–56.** How do you and your family prepare for the Lord's Day so that it's a day of worship and rest?

24. **24:1–12.** (a) What difference does Christ's resurrection make?

(b) When you share the gospel, how do you explain the importance of Christ's resurrection (see 1 Cor. 15:12–20)?

25. **24:13–47.** Why is it important that we see Christ in all of Scripture?

26. **24:48–53.** How do you need to grow as a worshiper of God, a worker for His glory, and a witness for His great name?

Putting It All Together...

What do you think of when you hear the word *suffering*? Maybe you think of the physical pain you or a loved one has experienced, a traumatic experience you have endured, or a relational difficulty that seems insurmountable. Perhaps you recall a mocking word a coworker spoke when you tried to share the gospel or an unkind letter from a family member who no longer wanted to hear about your faith. Maybe you think about the suffering you have watched your child endure as he struggles to keep up with his classmates academically. Or perhaps you think of your elderly parent enduring dementia. Regardless, *suffering* is a word we don't like to hear. Whether it's our own suffering or that of someone else, we don't get excited about it. In fact, we spend a great deal of time and money trying to avoid it. But suffering is inevitable in a fallen world. And Scripture informs believers that they should expect suffering and even rejoice in it: "Beloved, do not think it strange concerning the fiery trial which is to try you, as though some strange thing happened to you; but rejoice to the extent that you partake of Christ's sufferings, that when His glory is revealed, you may also be glad with exceeding joy" (1 Peter 4:12). Thankfully, our suffering has a purpose. It conforms us more and more to Christ.

Jesus sets the pattern for the Christian life. Suffering comes before glory. The unjust trials He underwent and His crucifixion came before His resurrection and ascension. How did He endure such suffering? He kept His eyes on His Father, submitting to His will and recognizing that glory would follow suffering. You and I must do the same.

I. Condemned by Sinful Men (22:63–23:25)

The men who were holding Jesus in custody at the high priest's house (see Luke 22:52, 54) were mocking and beating Him. They thought it would be fun to play a game, putting a blindfold on Jesus and making Him guess which one of them struck Him while they called out "Prophesy!" to ridicule His office of prophet (see Luke 1:76; 13:33; 24:19).

A comparison of the gospel accounts seems to show that another trial went on the same night Jesus was betrayed by Judas and beaten by sinful men. The band of soldiers and the officers of the Jews first led Jesus to Annas, the father-in-law of the high priest, Caiaphas (John 18:13). Jesus also underwent a trial that night with Caiaphas presiding (Matt. 26:59–66; Mark 14:55–64). But Jewish law forbade the high council in Jerusalem to try a case at night.[1] So "*as soon as it was day*, the elders of the people, both chief priests and scribes, came together and led Him into their council" (Luke 22:66; emphasis added).

This council was the Sanhedrin, which was the highest court of law in Israel, made up of seventy elders plus the high priest. This would be Jesus's last stop before being handed over to the Romans, for the Jews had no right to execute the death penalty; only the Romans could sentence a person to death.[2]

The key issue before the Sanhedrin was whether or not Jesus *claimed* to be the Christ. Sadly, they did not believe Jesus is the Christ, which is why Jesus answered as He did: "If I tell you, you will by no means believe." He went on to say, "And if I also ask you, you will by no means answer Me or let Me go" (Luke 22:67–68). Remember that when Jesus asked them whether the baptism of John was from heaven or from man, they answered that they did not know where it came from (20:4–7). And when

---

1. Ryken, *Luke*, 2:537.
2. Ryken, *Luke*, 2:538.

He asked them how they could say that the Christ is David's son, they did not reply (vv. 41–44). Jesus knew exactly who He was dealing with, so He answered by alluding to two Old Testament passages, Psalm 110:1 and Daniel 7:13. By doing so, He acknowledged not only that He is the Christ but that He is the Son of God, who would be seated at the right hand of God.

When they challenged whether He was claiming the title Son of God for Himself, Jesus said, "You rightly say that I am." He was responding that they were saying the title correctly, but they didn't comprehend what it meant. This claim to be the Son of God was enough evidence for the Sanhedrin. They took Him to the Romans.

Pontius Pilate, a governor, was the local Roman authority.[3] He was responsible for finances in that region and for keeping law and order.[4] The Sanhedrin accused Jesus of three things before Pilate. First, they accused Him of misleading the nation of Israel, which was false. He was the final Prophet, Priest, and King who had come to save God's people. Second, they accused Him of forbidding them to pay tribute to Caesar, which was also false (see Luke 20:19–26). Third, they accused Him of saying that He is Christ, a King, which was true. Jesus is the Christ, the King of kings.

This final accusation was what drew Pilate's attention because if Jesus said He was a king, He could be a potential threat to Rome. Pilate asked Jesus, "Are You the King of the Jews?" Jesus answered, "It is as you say" (Luke 23:3). In other words, Jesus is the King of the Jews, but not in the way Pilate thought.

Jesus's answer, evasive as it was, led Pilate to declare to the chief priests and crowds that Jesus was not guilty. Instead of accepting his verdict, the chief priests and crowds spoke fiercely to Pilate, accusing Jesus of stirring up people with His teaching. If they could convince Rome that He was a political threat, they would win. But Pilate didn't want the responsibility for making a decision, so he inquired about where Jesus was born. On learning that He was a Galilean belonging to Herod's jurisdiction, he sent Him over to Herod, who was in Jerusalem for the Passover, to undergo the next step in His trials.

Herod (Antipas) was the son of Herod the Great, who had ordered all male babies two years old and younger to be killed when he heard of Jesus's birth (Matt. 2:16–18). Sadly, he wasn't much different from his father. On one occasion, he granted his daughter her request for John the Baptist's head on a platter (14:1–12). On another occasion, some Pharisees told Jesus that Herod wanted to kill Him (Luke 13:31). Herod was exceedingly glad that he could finally see Jesus. He was not interested in Jesus as King or Savior. Not surprisingly, then, Jesus would not answer his questions. So Herod quickly joined the chief priests and scribes in mocking Him. He arrayed Jesus in splendid clothing fit for a king, which He claimed He was, and sent Him back to Pilate for the final trial. Notably, Herod and Pilate, who had been enemies, became friends with each other over Jesus's trials, fulfilling the words of Psalm 2:2.

---

3. Ryken, *Luke*, 2:548.
4. Bock, *Luke*, 2:1808.

Jesus's trials ended with Pilate. Since this was the second time that Jesus had appeared before him, Pilate summarized what occurred at the first trial to the chief priests, the rulers, and the people. Interestingly, this time he mentioned their first accusation that Jesus was one who was misleading the people. He reminded them that after he had examined Jesus, he did not find Jesus guilty of *any* of the charges against Him. And Pilate reminded them that Herod didn't either because he had sent Jesus back to him. He tried to reason with them, saying that Jesus had not done anything deserving of death, so he would punish and release Him. Punishment before release was customary, especially when the ruler was trying to appease the people. But the chief priests, the rulers, and the people would not accept Pilate's verdict.

With escalated voices, the people demanded that Pilate take Jesus away to be crucified and release Barabbas instead, a fulfillment of Isaiah 53:8. Barabbas had been thrown into prison for starting a rebellion in the city and committing murder. Pilate, still desiring to release Jesus, addressed the demanding crowd once more. But they would hear nothing from him. Instead, they demanded that Jesus be crucified. Again, Pilate questioned their desire because He had done no evil, and he again stated his intention to punish and release Him. But the crowd was relentless, and their voices prevailed over Pilate's. So Pilate released a rebellious murderer and delivered Jesus into the hands of sinful men (see Isa. 53:6, 12).

Our world so often puts Jesus on trial when we should be the ones on trial. Like Barabbas, we are the guilty and rebellious ones. Yet God the Father loved the world so much that He put His Son on the cross. For those who trust in Christ alone for salvation, the blood of Jesus covers their names, and their verdict reads, "not guilty anymore."

II. Crucified, Dead, and Buried (23:26–56)

The chief priests, the rulers, and the people led Jesus away from Pilate and Jerusalem toward the outskirts of the city to the place called Calvary. They laid hold of Simon, a Cyrenian (a man from North Africa)[5] who was coming in from the country, to carry Jesus's cross. Jesus was likely too weak from all of the beatings (Luke 22:63–65) to carry His own cross without the possibility of dying, something the people didn't want. Sadly, they wanted to make a public spectacle of Him and watch Him die the slow, cruel death of crucifixion.

Notice the great exchange that Jesus was making.[6] Simon should have not only carried the cross but he should have died on it. Here is a picture of every sinner carrying his or her huge load of sin that is too heavy and too great to bear. Jesus, the Righteous One, does the unimaginable. He became sin so that we might become righteous (2 Cor. 5:21).

---

5. Ryken, *Luke*, 2:570.
6. Ryken, *Luke*, 2:570.

A great multitude of the people followed Him, and women were mourning and lamenting for Him. But Jesus pointed out that their mourning was misplaced. They should have been weeping for themselves and their children. Jesus predicted the coming destruction of Jerusalem in AD 70 (see also Luke 21:5–9, 20–24). In that day it would be better for those who had no children because the destruction would result in a lack of resources (see Lam. 4:4). The destruction would be so great that the people would cry for the mountains to fall on them and the hills to cover them (see Hos. 10:8).

Jesus told these daughters of Jerusalem a proverb: "If they do these things in the green wood, what will be done in the dry?" (Luke 23:31). The green wood represents Jesus, the true Israel, and the dry wood represents rebellious Israel (see Jer. 11:16). If righteous Jesus (the green wood) is about to be hurled into the fire of crucifixion, how much worse will it be for rebellious Israel (the dry wood) when deserved judgment comes to them? They will be destroyed.[7]

Two criminals were led away with Jesus to be crucified. One would be hung on a cross on Jesus's right side and the other on His left side. From the cross Jesus cried out, "Father, forgive them, for they know not what they do" (Luke 23:34; see Isa. 53:12). While Jesus hung on the cross in naked shame, the rulers cast lots to divide His garments, a fulfillment of Psalm 22:16–18. The rulers were scoffing at Jesus (see Ps. 22:7–8), and the soldiers were mocking Him. Ironically, in the midst of awful accusations and misplaced mocking, the inscription that hung over Jesus was true: "THIS IS THE KING OF THE JEWS" (Luke 23:38; see 1:32–33).

The two criminals came to the cross having pursued the same lifestyle. They were both rebels in need of a Savior. But their lives could not have ended more differently—one was eternally lost, the other was eternally saved. The one who remained in sin and rebellion refused to repent and respect the Son of God; instead, he railed at Him in mockery. The other criminal called him to account and recognized the injustice of Jesus's punishment. He believed that Jesus is King and wanted to be in His kingdom.

Jesus turned with compassion to the criminal who asked to be remembered by Him and granted his request. He promised him that he would be with Him in paradise that very day (see Gen. 2:8; Rev. 2:7). Jesus, the second Adam and the true Israel, gives everyone who repents of their sin and believes in Him for salvation the promise of being with Him immediately after their physical death in this world. When we die our souls go to be with Jesus, while our bodies wait for the resurrection day when Christ returns again. It is never too late, as long as you are still living on this earth, to place your trust in Christ. Dear reader, which criminal will you be like, the one who believed or the one who remained in rebellion?

The crucifixion began at the third hour, or nine in the morning (Mark 15:25). From the sixth hour, noon, until the ninth hour, three in the afternoon, darkness was over the earth. The sun was darkened. This was not a natural phenomenon, such as an eclipse, because it was the time of the Passover, when there would have been a full

---

7. Ryken, *Luke*, 2:575.

moon.[8] This was God's doing. He was pouring out His wrath against sin on His only beloved Son. The prophets used such imagery of darkness to speak about God's judgment (Joel 2:10; Amos 8:9; Zeph. 1:15), and here was the greatest hour of judgment when the greatest exchange in history took place—our sin for Christ's righteousness.

The second event that was solely God's doing was tearing the curtain of the temple in two. It was torn from top to bottom (Matt. 27:51). No human could have done this. The curtain was about thirty feet wide, thirty feet high, and almost an inch wide. It was made of very heavy, tightly woven material. The weight would have been hundreds, perhaps even thousands, of pounds.[9] Significantly, God the Father was declaring that the last and final sacrifice was being made to open the way to the Holy of Holies. The spotless Lamb of God had finally taken His place on the altar to make the atoning sacrifice for God's people (see Heb. 6:19–20; 9:26).

Immediately before His final breath, Jesus cried, "Father, into Your hands I commit My spirit" (Luke 23:46), a fulfillment of Psalm 31:5. Jesus was fully submitted to His Father's will, as His prayer had already displayed in Gethsemane (see 22:42).

It is significant that God used Christ's death to bring a Gentile centurion to saving faith. When the centurion saw Jesus die and heard what He said, he praised God and declared Jesus's innocence. God also used Christ's death to turn a people's dancing into mourning. Rather than laughing at Jesus, they beat their breasts and returned to Jerusalem. As for Christ's acquaintances and the women who followed Him from Galilee—Mary Magdalene, Mary the mother of James and Joseph, and the mother of the sons of Zebedee (Matt. 27:55–56), as well as Jesus's mother and the apostle John (John 19:26)—they saw redemptive history unfold before their very eyes. Dear friend, what we think about Jesus and the cross is of greatest importance. If we believe in Him as our Lord and Savior, we will be saved, but if we reject Him, we will spend an eternity in hell.

Not every person who was a member of the council was against Jesus. There was one man, Joseph, who was from the Jewish town of Arimathea,[10] who was good and righteous and had not consented to the council's decision because he was looking for the kingdom of God. With great boldness and courage, he asked Pilate for Jesus's body. Pilate must have agreed to his request because Joseph took Jesus's body down from the cross, wrapped it in a linen shroud, and laid it in a tomb cut in stone. Significantly, this tomb had never been used, so we can be certain it was Jesus who rose from it.

The day of burial was the day of Preparation, for the Sabbath was beginning. Perhaps Joseph did not have enough time to prepare the body as he wanted, and that is why the women prepared spices and ointments, planning to return to the tomb the morning after the Sabbath (see Luke 24:1). Notably, these women showed their love for Jesus by keeping the fourth commandment (Ex. 20:8–11; 1 John 5:3). They had

---

8. Ryken, *Luke*, 2:608.
9. Ryken, *Luke*, 2:611.
10. The location of Arimathea is unknown. Morris, *Luke*, 349.

learned from His example, and even when they had the greatest excuse in history to break His command, they obeyed it.

Do you recognize the Lord's Day as one of worship and rest? It is important that we gather corporately on the Lord's Day to hear the preaching of God's word and pray. It is also a day for us to rest from our work and acknowledge our Provider. By keeping the Sabbath holy, we are honoring the Lord as both Creator and Redeemer (Ex. 20:8–11; Deut. 5:12–15).

III. Christ Is Risen (24:1–12)

After keeping the Sabbath day holy, the women who had followed Jesus from Galilee to Jerusalem as well as certain other women were up at early dawn on the first day of the week to go to the tomb, taking the spices they had prepared. Surprisingly, the stone was rolled away from the entrance to the tomb and Jesus's body was nowhere to be seen. Greatly perplexed, they received another surprise—two angels stood by them (see Luke 24:23). Afraid, they bowed their faces to the ground in respect and godly fear. Like the angels in Luke 1–2, these angels had an important message.

First, they revealed the women's misunderstanding by asking a question: "Why do you seek the living among the dead?" (Luke 24:5). Second, they proclaimed that Jesus had risen. Third, they reminded them of Jesus's teaching in Galilee, that the Son of Man must be delivered into the hands of sinful men and be crucified and on the third day rise (see 9:22, 44).[11]

Remembering Jesus's words, they told all they had heard to the eleven apostles and to all the rest. Mary Magdalene, Joanna, Mary the mother of James, and at least two other women must have felt discouraged when their message was received with unbelief, as if they were telling idle tales. But there was one apostle whose curiosity was raised.

Peter had previously denied he knew Jesus; perhaps he didn't want to deny He had risen. He rose and ran to the tomb, stooped down, saw the linen cloths lying alone, and departed, marveling that Jesus had risen from the dead. Notably, Peter wasn't the only one at the tomb. The apostle John went with Peter, reaching the tomb first, and believed the women's report.

How encouraging that the Lord gave women the privilege of being the first to proclaim the gospel. By doing so, He recognized their loyalty and devotion, dignity and worth, and capability of proclaiming the good news. The response that they initially received should also help us as we proclaim the gospel. People will often respond with skepticism, doubt, and unbelief. We must not place our hope in how well we proclaim the gospel but in the Lord who opens blind eyes to see.

---

11. Interestingly, Luke 9:22 is addressed to Jesus's disciples, so either the disciples told the women or Jesus taught the same truth at another time because these women remembered Jesus's words and the angels said, "Remember how *He spoke to you*" (24:6; emphasis added).

IV. Conversation on the Way to Emmaus (24:13–35)

Two of the people who were with the eleven apostles when they heard the women's report left Jerusalem for Emmaus, a village seven miles away. They had probably been in Jerusalem for the feast of Passover and were now making the return journey, about a two- or three-hour walk.[12] As they walked, they talked about all the things that had happened to Jesus. Since they had not believed the women's report, they were very sad. They had hoped Jesus would redeem Israel, but now those hopes were dashed.

In a striking turn of events, Jesus joined them on their journey, but God kept their eyes from recognizing Him. Jesus questioned their topic of conversation, which brought their walking to a complete stop and revealed their sadness. Luke names only one of the travelers, Cleopas, and he answered Jesus with surprise. He couldn't believe Jesus had not heard the news. But Jesus pressed on with His questions. So Cleopas and the other follower answered Him with a summary of what had happened and how they had interpreted the events.

They claimed that Jesus was a prophet who was mighty in deed and word before God and all the people. Then they blamed Israel's chief priests and rulers for Jesus's death and admitted that they had hoped Jesus was going to redeem Israel. Since it had now been three days since all of this happened, their doubt and dashed dreams seem to be confirmed. Finally, they told Him of the women's report, their astonishment, and that Jesus's body was missing from the tomb.

Jesus then admonished them (Luke 24:25). They should have known from the Old Testament that these events must take place, but they did not understand. Then He slipped in another question, implying that it was necessary for Christ to first suffer and then enter glory (see 22:69; Acts 2:29–36).

Beginning at Moses and all the Prophets, Jesus showed them what the Scriptures taught about Him.[13] When the Lord opened up my eyes to understand the truth of Luke 24:27, I wept.[14] Studying the Old Testament came alive for me in a way it never had before. I was overwhelmed with seeing Christ on every page of Scripture. It deepened my love for the Lord, increased my understanding of Scripture, and made my teaching more effective. If you get to the end of a passage in the Old Testament and you haven't seen Christ, go back and look again! Our study is not complete until He is at the center of our interpretation.

As the Lord interpreted the Scriptures to Cleopas and the other follower, their hearts were burning within them (Luke 24:32). No wonder they strongly urged Him to stay with them when they reached Emmaus. Remarkably, He did. When Jesus was at the table with them, He took the bread, blessed it, broke it, and gave it to them (see

---

12. S. G. De Graaf, *Christ's Ministry and Death*, vol. 3 of Promise and Deliverance (St. Catharines, Ont.: Paideia Press, 1979), 449.

13. For a more detailed discussion of how Jesus is revealed in the Old Testament, see "A Christ-Centered Interpretation of Luke" in the introduction, pp. xvii–xix.

14. I am indebted to Edmund Clowney (1917–2005), whose numerous books, class lectures, and sermons taught me how to see Christ in all the Scriptures.

also 9:16; 22:17–20). Then God opened their eyes to recognize their guest. But they had no sooner recognized Him when He vanished from their sight. Jesus's resurrection body had supernatural abilities to do supernatural things.

Now Cleopas and the other follower understood why their hearts had burned within them while He talked with them and explained the Scriptures to them. The One to whom all Scripture points had been preaching to them! They were so excited and energized that they forgot the day was almost over and they had already walked seven miles from Jerusalem. They immediately returned to Jerusalem to tell the eleven and the others with them about their encounter with Jesus.

This is how all encounters with Jesus should end—in sharing with others. In our excitement of seeing Christ in all of Scripture and having a fresh encounter with Him in the written Word, we should want to share with those around us. The Emmaus disciples were not met with skeptics, as the women were; they were not accused of telling idle tales. Instead, they were met with the proclamation of the gospel—the Lord has risen indeed! Significantly, Jesus had also appeared to Simon Peter, the disciple who had denied Him and would have needed to know His reassurance and love (see also 1 Cor. 15:5).

V. Comprehend the Scriptures (24:36–43)

It must have been very late when Cleopas and the other follower arrived back in Jerusalem. Remember, it was still the day of Jesus's resurrection. As all of them were talking about the events of the day and sharing the excitement of their eyes being opened to the gospel, Jesus suddenly appeared among them and said, "Peace to you" (Luke 24:36).

Startled, frightened, and thinking that they were seeing a spirit, the disciples were far from experiencing peace. But Jesus questioned their doubting hearts, showed them His hands and feet, invited them to touch Him, and then ate a piece of fish in front of them. He wanted His followers to know and believe that He was the risen Christ, their Master whom they had come to know and love. This is the purpose of Luke's gospel also—that we might have certainty of our faith. The Holy Spirit, writing through Luke, wants us to know for sure that Jesus is the resurrected Christ, the firstfruits of all of God's children who will one day receive resurrected bodies as well (1 Cor. 15:20–23).

As the Lord stood there extending peace to His followers, He was fulfilling His purpose. Jesus came to guide people into peace (Luke 1:79). The angels announced to the shepherds that He would bring peace among God's people (2:14). Through His blood shed on the cross, Christ has made peace between God and humankind (Col. 1:18–20). But for those who refuse to trust in Christ alone for salvation, He has brought division (Luke 12:51). When Christ returns He will divide believers from unbelievers. Today is the day we must repent of our sins and run to Christ. He is the only One who can save us from the wrath to come.

VI. Carried into Heaven (24:44–53)

Luke 24 reads as if it were an account of one very long day. But we know that Jesus appeared to His disciples over a course of forty days before ascending into heaven (Acts 1:3), so there is most likely a time lapse between verses 43 and 44.[15] In Luke 24:44–53, Jesus is addressing all of His disciples. In some ways, He repeated the sermon that He gave to Cleopas and the other follower on the Emmaus Road, but there are important additions (see vv. 47–49). The words that Jesus spoke to His disciples while He was with them concerning the Law, the Prophets, and the Psalms can be found throughout the book of Luke (see for example 3:4–6; 4:18–19; 7:27; 9:22; 17:22; 18:31–33; 20:17, 41–44; 22:22). Here the Lord opens His disciples' eyes so that they can understand the Scriptures.

Jesus speaks of the prophecies and the necessity of His suffering. There are several Old Testament texts that are used in the book of Luke that point to Jesus's suffering.[16] There are also several that display Christ's resurrection.[17]

Jesus also focused on proclaiming repentance and forgiveness of sins to the nations (see Isa. 49:6). This was not what the Jews expected. They believed that the nations would come to Jerusalem (see Isa. 2:2–5), but Christ was sending them out from Jerusalem to the nations of the world to proclaim the gospel.[18] They were to be witnesses of the good news of the gospel for those who repent and believe in Jesus as Lord and Savior.

Jesus told them that He would send the promise of His Father to them, the Holy Spirit (see Acts 1:4–5, 8; 2:4). The third person of the Trinity was the key to their witness work. In fact, they were to stay in Jerusalem until they had received the Holy Spirit, which occurred on the day of Pentecost (Acts 2). This was foretold in the Old Testament (see Joel 2:28; see also Isa. 32:15; Ezek. 39:29).

Luke concludes his gospel by telling us that Jesus led His disciples out as far as Bethany, which is at the Mount of Olives (Luke 19:29), about two miles from Jerusalem, and home to Lazarus, Mary, and Martha (John 11:1, 18). Jesus, the true and final Priest, blessed His people as He ascended to His Father (see Lev. 9:22).

Filled with newfound understanding and joy, the disciples worshiped their Lord and Savior. They returned to Jerusalem to continually bless God in the temple and await the promise of the Holy Spirit. This is what true knowledge of the Scriptures and a personal relationship with the Lord should always result in—worship that leads to witness. Significantly, it was not just the men who were devoted to prayer. They were together with the women, Mary the mother of Jesus, and Jesus's brothers (Acts

---

15. Ryken, *Luke*, 2:677–78.

16. See, for example, Ps. 118:22 in Luke 20:17; Isa. 53:12 in Luke 22:37; Ps. 31:5 in Luke 23:46; Pss. 22:7, 18; 69:21 in Luke 23:34–36.

17. See Psalm 16:8–11 in Acts 2:25–28 and 13:35, as well as Isaiah 55:3 in Acts 13:34. Pao and Schnabel, "Luke," 401.

18. Pao and Schnabel, "Luke," 401.

1:14). Oh, that our churches would be filled with men and women who, in one accord, devote themselves to prayer in humble reliance on the Holy Spirit!

How does the gospel of Jesus Christ transform our suffering? Instead of anxiety and fear, despair and hopelessness, it gives us hope. Jesus died so that you and I might live. He rose from the grave as the firstfruits of the resurrection. He ascended into heaven to prepare a place for us and intercede for us until we enter into glory. In the midst of your hardship and heartache, don't despair. Submit to the Father's will, cling to Christ, and receive comfort from the Holy Spirit. One day soon you will enter into glory, where "God will wipe away every tear from [your] eyes; there shall be no more death, nor sorrow, nor crying. There shall be no more pain, for the former things have passed away" (Rev. 21:4).

Processing It Together...

1. What do we learn about God in Luke 22:63–24:53?

2. How does this reshape how we should view our present circumstances?

3. What do we learn about God's Son, Jesus Christ?

4. How should this impact our relationship with God and with others?

5. What do we learn about God's covenant with His people?

6. How are we to live in light of this?

7. How can we apply Luke 22:63–24:53 to our lives today and in the future?

8. How should we apply this passage in our churches?

9. Look back at "Put It in Perspective" in your personal study questions. What did you find challenging or encouraging about this lesson?

10. Look back at "Principles and Points of Application." How has this lesson impacted your life?

Bibliography

Bock, Darrell L. *Luke 1:1–9:50*. Baker Exegetical Commentary on the New Testament. Grand Rapids: Baker, 1994.

———. *Luke 9:51–24:53*. Baker Exegetical Commentary on the New Testament. Grand Rapids: Baker, 1996.

Bonhoeffer, Dietrich. *The Cost of Discipleship*. New York: Touchstone, 1995.

Carson, D. A., and Douglas J. Moo. *An Introduction to the New Testament*. Grand Rapids: Zondervan, 2005.

De Graaf, S. G. *The Failure of Israel's Theocracy*. Vol. 2 of Promise and Deliverance. St. Catharines, Ont.: Paideia Press, 1978.

———. *Christ's Ministry and Death*. Vol. 3 of Promise and Deliverance. St. Catharines, Ont.: Paideia Press, 1979.

The ESV Study Bible. Wheaton, Ill.: Crossway, 2008.

Morris, Leon. *Luke*. Tyndale New Testament Commentaries. Downers Grove, Ill.: IVP Academic, 1988.

Pao, David W., and Eckhard J. Schnabel. "Luke." In *Commentary on the New Testament Use of the Old Testament*, edited by G. K. Beale and D. A. Carson (Grand Rapids: Baker Academic, 2007), 251.

Ryken, Philip Graham. *Luke*. Vol. 1, *Chapters 1–12*. Reformed Expository Commentary. Phillipsburg, N.J.: P&R, 2009.

———. *Luke*. Vol. 2, *Chapters 13–24*. Reformed Expository Commentary. Phillipsburg, N.J.: P&R, 2009.

Ryle, J. C. *Luke*. Crossway Classic Commentaries. Wheaton, Ill.: Crossway, 1997.

Sproul, R. C. *A Walk with God: Luke*. Fearn, Ross-shire, Scotland: Christian Focus, 2011.

The Westminster Confession of Faith and Catechisms, as adopted by the Presbyterian Church in America with Proof Texts. Lawrenceville, Ga.: Christian Education and Publications, 2007.